Quantum Technology Applications, Impact, and Future Challenges

This book presents a comprehensive exploration of quantum computing, exploring its wide-ranging applications across industries, elucidating its transformative impact on diverse sectors, and addressing the forthcoming challenges and future directions within this rapidly evolving field.

Quantum Technology Applications, Impact, and Future Challenges explores the current state of quantum hardware and software, providing readers with a clear understanding of the challenges and opportunities posed by this technology. It also examines how quantum computing is being used today in industries such as energy, finance, healthcare, and logistics, offering real-world examples of the potential impact of this technology. Readers will gain an understanding of quantum computing's potential applications and its profound implications for businesses, individuals, and society at large. Through a blend of theoretical insights, practical examples, and thought-provoking discussions, this book equips readers with the knowledge and vision to navigate quantum technology with confidence. Authored and edited by leading academics and industry experts in the field, the book offers authoritative insights and perspectives, ensuring readers receive credible and up-to-date information on quantum computing advancements and applications.

This book navigates readers through the intricate landscape of quantum computing and communications, offering valuable perspectives for scholars, researchers, and practitioners alike.

Quantum Technology Applications, Impact, and Future Challenges

Edited by
Mohammad Hammoudeh, Clinton Firth,
Harbaksh Singh, Christoph Capellaro,
and Mohamed Al Kuwaiti

CRC Press
Taylor & Francis Group
Boca Raton London New York

CRC Press is an imprint of the
Taylor & Francis Group, an **Informa** business

Designed cover image: © Shutterstock

First edition published 2025
by CRC Press
2385 NW Executive Center Drive, Suite 320, Boca Raton FL 33431

and by CRC Press
4 Park Square, Milton Park, Abingdon, Oxon, OX14 4RN

CRC Press is an imprint of Taylor & Francis Group, LLC

ISBN: 978-1-032-88330-4 (hbk)
ISBN: 978-1-032-88326-7 (pbk)
ISBN: 978-1-003-53724-3 (ebk)

DOI: 10.1201/9781003537243

Typeset in Times LT Std
by KnowledgeWorks Global Ltd.

Contents

Preface

Welcome to *Quantum Technology Applications, Impact, and Future Challenges.* In an era defined by rapid technological advancement, the convergence of quantum computing and quantum communications is poised to redefine industries, reshape cybersecurity, and unlock new dimensions of computational power. This book serves as your guide to understanding and navigating this exciting landscape. As we embark on this journey, we invite you to explore the dynamic interplay between the ethereal realm of quantum computing and the practical landscapes of industries ranging from energy to cybersecurity, networking, optimization, and beyond.

This novel approach to computation has ignited a spark of innovation that resonates across sectors, beckoning us to reimagine what is possible. This book emerges as a response to the approaching deadline of quantum technology readiness and its potential impact on industries. It seeks to demystify the complex interplay between quantum concepts and practical applications, offering a roadmap for individuals and organizations to harness the power of this new paradigm. We aim to guide readers through the theoretical underpinnings, real-world use cases, and speculative visions that define the quantum-industry nexus.

Our book is a collaborative endeavor, featuring contributions from experts who span disciplines, industries, and visions. It stands as a testament to the collective curiosity that motivates us, inspiring us to explore the unknown and shape the future.

As you read through this book, we invite you to approach with an open mind, as quantum-industry convergence is a realm of transformation. With each chapter, we endeavor to brighten a corner of this expansive landscape, offering insights, knowledge, and reflections that can guide your path forward.

Dr. Mohamed Al Kuwaiti
Head of Cyber Security for the UAE Government

Overview

This book presents a comprehensive exploration of quantum computing, exploring its wide-ranging applications across industries, elucidating its transformative impact on diverse sectors, and addressing the forthcoming challenges and future directions within this rapidly evolving field. Through in-depth analyses and practical case studies, it navigates readers through the intricate landscape of quantum computing, offering valuable perspectives for scholars, researchers, and practitioners alike.

The *Quantum Technology Applications, Impact, and Future Challenges* book takes readers on a journey exploring both the present and future applications of quantum technologies. This book provides a reference for both novice and seasoned enthusiasts, offering a guide to navigating the complex landscape of quantum technology adoption. From its fundamental applications to future use cases, each chapter unveils quantum technology's vast potential and transformative influence across a myriad of sectors.

Through a series of carefully crafted chapters, readers will dive into the fundamental principles of quantum computing, unravel the intricacies of quantum machine learning, and uncover the practical applications reshaping industries worldwide. From clarifying the revolutionary impact of quantum computing on energy systems to dissecting the convergence of quantum and classical computing architectures, each chapter provides a comprehensive examination of key topics shaping the quantum landscape.

The readers will discover how quantum algorithms are revolutionizing optimization and machine learning, explore the implications of quantum data centers and quantum-as-a-service models, and peer into the post-quantum era with insights into future directions and challenges. By adopting *Quantum Technology Applications, Impact, and Future Challenges*, readers will gain an understanding of quantum computing's potential applications and its profound implications for businesses, individuals, and society at large. Through a blend of theoretical insights, practical examples, and thought-provoking discussions, this book equips readers with the knowledge and vision to navigate quantum technology with confidence.

About the Editors

Mohammad Hammoudeh is the Saudi Aramco Cybersecurity Chair Professor at King Fahd University of Petroleum and Minerals. His research interests include quantum communication technologies, quantum-safe encryption methods, and quantum adoption strategies in both IT and OT systems. He has hands-on experience in working with quantum hardware and algorithms. He developed practical ways of evaluating the real applications of new technologies in cyberspace such as quantum computing, digital twins, and blockchains.

Clinton Firth is a Partner at PwC focusing on digital, cyber, and resilience. He is an experienced cybersecurity consulting executive, holding many senior and global roles for large consulting and system integrator firms. He has diverse experience working with commercial, government, and defence clients. Clinton leads a passionate team of industry specialists to address some of the most complex technology trust problems of our time.

Harbaksh Singh is a seasoned leader with 21+ years of experience in the IT industry and has worked with Telecom organizations like Bharti Airtel, COLT, and British Telecom. He is currently working as Cybersecurity Architect at Ernst & Young. He has a double masters and is a long-standing member of IEEE. He is a musician at heart and likes to stay updated on AI, tech-gadgets, and cars in his free time.

Christoph Capellaro received his Ph.D. in mathematics at the Technical University Munich. He started his career in corporate R&D at Siemens and is now working with EY Consulting in Germany. His focus is on C-level advisory and major transformation projects in the context of cybersecurity and IT governance. Latest engagements are with financial institutions as well as industrial enterprises to improve cyber resilience while adopting latest technology like cloud and AI. Christoph holds several patents in cryptography and has authored articles and books on security management, digital currencies, and IT compliance. He is a passionate chess and piano player and mountain enthusiast. Dr. Al Kuwaiti was appointed by the Cabinet as Head of Cyber Security for the UAE Government in 2020. As Head of Cyber Security for the UAE Government by investiture, Dr. Al Kuwaiti has legal authority over all aspects pertaining to securing the cyberspace for the entire nation.

Dr. Al Kuwaiti holds a Doctorate in Computer Engineering and Network Security from George Washington University in the U.S. and a master's degree in Telecommunications and Computer Networks. He also holds an M.A. degree in International and Civil Security. Dr. Al Kuwaiti is an honorable member of the Society of Engineers, IEEE Society, Golden Key National Honor Society, and Computer Society. His research interests are detecting, monitoring, and responding to cyber warfare, network forensics, corporate governance and processes, and national cyber policy.

Contributors

Syed Farhan Ahmad
NC State University

Abdulelah S Alghamdi
Saudi Aramco

Guzmán Calleja
EY Company

Christoph Capellaro
EY Company

Khaled Chait
University of El Oued

Hanan Faour
Manchester Innovation and Technology
Academy

Pascal Halffmann
ITWM Fraunhofer

Mohammad Hammoudeh
King Fahd University of Petroleum and
Minerals

Ramkumar Harikrishnakumar
Wichita State University

Mostefa Kara
National Higher School
of Mathematics

Abdelkader Laouaid
University of El Oued

Rafael Martín-Cuevas
EY Company

Shivam Sharma
ITWM Fraunhofer

Harbaksh Singh
EY Company

Wissam Steitie
Manchester Innovation and Technology
Academy

Danish Vasan
King Fahd University of Petroleum and
Minerals

HyeJi Yang
Harvard University

1 Quantum Computing for Future Energy Systems

Syed Farhan Ahmad, Hye Ji Yang,
and Ramkumar Harikrishnakumar

1.1 FUTURE ENERGY SYSTEMS

Future energy systems refer to innovative and sustainable methods of generating, storing, and distributing energy to meet the world's growing demand while minimizing environmental impact. These systems often incorporate renewable energy sources such as solar, wind, and hydropower to reduce reliance on fossil fuels. By integrating advanced technologies like energy storage systems and smart grids, future energy systems aim to increase efficiency and reliability while meeting global energy needs.

Additionally, future energy systems prioritize reducing greenhouse gas emissions and promoting a transition towards a cleaner and more sustainable energy landscape. Overall, the goal is to create a more resilient and flexible energy infrastructure that can adapt to changing demands and environmental challenges. By embracing innovation and sustainability, future energy systems strive to ensure a reliable and affordable supply of energy for generations to come. The field of future energy systems provides answers to some of the open problems posed by [1]: How can we responsibly develop hydrocarbon energy? How do we mitigate the impacts of existing energy technology? How do we efficiently harness renewable energy? How will new energy technologies reshape our world?

1.2 STATE OF THE ART QUANTUM COMPUTE RESOURCES

Superconducting quantum computers utilize superconducting circuits to create qubits, which are the building blocks of quantum information processing. These systems have shown promise in scaling up to larger numbers of qubits, making them a leading candidate for future quantum computing applications. Some of the prominent companies involved in developing superconducting quantum systems are IBM, Google, and Rigetti.

IBM has recently released Condor, a 1,121 superconducting qubit quantum processor based on their cross-resonance gate technology. The Condor chip design pushes the limits of size and yield by adding 50% more qubits, making qubit fabrication and laminate size better, and adding over a mile of high-density cryogenic flex IO wiring inside a single dilution refrigerator.

Hardware alone cannot achieve quantum-centric supercomputing. It requires performant software for generating and manipulating quantum circuits and middleware for executing hybrid quantum-classical workflows in a heterogeneous computing environment, and that is where the IBM Qiskit package comes into play.

Trapped ion quantum computers use individual atoms as qubits, which are manipulated using lasers to perform quantum operations. This approach allows for high-fidelity quantum operations and long coherence times, making trapped ion systems a promising candidate for scalable quantum computing in the future. The advantages of using trapped ions for quantum information processing include long coherence times and high-fidelity operations. However, disadvantages include the need for complex control systems and susceptibility to environmental noise.

Silicon Spin quantum computers use the spin of individual electrons in silicon as qubits, offering the potential for scalability and compatibility with existing semiconductor technology. This approach aims to address the challenges of trapped ion systems by utilizing the advantages of silicon-based platforms for quantum information processing. By leveraging the well-established infrastructure of silicon technology, researchers are hopeful that silicon spin quantum computers can overcome some of the hurdles faced by other quantum computing architectures. Additionally, the use of silicon as a material for qubits may also enable easier integration with classical computing systems, paving the way for hybrid quantum-classical computing solutions.

Intel has been actively exploring silicon spin qubits as a potential solution for scalable quantum computing. With their expertise in silicon technology, Intel is well-positioned to make significant advancements in the field of quantum computing using this approach.

Photonic quantum computers are another promising architecture that could offer advantages in terms of scalability and error correction. Companies like Xanadu are working on developing photonic quantum computers that could revolutionize the industry. These computers utilize photons to perform quantum operations, which could potentially lead to more stable and efficient quantum computing systems. As research in this area continues to progress, photonic quantum computers may become a key player in the future of quantum computing technology.

Neutral atom quantum computers are also gaining attention for their potential to overcome some of the challenges faced by other quantum computing architectures. By using individual atoms as qubits, these systems offer high levels of control and precision in quantum operations. As advancements in neutral atom quantum computing continue, they could become a significant player in the evolution of quantum technology. Atom computing is one of the leading organizations driving innovation in neutral atom quantum computing. The computing resources that researchers use for their work will be referred to throughout this chapter.

1.3 QUANTUM COMPUTING FOR SMART GRIDS

A growing number of organizations have committed to going net-zero following COP28, which took place in Dubai in 2023. Electricity generation based on fossil fuels is becoming less common, and Distributed Energy Resources (DERs) will be essential parts of smart networks of the future. DER figures indicate that DERs are projected to continue to rise in number in the future. There are two main obstacles to overcome when integrating such an enormous amount of DERs into a smart grid:

first, the complexity of control and optimization approaches; and second, the security risks associated with these cyber–physical devices.

Due to the fact that quantum technologies offer unrivalled computational capabilities for emerging complexities, as well as quantum-safe algorithms that are not susceptible to cryptographic vulnerabilities, quantum technologies appear to be a solution to these challenges.

The following portion of this section provides a comprehensive summary of the current research conducted on the subject of quantum computing, specifically in relation to smart grids. Additionally, this section addresses some prospective areas of research in the field of smart grids.

1.3.1 POWER FLOW/LOAD FLOW ANALYSIS

Load flow analysis, also known as power flow study, is a crucial aspect of power system planning and operation. It involves the computation of voltages, currents, and real and reactive power flows in a power system under steady-state conditions.

Power flow equations, if solved by the classical direct iterative algorithms, scale with $O(N)$ for an $N \times N$ system and this number grows further if uncertainties are taken into account. The authors in Ref. [2] demonstrate Quantum Power Flow (QPF) algorithms to meet the growing needs of power flow calculation and support fast and resilient power system operations. The authors' contributions are three-fold:

I. Establishing a quantum-state-based fast decoupled model empowered by Hermitian and constant Jacobian matrices.
II. Devising an enhanced Harrow–Hassidim–Lloyd (HHL) algorithm to solve the fast decoupled QPF.
III. Further improving the HHL efficiency by parameterizing quantum phase estimation and reciprocal rotation only at the beginning stage.

The proposed HHL circuit architecture primarily comprises quantum phase estimation and inverse rotations to facilitate efficient quantum computations. The parameters of the quantum circuit are trained classically using a classical loss function and optimizer. The authors verified the effectiveness and efficiency of QPF on a five-bus test system in normal and stressed conditions. QPF is implemented using IBM's Qiskit, and the experiments are run on both a simulator and IBM quantum computing resources. Their test results validate the accuracy and efficacy of QPF and demonstrate QPF's enormous potential in the era of quantum computing.

1.3.2 CYBERSECURITY IN MICROGRIDS

The maintenance of regular grid operations and the attainment of desirable benefits, such as rapid recovery during a main grid blackout, enhanced system stability and resilience, and cost-effective power delivery to customers, heavily rely on the criticality of data transfer security in smart microgrids. At present, smart grids rely on classical encryption technologies for their security, rendering them susceptible to potential security assaults [3].

The authors in Ref. [4] employ Quantum Key Distribution (QKD) as a solution to the challenges faced by microgrids in the quantum era. They devise a novel Python-based QKD simulator capable of simulating QKD protocols and demonstrate how to build a quantum-secure microgrid testbed in a real-time digital simulator environment.

1.3.3 UNIT COMMITMENT

Unit Commitment (UC) is a critically important problem for operational optimization within power systems. Combinatorial complexity arises in the UC problem due to the existence of binary commitment choice variables. Furthermore, it is anticipated that complexity will rise in the future due to efforts to enhance the penetration of intermittent renewable energy sources, necessitating the search for new sources of disruptive solution techniques.

Within the UC problem, the generation cost is minimized subject to unit-wise constraints (e.g., generation capacity, ramp-rated, and minimum up/downtime.) as well as the system-wide constraints (e.g., system demand, reserve, and transmission capacity). The authors in Ref. [5] present a quantum distributed method for solving UC problems in quantum computing frameworks. The Quantum Approximate Optimization Algorithm (QAOA) is presented in the paper and the Quantum Alternate Direction Method of Multipliers (QADMM) is then developed as a heuristic algorithm to solve the distributed UC problem. Comparing the obtained results with those from its classical counterpart ensured the superiority of quantum computers in terms of computing performance.

1.4 QUANTUM COMPUTING FOR SUSTAINABLE BUILDING DESIGN

Sustainable building requires heavy data analysis and intricate simulations to mitigate its negative impact on the environment throughout the building's design, construction, and operational phases. Therefore, quantum computing's potential to solve complex optimization problems will significantly influence sustainable building practices in various ways in the future.

1.4.1 STRUCTURAL OPTIMIZATION

Structural design of buildings requires heavy structural integrity assessments and behavioural simulations to achieve the most optimal solution. Quantum computers could accelerate calculating computationally intensive analyses which involves diverse loading scenarios and environmental factors. Quantum machine learning could quickly process climate data analysis of the site by identifying its patterns, anomalies, or trends, which are integral factors in structural optimization [6]. With these analyses, resilient infrastructure can successfully perform under severe weather and natural disasters.

1.4.2 SUSTAINABLE ENERGY IN SMART BUILDINGS

Sustainable buildings need to monitor and conduct various types of analyses such as energy simulation, daylight analysis, and thermal comfort assessments. Quantum computing could help process vast amounts of data and even monitor real-time energy consumption through quantum sensors. It could help in analysing indoor air quality, water, and electricity usage more efficiently. Through quantum computing, more energy-efficient and sustainable Heating, Ventilation, and Air Conditioning (HVAC) systems are being designed for complex buildings. With these new solutions, new HVAC network designs surpassed the current data-driven method [7].

1.4.3 SUSTAINABLE MATERIALS FOR SMART BUILDINGS

Quantum computing could help in creating new advanced building materials and finding new solutions to decarbonization. One of the main construction materials, cement, has significantly high CO_2 emission levels. Quantum computers could simulate and compound new properties and potentially help in engineering novel sustainable materials with improved strength, durability, or insulation [8]. Quantum sensors could also help in monitoring the structural health of buildings with real-time data on material conditions and predict their longevity. These ultra-sensitive sensors could detect minor changes and corrosion in the material and prevent larger damages [9].

1.5 QUANTUM COMPUTING FOR TRANSPORTATION

A range of cutting-edge technologies are integrated into the intelligent transportation system to support and monitor road traffic systems and hasten the urbanization of different nations. One such technology is quantum computing, which finds use in the transportation sector in three different application areas: facility layout, transportation operation management, and path planning. Here we will briefly discuss two case studies: one on rebalancing bike-sharing systems, and the other, for incident detection.

1.5.1 BIKE-SHARING SYSTEMS

Smart mobility is a fundamental element of the smart city idea, which is currently being investigated on a global scale. The bike-sharing system seeks to offer an alternate means of transportation for smart mobility, and it is gaining significant traction in urban regions. The utilization of bikes for short-distance transportation contributes to the mitigation of traffic congestion, the reduction of carbon emissions, and the mitigation of overcrowding risks.

A critical part of a bike-sharing system operation is the effective management of rebalancing vehicle carrier operations that ensure bikes are restored in each station to their target value during every pick-up and drop-off operation. In Refs. [10, 11], the authors present potential applications of quantum Bayesian networks, which are quantum-equivalent to classical Bayesian networks for probabilistic rebalancing cost prediction under uncertainty. A demonstration using IBM Qiskit is presented, and the results are compared classically using Netica for a case study involving rebalancing across three bike stations.

In [10], when the number of potential choice variables expands, conducting a comprehensive search becomes computationally costly or occasionally impractical on a classical computer. In this scenario, the authors propose the utilization of a hybrid quantum-classical methodology, wherein a classical optimizer is employed to determine the values of decision variables and the overall cost associated with a decision can be derived through the application of a Quantum Bayesian Network (QBN).

1.5.2 INCIDENT DETECTION

The efficiency and reliability of real-time incident detection models directly impact the affected corridors' traffic safety and operational conditions. The researchers in Ref. [12] have devised a quantum neural network hybrid methodology to detect events by utilizing the data from connected vehicles. The evaluation of their framework is conducted by utilizing data obtained from a microsimulation tool, which encompasses several incident scenarios. The findings indicate that a hybrid neural network containing a four-qubit quantum layer outperforms all other baseline models when there is a lack of training data.

1.6 QUANTUM COMPUTING FOR LOW-CARBON FUELS AND DECARBONIZATION

1.6.1 CARBON CAPTURE

Carbon capture involves the capture of Carbon Dioxide (CO_2) emissions originating from significant point sources, including power stations and various industrial sites. The objective of carbon capture is to decrease the release of greenhouse gas emissions, thereby addressing the issue of climate change.

There are three major technologies that are utilized for Carbon Capture and Storage (CCS) [13]: pre-combustion carbon capture, which refers to the process of capturing CO_2 prior to its release into the atmosphere; post-combustion carbon capture which refers to the process of capturing CO_2 after its emission into the Earth's atmosphere; and finally, oxyfuel combustion which involves burning fuel in an atmosphere of nearly pure oxygen, which produces a highly concentrated form of CO_2 that is easier to collect.

Direct Air Capture (DAC) [14] is a technology that captures CO_2 directly from the ambient air. This differs from most CCS technologies, which capture CO_2 from the flue gases of large point sources such as power plants. In DAC, giant fans suck air into a device called a collector, where the CO_2 is then separated out through means similar to post-combustion capture.

Carbon capture, utilization, and storage [14] is an emerging technology that aims to reduce greenhouse gas emissions and mitigate climate change. It involves capturing CO_2 from large point sources such as power plants and other industrial facilities, and then either storing it underground or reusing it.

The authors in Ref. [15] present a hybrid quantum-classical method for calculating potential energy surface scans, which are essential for designing metal-organic frameworks for DAC applications. The electronic structure of CO_2–Mg^{2+} was analysed in this work using a Perfect Intermediate-Scale Quantum approach. The quantum computing approach yields similar results to that of classical for small problem sizes but an attempt to scale up the model to involve more molecular orbitals and hardware implementation revealed drawbacks of current quantum computers.

1.6.2 ENERGY-EFFICIENT AMMONIA PRODUCTION

Industrial ammonia production is currently the most energy-demanding chemical process worldwide and contributes up to 3% to global CO_2 emissions. Therefore, the development of more energy-efficient pathways for ammonia production is an attractive proposition [16]. But this requires modelling quantum dynamics for a coupled system larger than what is currently supported on available quantum hardware. The authors of [17] analyse the scaling limitations of variational quantum eigensolver on current quantum computing hardware. Titanium hydride was chosen as a relatively simple chemical system that incorporates d orbitals and strong electron correlation. Their results suggest that until substantial advancements in error correction algorithms and hardware are made, it is probably going to be prohibitive to get good simulation results on today's quantum hardware.

1.7 CONCLUSION

This chapter emphasized the capacity of quantum computing to transform energy systems by optimizing energy distribution, expanding transportation efficiency, improving sustainable design processes, and promoting clean fuel technologies. The case studies yielded significant insights into the pragmatic application of quantum computing solutions in tackling intricate difficulties within various industries. This report additionally included a summary of multiple real-world case studies to illustrate the extensive use of QC across diverse scientific domains. The technology is in its nascent stage and cannot be used to show any quantum advantage over classical computers yet. However, the successful outcomes presented serve as compelling evidence for the promising future of quantum computing in driving innovation and sustainability.

REFERENCES

1. *Future Energy Systems*. University of Alberta. Accessed: Mar. 22, 2024 [online]. Available: https://www.futureenergysystems.ca/
2. F. Feng, Y. Zhou, and P. Zhang, "Quantum Power Flow," *IEEE Trans. Power Syst.*, vol. 36, no. 4, pp. 3810–3812, Jul. 2021. doi: 10.1109/TPWRS.2021.3077382.
3. M. Farrokhabadi *et al.*, "Microgrid Stability Definitions, Analysis, and Examples," *IEEE Trans. Power Syst.*, vol. 35, no. 1, pp. 13–29, Jan. 2020. doi: 10.1109/TPWRS.2019.2925703.
4. Z. Tang, Y. Qin, Z. Jiang, W. O. Krawec, and P. Zhang, "Quantum-Secure Microgrid," *IEEE Trans. Power Syst.*, vol. 36, no. 2, pp. 1250–1263, Mar. 2021. doi: 10.1109/TPWRS.2020.3011071.

5. N. Nikmehr, P. Zhang, and M. A. Bragin, "Quantum Distributed Unit Commitment: An Application in Microgrids," *IEEE Trans. Power Syst.*, vol. 37, no. 5, pp. 3592–3603, Sep. 2022. doi: 10.1109/TPWRS.2022.3141794.

6. A. Nammouchi, A. Kassler, and A. Theocharis, "Quantum Machine Learning in Climate Change and Sustainability: A Short Review," *Proc. AAAI Symp. Ser.*, vol. 2, no. 1, pp. 107–114, Jan. 2024. doi: 10.1609/aaaiss.v2i1.27657.

7. *Revolutionizing Sustainable Building Design: Quantum Computing Takes the Lead.* Accessed: Mar. 22, 2024 [online]. Available: https://www.iot-mesh.io/vinci-energies-uptownbasel-diane-quantumbasel-d-wave/

8. *Quantum Computing Just Might Save the Planet.* Accessed: Mar. 22, 2024 [online]. Available: https://www.mckinsey.com/capabilities/mckinsey-digital/our-insights/quantum-computing-just-might-save-the-planet

9. Sarah Moore, *Utilizing Quantum Computing in the Construction Industry.* Accessed: Mar. 22, 2024 [online]. Available: https://www.azobuild.com/article.aspx?ArticleID=8376

10. R. Harikrishnakumar, S. E. Borujeni, S. F. Ahmad, and S. Nannapaneni, "Rebalancing Bike Sharing Systems under Uncertainty Using Quantum Bayesian Networks," in *2021 IEEE International Conference on Quantum Computing and Engineering (QCE)*, Broomfield, CO: IEEE, Oct. 2021, pp. 461–462. doi: 10.1109/QCE52317.2021.00078.

11. R. Harikrishnakumar, S. F. Ahmad, and S. Nannapaneni, "Comparing Quantum Optimization Solvers for Rebalancing Analysis of Bike Sharing System," in *2022 IEEE International Conference on Quantum Computing and Engineering (QCE)*, Broomfield, CO: IEEE, Sep. 2022, pp. 753–755. doi: 10.1109/QCE53715.2022.00106.

12. Z. Khan *et al.*, *Hybrid Quantum-Classical Neural Network for Incident Detection*, 2021. doi: 10.48550/ARXIV.2108.01127.

13. M. Shen *et al.*, "Carbon Capture and Storage (CCS): Development Path Based on Carbon Neutrality and Economic Policy," *Carbon Neutrality*, vol. 1, no. 1, p. 37, Nov. 2022. doi: 10.1007/s43979-022-00039-z.

14. F. Wang, F. Wang, K. B. Aviso, R. R. Tan, Z. Li, and X. Jia, "Bi-Objective Synthesis of CCUS System Considering Inherent Safety and Economic Criteria," *Process Integr. Optim. Sustain.*, vol. 7, no. 5, pp. 1319–1331, Nov. 2023. doi: 10.1007/s41660-023-00344-9.

15. K. S. Dogahe, T. Sarac, D. De Smedt, and K. Bertels, *"Toward" Metal-Organic Framework Design by Quantum Computing*, 2023. doi: 10.48550/ARXIV.2309.05465.

16. R. González-Cabaleiro, J. A. Thompson, and L. Vilà-Nadal, "Looking for Options to Sustainably Fixate Nitrogen. Are Molecular Metal Oxides Catalysts a Viable Avenue?," *Front. Chem.*, vol. 9, p. 742565, Sep. 2021. doi: 10.3389/fchem.2021.742565.

17. J. M. Clary, E. B. Jones, D. Vigil-Fowler, C. Chang, and P. Graf, "Exploring the Scaling Limitations of the Variational Quantum Eigensolver with the Bond Dissociation of Hydride Diatomic Molecules," *Int. J. Quantum Chem*, vol. 123, no. 11, p. e27097, Jun. 2023. doi: 10.1002/qua.27097.

2 Application of Quantum Computing in the Energy Industry, Decarbonization, and Sustainability

Christoph Capellaro, Rafael Martín-Cuevas,
Guzmán Calleja, Pascal Halffmann,
and Shivam Sharma

2.1 INTRODUCTION

We are only at the beginning to understand the impact quantum computing will have on our society. This chapter illustrates this by picking examples from various industries where we can already see significant change being stipulated by this technology. With green energy taking an even higher percentage of energy production, predictions on the energy market gain in importance. Quantum Machine Learning (QML) offers promising solutions to improve energy supply and demand forecasts in a volatile market. In addition, Quantum Annealing can be used to solve the Unit Commitment Problem (UCP) in the energy sector, asking about the most cost-effective energy production unit to supply a scheduled demand. Optimizing investment portfolios is a highly sought-after task in the financial sector. Of course, quantum computing also offers approaches in this regard. A number of different approaches are currently studied in this field of application.

The global urgency to combat climate change and achieve sustainability goals has grown exponentially in the last decade, prompting widespread efforts across multiple sectors. Quantum computing, an emerging technology built on the principles of quantum physics, has immense potential to make a transformative impact on such initiatives. With its promise to process information and solve complex problems at a scale unfeasible for classical computers, quantum computing is poised to offer innovative solutions in the pursuit of a sustainable future.

Quantum computing has the potential to revolutionize the financial services industry, offering faster data processing, optimizing portfolio management, and enhancing risk analysis. Current applications for quantum computing in financial services include portfolio optimization, fraud detection, index tracking, and demand forecasting, among several others. In this chapter, we dive into these applications,

DOI: 10.1201/9781003537243-2

highlighting how and where financial companies could take advantage of quantum computing to improve their current tactics to address these challenges. The large-scale implementation of quantum computing still faces several challenges, including the fragility and high cost of quantum machines, understanding and interpreting quantum results, and the integration with current classical systems, but despite these hurdles, preparing companies' structures for when the technology is ready is crucial. And there are still ways to start getting ready for the transformation today.

Quantum computing also poses a serious threat to financial institutions. This makes it necessary to develop a strategy to replace existing cryptographic procedures with those being quantum resistant. Regulators have set timeframes for the introduction of Post Quantum Cryptography (PQC). The areas of application of cryptographic procedures in the financial sector are diverse. Financial institutions typically have quite a number of communication relationships and data interfaces whose protection mechanisms are defined by different bodies. Depending on the cryptographic procedures currently used and their application environments, different paths must be taken for the migration to PQC. This makes it necessary to develop an institution-specific PQC migration strategy and to cooperate with partners, customers, and authorities. We conclude this chapter with some remarks on using QML in the financial sector and an outlook on applications in the healthcare, pharma, and defence industries.

2.2 APPLICATION OF QUANTUM COMPUTING IN THE ENERGY INDUSTRY

Energy trading is a vital component of the global energy sector, instrumental in balancing supply and demand, mitigating price volatility, and managing market risks. It encompasses several market types, including Futures Markets, Day-Ahead Markets, and Intraday Markets, each catering to specific trading strategies and operational requirements. In this intricate and fast-paced domain, QML emerges as a transformative force, offering novel approaches to address the longstanding challenges inherent in energy trading.

2.2.1 ENERGY MARKET ANALYSIS

Futures Markets involve contractual agreements for buying or selling energy at a predetermined price. These markets are critical for hedging against price fluctuations, allowing entities to secure future transaction prices.

2.2.1.1 Quantum Enhancement of Market Analysis

The procurement process for municipal utilities and large industries involves complex decision-making, where entities like EU municipalities procure energy from the European Energy Exchange (EEX) based on the average monthly consumption of households. This scenario is akin to a portfolio optimization problem within the mean-variance analysis framework, aiming to optimize the mix of energy contracts to achieve a desired balance between cost minimization and reliability.

2.2.1.2 Mathematical Formulation

The procurement challenge can be mathematically formulated as a problem of minimizing the total cost of procured energy while meeting the demand, represented as:

$$\min \sum_{i=1}^{n} c_i x_i$$

Subject to:

$$\sum_{i=1}^{n} x_i = D$$

$$x_i \in \{0,1\} \, \forall i$$

where c_i is the cost of energy for day i, x_i is a binary variable indicating whether to procure energy on that day ($x_i = 0$) or not ($x_i = 1$), and D is the total demand that needs to be met.

The constraint ensures that the selected sources meet the demand, while the objective function aims to minimize the total cost.

The procurement challenge can be reformulated within the Quadratic Unconstrained Binary Optimization (QUBO) framework for quantum computing, where the goal is to minimize a quadratic polynomial of binary variables:

$$\min_x \left(x^T Q x \right)$$

The energy procurement problem can be mapped to a QUBO matrix where the diagonal elements represent the costs and penalties for not meeting demand, and the off-diagonal elements can encode the interactions which would be specific to the way the constraint optimization problem is formulated.[1]

2.2.1.3 Conceptual Case Study

This section outlines a conceptual case study where a municipal utility, Stadtwerke, faces the challenge of optimizing its energy procurement strategy over a two-month period. The utility must make procurement decisions at the start of each month, balancing cost efficiency with the need to meet forecasted demand.

The temporal framework and decision dynamics require the consideration of:

- *Time Horizon:* The scenario spans two months, with decisions made at the beginning of each month.
- *Decision Points:* The first day of each month serves as a decision point for determining the volume of electricity to be procured.
- *Strategic Objective:* The primary aim is cost-effective procurement that aligns with the anticipated electricity demand.

The decision variables and the objective function are as follows:

- c_1, c_2: Projected electricity prices for the first and second months.
- x_1, x_2: Binary decision variables representing procurement actions in each month.

The procurement strategy's core is captured by a linear objective function designed to minimize total costs:

$$\min(c_1 x_1 + c_2 x_2)$$

For the transition to a formulation, we consider the binary essence of x_1 and x_2. The linear terms are adeptly recast into quadratic terms, adhering to the binary variable property $x_i^2 = x_i$. Consequently, the QUBO matrix Q for this scenario is structured with c_1 and c_2 as its diagonal elements, signifying the costs linked to each decision variable.

To employ quantum computing for this optimization problem, the objective function is translated into the QUBO format. The binary nature of the decision variables allows their linear terms to be expressed in quadratic form, leading to a QUBO matrix Q together with c_1 and c_2 as its diagonal elements:

$$Q = \begin{bmatrix} c_1 & 0 \\ 0 & c_2 \end{bmatrix}$$

The QUBO objective function then becomes:

$$\min(x^T Q x) = \min(c_1 x_1^2 + c_2 x_2^2)$$

The energy procurement process is subject to numerous real-world complexities, including fluctuating prices, contractual obligations, and the integration of renewable energy sources. To accurately reflect these dynamics, the QUBO model can be expanded to include a broader array of variables and constraints, such as different energy sources, contract types, and time slots within each procurement period. This enhanced model can capture regulatory requirements, supply reliability metrics, and environmental considerations, providing a more nuanced and comprehensive optimization framework.

2.2.2   UNIT COMMITMENT PROBLEM IN ELECTRICAL POWER PRODUCTION

The UCP stands as a critical optimization problem in the energy sector,[2] tasked with determining the most cost-effective schedule for power generation units to meet demand over a given time horizon. The significance of optimizing this schedule cannot be overstated—it is at the heart of ensuring that energy production is not only reliable and efficient but also cost-effective. However, the task is far from straightforward due to the complex interplay of factors that must be considered, including the variability of demand, operational constraints of power plants, fuel costs, and increasingly, the integration of renewable energy sources, see Figure 2.1 for a typical network of different consumer and producers of electricity connected via an electricity grid.

The urgency and complexity of UCP have only been amplified by recent global events, such as the Ukraine crisis, which underscored the fragility and sensitivity of energy markets. This situation highlighted how geopolitical tensions can swiftly impact energy supply chains, leading to fluctuations in fuel availability and costs. Such dynamics make the energy production landscape more volatile, underscoring

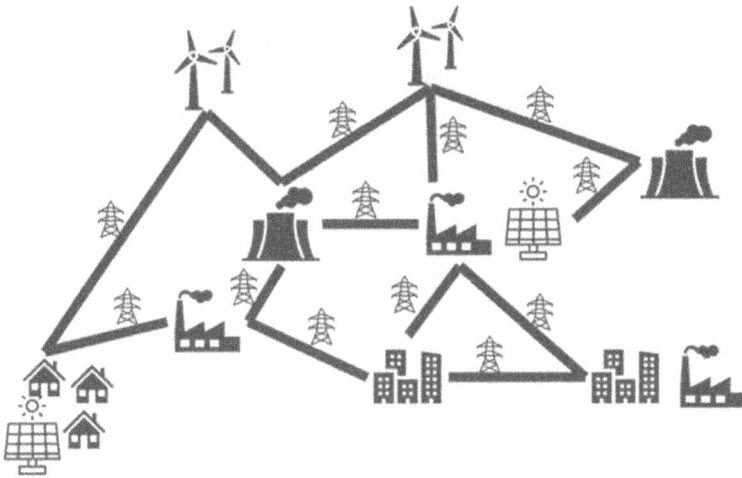

FIGURE 2.1 A typical electricity grid, illustrating connections between producers (coal, wind, solar) and consumers (cities, industrial areas) via power lines. With the growth of renewable energy sources, "prosumers"—such as households that both consume and generate electricity—are also becoming integral parts of the grid.

the importance of having a flexible and responsive power generation scheduling system that can adapt to rapid changes while minimizing costs. Moreover, the rise of renewable energies introduces new dimensions of complexity and unpredictability into the UCP. Renewable energy sources like wind and solar power are inherently intermittent, leading to a mismatch between supply and demand that can occur without warning. As the share of renewables in the energy mix continues to grow, driven by the global push toward sustainability and reduced carbon emissions, the task of effectively integrating these sources into the power grid while maintaining operational efficiency and cost-effectiveness becomes increasingly daunting.

Let us formally introduce the UCP. The UCP aims to optimizing the scheduling of electricity generation units to meet forecasted demand efficiently, see Figure 2.1. Here optimizing can mean both minimizing energy production costs as well as maximizing energy production revenues. It entails deciding which power plants to run, when to run them, and at what output levels, considering various technical and economic constraints. There are numerous variants of the UCP featuring different objectives, constraints, or meta requirements. We refer to Padhy's survey on Unit Commitment[3] for an overview and focus on the most common features in the following. In general, a UCP consists of the following:

- A specified planning horizon, typically 24 hours and discretized in 1 hour or 15-minute steps, for which the electricity planning has to be determined.
- A load profile (demand) for the upcoming time horizon that has to be satisfied. For every time step of the time horizon, the demand is specified. Since the demand cannot be fixed a priori, usually a forecasted profile (or a set of load scenarios) is used.

- A set of power plants or electricity generation units with their production capacities. Roughly there are three different types: thermal units (such as coal, gas, and even nuclear power plants burning a sort of fuel for producing electricity), hydro units (hydropower dams), and renewable energy units (such as wind farms and solar parks). All have distinct features, while the output of renewable energy units is dictated by the availability of wind or sunshine and, thus, is not fully controllable, thermal units can be adjusted to energy demand but the control is subject to complex technical constraints (e.g., minimum up and down time: if switched on/off the unit has to be kept on/off for a certain amount of time).
- The underlying energy grid network specifying production and consumption nodes as well as the power lines and their capacities in between.

This leads to an optimization problem with the following features:

- *Decision Variables:* They specify the production status (on/off, switched on/off) of the power units at each time step, the production amount of the power units at each time step, and the energy flow through the energy grid network.
- *Objective:* Minimize the production costs (including fixed cost components and variable components depending on the amount of energy produced), maximize the profit, and minimize the carbon emissions, among others.
- *Constraints:* Satisfy the load profile, the constraints of the energy grid, and the constraints by the different power units.

Figure 2.2 provides an example outcome of the UCP, showing energy production by different types of power units over a 24-hour period. Energy demand is consistently met at each hour. As an illustrative example, we present the optimization model of a UCP that minimizes the costs of a set of thermal units, while satisfying

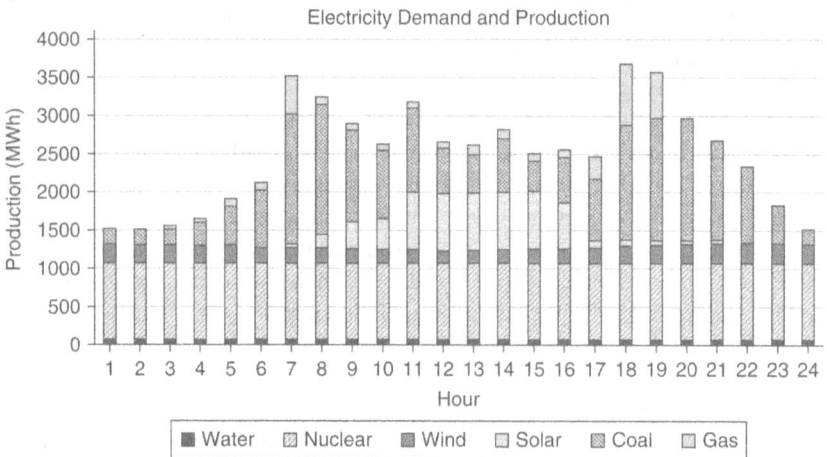

FIGURE 2.2 Exemplary outcome of the unit commitment problem showing the energy production by various types of power units over 24 hours. The demand is met at every hour.

the load profile, minimum and maximum power generation, and respecting minimum up and down time constraints,[4] without any electricity grid:

$$\text{Minimize} \quad \sum_{t=1}^{T}\sum_{i=1}^{N}\left(C_{\text{start},i}\cdot y_{i,t}+C_{\text{run},i}\cdot P_{i,t}\right)$$

$$\text{subject to} \quad \sum_{i=1}^{N}P_{i,t}=D_{t},\forall t$$

$$P_{\min,i}\cdot u_{i,t}\leq P_{i,t}\leq P_{\max,i}\cdot u_{i,t},\forall i,t$$

$$u_{i,t}-u_{i,t-1}=y_{i,t}-z_{i,t},\forall i,t$$

$$\sum_{\tau=t}^{t-1+U_{\min,i}}y_{i,\tau}\leq u_{i,t-1},\forall i,t\leq T-U_{\min,i}+1$$

$$\sum_{\tau=t+1-D_{\text{mini},i}}^{t}y_{i,\tau}\leq 1-u_{i,t-D_{\text{mini},i}},\forall i,t\geq D_{\min,i}+1$$

Here, $C_{\text{start},i}$ and $C_{\text{run},i}$ represent the start-up and running costs of unit i, $y_{i,t}$ is the binary variable indicating whether unit i starts up at time t, $P_{i,t}$ is the power generated by unit i at time t, D_t is the demand at time t, $P_{\min,i}$ and $P_{\max,i}$ denote the minimum and maximum generation capacities of unit i, $u_{i,t}$ is a binary variable representing whether unit i is on or off at time t, and $U_{\min,i}$ and $D_{\min,i}$ are the minimum up and down times of unit i. There are numerous other model formulations for various types of UCP, Knueven et al.[5] provide an overview.

Given the critical significance of optimizing costs and revenues within the energy sector, the UCP has been the subject of extensive research. A myriad of algorithms, harnessing state-of-the-art optimization techniques such as decomposition methods and Branch-and-Bound, have been developed, reflecting the depth of academic and practical engagement with the UCP. Furthermore, the evolution of commercial optimization solvers like CPLEX or Gurobi ushered in a new era of efficiency, offering optimal solutions for simplified versions of the UCP within remarkably short time frames. For instance, deploying these advanced solvers on practical and relevant datasets[6] allows for the resolution of UCPs involving 24 time steps and 3,000 power units in under 5 minutes on conventional computing hardware.

Despite these advancements, the inherently NP-hard nature of the UCP signifies that solution times escalate exponentially as the problem size increases, underlining a fundamental computational challenge. More realistic models that incorporate the energy grid extend algorithmic run times significantly. The anticipated shift in energy production toward smaller, more adaptable thermal units, alongside an increased reliance on energy storage and renewable sources, is poised to multiply the number of power units, introducing additional layers of complexity to the UCP. Current models predominantly focus on a singular objective of cost minimization, overlooking other critical dimensions such as sustainability and energy independence.

This narrow focus belies the multifaceted nature of modern energy challenges, where balancing competing objectives adds a layer of complexity that cannot be understated.

Furthermore, the stochastic variability inherent in renewable energy sources, such as wind and solar power, poses a profound challenge. The unpredictable fluctuations in energy output from these sources inject a degree of uncertainty that traditional, deterministic algorithms are ill-equipped to manage. This gap in capability complicates the UCP, rendering the task of devising reliable and optimally efficient power generation schedules increasingly formidable.

In summary, the evolving energy landscape, marked by fast-paced markets, cost sensitivities, geopolitical influences, and the integration of renewable energies, necessitates a reevaluation of traditional approaches to UCP. The complexity and dynamism of modern energy systems demand innovative solutions capable of optimizing power generation schedules in the face of uncertainty and rapid market changes. This backdrop of classical approaches sets the stage for exploring the potential of quantum computing as a transformative tool in tackling the UCP, promising to revolutionize how energy providers navigate the challenges of ensuring efficient, reliable, and cost-effective power generation in an increasingly complex and unpredictable world.

2.2.2.1   Solving the UCP with Quantum Computing

In response to the evolving challenges within the energy landscape, characterized by rapidly shifting markets, sensitivity to costs, geopolitical factors, and the burgeoning integration of renewable energy sources, quantum computing emerges as a pivotal technological advancement, poised to redefine the methodologies employed in tackling the UCP. Its inherent suitability for addressing complex sears spaces in optimization problems, amplified by the complexities and uncertainties associated with renewable energy sources and fluctuating demand, positions quantum computing as an indispensable tool. Notably, the algorithms introduced earlier which are designed for tackling optimization problems, offer a promising approach to resolving the intricacies of the UCP.

The selection of an appropriate algorithm for solving the UCP via quantum computing requires a meticulous evaluation of the available options, given the current landscape of quantum technology. While Quantum Annealing, Grover's Algorithm, and other quantum computing approaches such as the Variational Quantum Eigensolver (VQE) and the Quantum Approximate Optimization Algorithm (QAOA) present potential pathways, each comes with its unique set of challenges and limitations when applied to the UCP. Grover's Algorithm, for instance, is currently deemed impractical for most applications, and the current versions of VQE and QAOA, when tested against even simplified versions of the UCP, face difficulties due to the limited number of qubits, their connectivity, and issues related to error rates and coherence times on existing and established quantum hardware. Given that even basic toy examples of the UCP necessitate between 10 and 30 binary variables, these methods cannot be applied to UCP on innovative hardware with error-corrected qubits, as the number of available qubits does not allow benchmarking various problem sizes. Consequently, Quantum Annealing emerges as the selected approach for tackling the UCP within the realm of quantum computing. The availability of over 5,000 qubits on platforms such as D-Wave, coupled with their robust connectivity, offers a substantial advantage, making Quantum Annealing the most feasible option for addressing the UCP in the current quantum computing era.

Quantum Annealing, like other quantum algorithms, requires the problem at hand to be structured as a QUBO problem. While the generic transformation method presented in the Chapter on Quantum Optimization offers versatility, it is not without its drawbacks, notably the introduction of auxiliary qubits to model inequality constraints as penalty terms. Given the scarcity of qubits and the reality that even simplified examples of the UCP necessitate at least 10 variables, more efficient methodologies are warranted. For example, the minimum up time constraint in the formulation above would result in a quadratic penalty term:

$$\left(\sum_{\tau=t}^{t-1+U_{\min,i}} u_{\tau,i} + encod\left(s\right) - y_{i,\tau} \cdot U_{\min,i} \right)^2 ,$$

where we get additional variables (s) for the transformation from an inequality to an equality constraint and we need an all-to-all connectivity between all variables in that constraint. Since the input model for the quantum annealer is allowed to be quadratic and the UCP is traditionally modeled as a mixed-integer linear problem, a natural idea is to model UCP as a quadratic problem with quadratic constraints that can be easily transformed into an unconstrained problem. We follow the approach presented by Halffmann et al.[7] For example, the minimum up time constraint can be modeled as a quadratic constraint as follows:

$$\sum_{\tau=t}^{t-1+U_{\min,i}} y_{i,\tau} \cdot u_{i,\tau} = y_{i,\tau} \cdot U_{\min,i}.$$

It can be quickly checked that this constraint is an alternative formulation of the minimum up time constraint. This can be transformed into a penalty term by subtracting the right-hand side from the left-hand side. The full model looks like this:

$$\min \quad \sum_{t=1}^{T}\sum_{i=1}^{I} C_{start,i} \cdot y_{i,t} + C_{run,i} \cdot P_{\max,i} \cdot u_{i,t}$$

$$+ A \cdot \sum_{t=1}^{T}\sum_{i=1}^{I} \left(P_{\max,i} \cdot u_{i,t} - D_t \right)^2$$

$$+ B \cdot \sum_{t=1}^{T}\sum_{i=1}^{I} \left(u_{i,t} \cdot \left(1 - u_{i,t-1}\right) + 2 \cdot y_{i,t} \cdot \left(u_{i,t-1} + 1 - u_{i,t}\right) - y_{i,t} \right)$$

$$+ C \cdot \sum_{t=1}^{T}\sum_{i=1}^{I} \left(y_{t,i} \cdot U_{\min,i} - \sum_{\tau=t}^{t-1+U_{\min,i}} y_{t,i} \cdot u_{\tau,i} \right)$$

$$+ D \cdot \sum_{t=1}^{T}\sum_{i=1}^{I} \left(\sum_{\tau=t}^{t+D_{\min,i}} (y_{t,i} + u_{t-1,i} - u_{t,i}) \cdot u_{\tau,i} \right),$$

Note that we have omitted the power output variables here for educational purposes and assumed that if the power unit is on, it produces energy with maximal capacity. This approach has clear advantages: we need fewer variables, thus, fewer qubits, and less connectivity between qubits, since fewer quadratic terms occur. So larger problems can be solved by quantum computers with fewer qubits available, bringing us closer to practical relevant problem sizes. Furthermore, the quadratic penalty terms are designed such that they have an a priori known range of values, therefore, it is rather easy to set the penalty factors A to D in advance such that penalties are high enough to ensure the feasibility of the solution obtained while preventing that the original objective function is underrepresented. Here, of course, knowledge about the importance and the interplay between the constraints is necessary. However, good estimators for penalty factors can be found using Machine Learning (ML). Alternatively, iterative procedures, where the problem is solved and given an infeasible solution is found, the penalty factors are adjusted, have been introduced to quantum algorithms. This has been a major step toward customized modeling for quantum computing algorithms and hardware.

Setting realistic expectations for the performance gains achievable through quantum computing in solving the UCP is paramount. The nascent state of quantum technology, characterized by its limited qubit availability and connectivity, presents challenges that currently restrict the immediate realization of its full potential. However, the theoretical underpinnings of quantum computing—notably its parallel processing capabilities and the ability to explore multiple solutions simultaneously—hint at significant improvements in computation times and optimization accuracy for complex problems like the UCP. The model above has been tested on real hardware, the D-Wave Advantage System with over 5,500 qubits, and compared against a commercial solver (Gurobi) performed on standard personal computing hardware. Datasets from https://power-grid-lib.github.io/ with various numbers of units, 24 time steps have been transformed such that power units run with maximum capacity when turned on. Figure 2.3 shows the performance of D-Wave vs. Gurobi. Clearly, at first glance, these results are no advertisement for quantum computing. However, the majority of the running time is bound by the embedding, and the mapping of the QUBO onto the hardware-specific network architecture of qubits and their connections. This is in itself a hard problem and accounts for another 90% of the total running time of the D-Wave solver even though an iterative approach regarding the penalty factors has been chosen and the annealer has been used several times with the embedding from the first run. The time on the actual D-Wave quantum annealer is, besides a small overhead, only given by the annealing time which is in the range of microseconds. Unfortunately, the annealer was not fit to solve problems with more than 50 units, simply due to the number of qubits available. However, if we extrapolate the curve, it is likely that we do not have an exponential increase like the performance curve of Gurobi. Regarding the solution quality, we report that for a few power units, D-Wave can produce optimal or near-optimal solutions. However, for the largest problems around 50 units, the solution quality drastically decreases. In summary, these early experiments and simulations suggest that quantum computing could drastically reduce the time required to find optimal or near-optimal solutions to the UCP, especially as the technology matures and becomes more accessible.

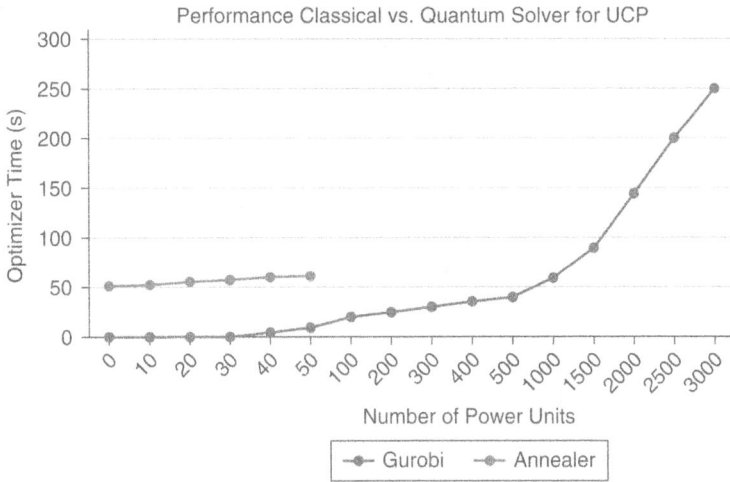

FIGURE 2.3 Comparison between the classical solver (Gurobi) and the quantum annealer (D-Wave) for instances of the UCP with 24 time steps and varying numbers of power units.

Until now, our focus has been primarily on a deterministic framework for the UCP, assuming both load profiles and renewable energy supplies are predictable and constant. However, the real-world scenario is fraught with uncertainties—electricity demand fluctuates subtly yet can be significantly influenced by foreseeable events (for instance, the surge during a major sports event like the FIFA World Cup). More unpredictably, solar power output is at the mercy of weather conditions, making it a challenge to forecast energy production reliably. The erratic movement of clouds, governed by the principles of chaos theory, adds layers of complexity to predicting the availability of solar energy.

Quantum computing presents unparalleled advantages in this realm, offering two distinct pathways to resilience: Firstly, it provides sophisticated tools for modeling and predicting weather-related variables, such as cloud cover, thereby enhancing the accuracy of solar power production estimates. This could be achieved by advanced QML algorithms, poised to revolutionize how we approach weather simulation and energy forecasting. Secondly, quantum computing introduces the possibility of solving robust optimization models that accommodate a spectrum of potential production outcomes rather than fixating on a singular, highly probable forecast. This approach not only acknowledges but harnesses the inherent uncertainty in renewable energy production, paving the way for more resilient and adaptive energy planning strategies.

Despite the recognized potential of quantum computing to transform our handling of uncertainty and stochastic parameters in energy systems, the exploration into this domain remains nascent. Pioneering works, such as the online learning framework proposed by Lim et al.,[8] illustrate the initial strides toward employing quantum computing for developing robust optimization solutions. However, these ventures are still in their infancy, underscoring a rich vein of opportunity yet to be fully mined. As the field progresses, leveraging the intrinsic stochasticity of quantum computing outputs could emerge as a key strategy for crafting solutions that inherently account for the unpredictability of renewable energy sources. The journey toward fully exploiting quantum computing's capabilities in this context is both promising and demanding, signifying a frontier ripe with potential for groundbreaking advancements in energy optimization.

2.2.2.2 Challenges and Outlook

As we navigate the promising frontier of quantum computing in the energy sector, particularly in addressing the UCP, it is crucial to recognize the challenges that lie ahead. Despite its potential to revolutionize energy optimization strategies, quantum computing is still in its infancy, and several hurdles must be surmounted to fully harness its capabilities.

One of the most significant challenges is the current state of quantum hardware. Quantum computers capable of solving complex optimization problems on a large scale are still under development. Improving qubit stability, error mitigation and correction, and coherence time are critical areas of ongoing research. Another challenge lies in the development of quantum algorithms themselves. While theoretical models have shown promise, translating these into practical, efficient algorithms that outperform their classical counterparts requires further innovation. In particular, classical state-of-the-art methods being crucial for the performance of classical approaches have barely been incorporated into quantum algorithms leaving room for directions of future research and performance gains.

Despite these challenges, the future of quantum computing in the energy sector is bright. Advancements in quantum hardware and algorithmic development are rapidly progressing, with significant investments from both the public and private sectors. As technology matures, we can anticipate a gradual transition from theoretical models to practical applications, where quantum computing plays a central role in optimizing energy production and grid management.

Furthermore, the advent of quantum computing promises not only to enhance the efficiency and sustainability of energy systems but also to drive innovations in other areas of the energy sector, such as new market strategies on the energy and electricity market (see Chapter 3) or material science for better energy storage solutions and improved solar cells. As we continue to push the boundaries of what is possible with quantum technology, the energy sector stands on the brink of a new era of optimization and innovation. In conclusion, while challenges remain, the potential of quantum computing to transform the energy sector is undeniable. Continued research, investment, and interdisciplinary collaboration are key to overcoming these hurdles and unlocking the full promise of quantum computing for energy optimization and beyond.

2.2.3 ENHANCING PORTFOLIO OPTIMIZATION WITH QUANTUM COMPUTING

Portfolio optimization is a critical concept in the realm of finance, central to constructing investment strategies that aim to maximize returns while managing risk. This process is vital for individual investors, fund managers, and financial institutions alike, as it informs the decision-making process regarding asset allocation and portfolio diversification. The essence of portfolio optimization lies in finding the most efficient combination of assets that aligns with an investor's risk tolerance, investment horizon, and financial goals.

The foundation of portfolio optimization is Modern Portfolio Theory (MPT), introduced by Harry Markowitz in the 1950s.[9,10] MPT revolutionized investment strategy through the introduction of quantifiable measures for risk and the correlation between assets. We refer to Elton et al.[11] for an overview of MPT. Markowitz's key insight was that a portfolio's risk and return characteristics should not be assessed by looking at individual assets in isolation but by considering how each asset's price movements relate to every other asset in the portfolio. This theory introduced the concepts of diversification, the risk-return trade-off, and the Efficient Frontier—a graphical representation of the most efficient portfolios offering the highest expected return for a given level of risk or the lowest risk for a given level of expected return.

The importance of portfolio optimization cannot be overstated.

In an ever-changing financial landscape marked by market volatility, economic shifts, and global events, the ability to construct resilient and efficient portfolios is indispensable. Portfolio optimization provides a structured framework to evaluate and manage investment risk, capitalize on diversification benefits, and systematically pursue optimal asset allocation strategies. This framework aids investors in making informed decisions that align with their financial objectives, whether it's capital preservation, growth, income, or a balanced approach. The prospects of applying portfolio optimization extend far beyond traditional asset management, such as real-time data analysis, advanced risk modeling, and the exploration of complex investment strategies. Furthermore, as financial markets evolve and new asset classes emerge, portfolio optimization remains a dynamic tool, continuously adapting to incorporate innovations in computational finance, data analytics, ML, and optimization.

The Markowitz portfolio optimization problem introduces a framework for constructing investment portfolios that efficiently balance risk and return. At its core, this mean-variance optimization model seeks to mathematically formulate the process of selecting the optimal mix of assets for an investment portfolio that efficiently balances risk and return. Harry Markowitz introduced this problem in his seminal work on MPT,[12] laying the foundation for what would become a pivotal framework in the field of finance and investment management. The optimization problem considers the returns of the assets as random variables, characterized by their expected returns and the covariance of their returns, which measures the degree to which the assets' returns move together. By optimizing the weights of the assets in the portfolio, investors can achieve diversification, reducing the overall risk of the portfolio without sacrificing potential returns.

The optimization problem in the mean-risk model is formulated as follows, incorporating a risk aversion coefficient to balance the trade-off between risk and return:

Objective:

$$\text{maximize } w^T R - \lambda \cdot w^T \sum w$$

Subject to:

$$\sum_{i=1}^{n} w_i = B,$$

$$w_i \geq 0, \text{ for all } i = 1, \dots, n.$$

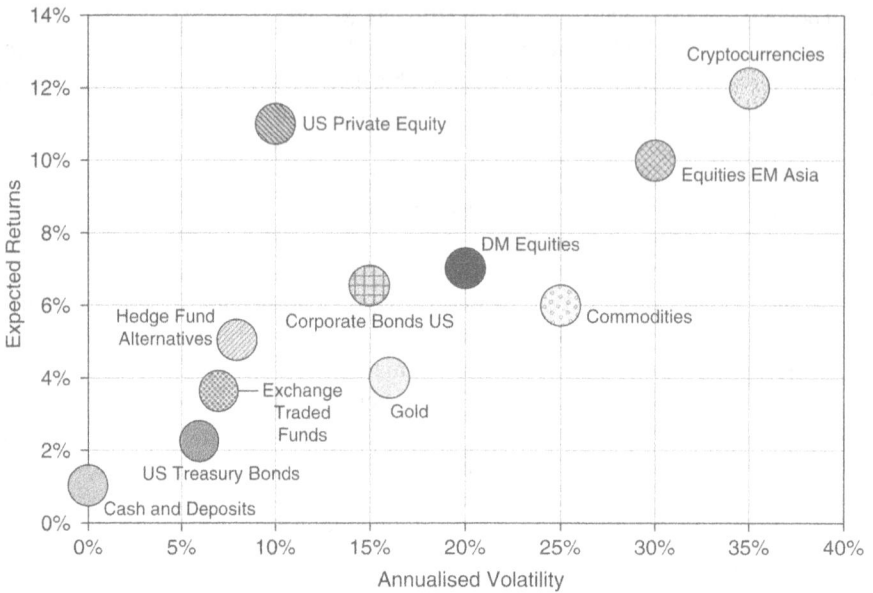

FIGURE 2.4 Exemplary asset visualized by their annualized volatility and expected return.

where w is the vector of asset weights in the portfolio, R is the vector of expected returns for each asset, Σ is the covariance matrix of asset returns, λ is the risk aversion coefficient, with higher values indicating a greater aversion to risk, B is the given budget that has to be spent, and n is the number of assets in the portfolio.

Figure 2.4 gives exemplary asset data for such a portfolio optimization problem.

The objective function consists of two parts: $w^T R$, the expected return of the portfolio, which is to be maximized, and $\lambda \cdot w^T \Sigma \, w$, the penalized term for portfolio variance (risk), which is to be minimized. The parameter λ allows investors to adjust the model according to their risk tolerance: a higher λ places more emphasis on minimizing risk, while a lower λ allows for greater risk in pursuit of higher returns. The constraint $\Sigma_{i=1}^{n} \, w_i = B$ ensures that the sum of the asset weights equals B, indicating that the entire budget is allocated. The non-negativity constraint on the weights w indicates that short selling is not permitted. An example of the outcome of the portfolio optimization problem is given in Figure 2.5.

Over the past decades, there has been considerable evolution and expansion in portfolio optimization techniques. Researchers and practitioners have developed numerous variants and extensions of the original model, aiming to address its limitations, adapt to changing financial landscapes, and incorporate advancements in financial theory and computational methods. These developments reflect the growing complexity of global financial markets, the emergence of new types of financial instruments, and a deeper understanding of investor behavior and risk factors beyond variance.

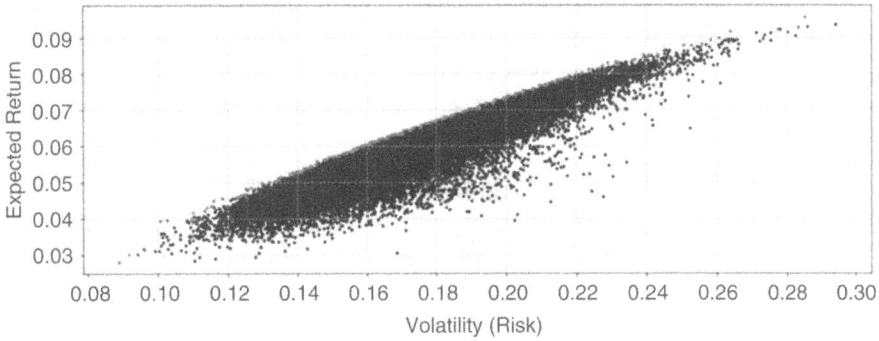

FIGURE 2.5 Visualization of portfolios by their volatility and expected return. The red dots indicate efficient portfolios, that is, there is no other portfolio that has both a smaller volatility and a higher return. These efficient portfolios can be found by varying the risk aversion coefficient λ.

Notable variants of the Markowitz model include:

- *Black-Litterman Model:* Integrates investor views with market equilibrium returns to overcome some of the sensitivity issues in the Markowitz model to input changes.
- *Multi-Factor Models:* Incorporate multiple risk factors, such as conditional Value-at-Risk (CVaR), momentum, liquidity, and dividend yield, to better capture the multifaceted nature of risk and return.
- *Copula-Based Models:* Use copulas to model the dependency structure between asset returns, allowing for more accurate risk assessment in portfolios.
- *Stochastic Programming and Robust Optimization Models:* Introduce randomness in the optimization process, hedge against model misspecification and parameter uncertainty, offering solutions, i.e., that are less sensitive to changes in assumptions.

Additionally, there exist various extensions that can be incorporated into portfolio optimization models such as:

- *Portfolio Optimization over Time:* Introduce a time component and examine the performance over a time horizon with either discrete trading time points or continuous trading.
- *Market Restrictions and Asset Properties:* Take market influences and special properties of assets (e.g., bonds) into account.
- *Regulatory and Accounting Requirements:* Add Solvency Capital Requirement (SCR) and International Financial Reporting Standard (IFRS) objectives or constraints.

These variants and extensions exemplify the ongoing effort to refine portfolio optimization methodologies, making them more relevant and applicable to the diverse needs of investors and the dynamic nature of financial markets. They demonstrate the adaptability of the foundational principles laid out by Markowitz, as well as the continued relevance of portfolio optimization in financial decision-making and theory. We refer to Best and Fabozzi[13] and Korn and Korn[14] for an overview of portfolio optimization models and best practices.

2.2.3.1 Quantum Portfolio Optimization

Quantum finance is an emerging field that stands at the crossroads of quantum computing and financial theory, aiming to leverage the principles of quantum mechanics to solve complex financial problems more efficiently than classical computing methods. This innovative discipline seeks to apply quantum algorithms and quantum computational techniques to various aspects of finance, including option pricing, portfolio optimization, risk management, and algorithmic trading. As outlined in a comprehensive review by Herman et al.,[15] quantum finance is poised to revolutionize the way financial markets operate, offering potentially faster and more accurate computations for financial modeling, derivative pricing, and risk assessment tasks that are notoriously difficult for classical computers to handle efficiently.

One of the key areas where quantum finance shows promise is in the realm of derivative pricing, particularly in the application of quantum algorithms for speeding up the Monte Carlo simulations used extensively in options pricing and risk analysis. These simulations, critical for assessing the value of financial derivatives under various market scenarios, can be computationally intensive and time-consuming with classical methods. Moreover, quantum finance is investigating the potential for QML algorithms to predict financial market trends and for quantum encryption to enhance cybersecurity in financial transactions. The integration of quantum computing into finance could thus not only improve computational tasks but also offer new methodologies for financial analysis and the development of innovative financial products and services. Quantum finance also explores the optimization of financial portfolios, where quantum algorithms could solve the Markowitz portfolio optimization problem more efficiently, especially as the number of assets grows large. This could enable investors to find the optimal asset mix with greater speed and precision, taking into account complex constraints and the nonlinear dynamics of financial markets.

The classical Markowitz portfolio optimization model has played a pivotal role as a benchmark problem in the exploration and testing of various optimization algorithms, including cutting-edge quantum computing techniques such as the VQE, QAOA, Grover's algorithm, and Quantum Walks. The model's popularity in these contexts is largely attributed to its straightforward yet quadratic structure, which provides a clear and manageable framework for evaluating the efficacy of optimization algorithms in handling complex financial problems. This quadratic nature of the Markowitz model, encompassing a quadratic objective function (portfolio variance) subject to linear constraints (such as budget constraints), allows for efficient exploration of the trade-offs between risk and return in portfolio selection.

As many quantum optimization algorithms require a quadratic unconstrained optimization (QUBO) model as input, it is rather simplistic to transform the Markowitz model to a QUBO if we restrict ourselves to 0/1 portfolio weights:

$$\text{maximize } w^T R - \lambda \cdot w^T \sum w - p \cdot \left(\sum_{i=1}^{n} w_i - B \right)^2,$$

where p is a penalty factor for the budget constraint. This QUBO can be solved via variational algorithms (VQE, QAOA) or quantum annealing. We refer to the chapter about an overview of quantum optimization algorithms and how to apply these.

Despite its utility in testing advanced quantum and classical optimization algorithms, it is crucial to note that the classical Markowitz portfolio optimization problem, in its basic form, is not categorized as NP-hard. The problem can be efficiently solved using classical algorithms, particularly quadratic programming techniques, thanks to its convex quadratic objective function and linear constraints. This efficiency arises because, for convex optimization problems, any local minimum is also a global minimum, enabling straightforward and reliable solutions. The scenario changes, however, when additional complexities are introduced into the Markowitz model, such as integer constraints (e.g., integer number of shares), cardinality constraints (limiting the number of assets in the portfolio), or transaction costs. These modifications can transform the portfolio optimization problem into a Mixed-Integer Quadratic Programming (MIQP) problem or a non-convex optimization problem, at which point the problem may become NP-hard, which is significantly more challenging to solve as computational resources and time required expand exponentially with increasing problem size.

In recent years, significant strides have been made in applying quantum computing techniques to portfolio optimization, demonstrating potential advantages over classical computing approaches, particularly in solving large-scale and complex optimization problems more efficiently. One of the landmark achievements in quantum portfolio optimization was presented by Rebentrost and Lloyd[16] in their work on applying quantum computing to financial problems, including portfolio optimization. They showcased the practical application of quantum algorithms both in the preparation of asset data for portfolio optimization as well as solving the optimization problem itself for a small number of assets, paving the way for future research on scaling these methods.

Building on these foundations, recent studies have demonstrated the capability of quantum computers to solve portfolio optimization problems with an increasing number of assets. For instance, Buonaiuto et al.[17] illustrated the application of quantum computing to solve a portfolio optimization problem involving up to 52 assets, marking a significant step forward in terms of problem size and complexity that can be addressed using quantum techniques. This work highlights not only the potential for scaling quantum portfolio optimization to more realistic market scenarios but also the practical challenges that need to be overcome, such as error rates and qubit connectivity.

Moreover, Egger et al.[18] provide a comprehensive overview of the current state and potential future applications of quantum computing within the finance sector. The chapter delves into the computationally challenging problems that arise in various aspects of financial services, including asset management, investment banking, and retail and corporate banking, highlighting how quantum computing could revolutionize problem-solving in these areas. A view on the active research into demonstrating Quantum Advantage in finance is given. The chapter serves as both an introduction to quantum computing for finance professionals and a survey of financial problem classes where quantum computing could offer significant improvements over classical computational methods. The authors categorize quantum algorithms based on the types of financial problems they solve—simulation, optimization, and ML—and map these to specific financial applications. Demonstrations of quantum algorithms on IBM Quantum back-ends are included, illustrating potential benefits for financial services.

These success stories in quantum portfolio optimization represent crucial steps toward realizing the practical benefits of quantum computing in finance. Although current quantum computers are in the early stages of development, and many challenges remain that must be addressed to fully realize their potential, the progress made thus far is promising.

One of the primary hurdles is the current limitation on the number of qubits available in quantum computers, which constrains the size and complexity of portfolio optimization problems that can be effectively solved. The scalability issue is crucial because financial markets often involve optimizing portfolios with hundreds or thousands of assets, requiring a quantum computational capacity that exceeds today's capabilities.

Another challenge lies in the error rates and noise inherent in current quantum computing systems, known as Noisy Intermediate-Scale Quantum (NISQ) devices. These errors can significantly impact the accuracy and reliability of the solutions to optimization problems, necessitating the development of sophisticated error correction and mitigation techniques to ensure that quantum computing can be practically applied to financial decision-making.

Additionally, there is a need for more development in quantum algorithms that can efficiently solve portfolio optimization problems. While algorithms like VQE, QAOA, and quantum annealing have shown promise, optimizing their performance for specific financial applications and ensuring they can outperform classical algorithms in real-world scenarios is a challenge that requires ongoing research and experimentation. Furthermore, the translation of traditional portfolio optimization models into formats suitable for quantum computing, such as QUBO formulations, introduces approximations and discretizations that may affect the fidelity of the solutions.

Lastly, the integration of quantum computing solutions into the existing financial infrastructure poses both technical and regulatory challenges. Financial institutions will need to adapt their systems and processes to incorporate quantum computing capabilities, and there will be a learning curve for practitioners to understand and trust these new tools.

2.2.3.2 Machine Learning for Improved QUBO-Formulation with Incorporation of Solvency II

Building upon the foundational insights into quantum computing's potential to transform finance, it becomes evident that while the classical Markowitz portfolio optimization problem offers valuable theoretical insights, its practical implications in today's financial landscape are somewhat limited. Traditional optimization techniques, leveraging classical computational resources, suffice for solving the standard Markowitz model efficiently. However, the financial industry's evolving complexity demands more sophisticated models that align closely with practical scenarios, stretching beyond the capabilities of conventional methods. A pertinent example of such complexity is observed within the insurance sector, especially for companies operating under the stringent regulatory frameworks of the European Union. These companies are mandated to calculate the Solvency Capital Requirement (SCR),[19] a critical metric designed to ensure that insurance firms maintain adequate capital to cover risks under adverse scenarios. The SCR calculation is notoriously intricate, relying on extensive simulations that are both time-consuming, often spanning days, and computationally demanding. The challenge is further compounded by the fact that even the approximation functions for SCR are far from straightforward, eschewing simple quadratic formulations for more complex mathematical representations.

This backdrop raises a crucial question: how can one devise a QUBO formulation for scenarios like the SCR calculation, where the problem at hand deviates significantly from the quadratic nature inherent in traditional portfolio optimization problems? Addressing this question is not just an academic exercise but a necessary exploration to harness quantum computing's power in providing efficient, scalable solutions for complex, real-world financial challenges. We delve into this discussion by showcasing the approach presented by Turkalj et al.[20] that utilizes ML to obtain a quadratic function to approximate the SCR.

The SCR is a critical metric mandated by regulatory authorities to ensure that insurance companies maintain sufficient capital reserves to cover their liabilities and mitigate the risk of insolvency. This requirement is a cornerstone of the insurance business model, which revolves around collecting premiums, investing them safely, and ensuring enough capital is on hand to meet future claims. Unlike hedge funds or investment banks that might pursue aggressive portfolio optimization strategies for maximum returns, insurance companies must navigate the delicate balance of optimizing their investment portfolios while adhering to stringent capital requirements to protect policyholders.

While the specific details and calculation methodologies for SCR can vary based on regulatory frameworks (such as Solvency II in the European Union), the key risk components typically include:

- *Market Risk*: Covers losses from fluctuations in market prices, including interest rates, equity prices, property values, and currency exchange rates.
- *Credit Risk*: Addresses losses that may arise from the default of counterparties or debtors, affecting the value of investments, receivables, and other financial assets.

- *Life Underwriting Risk*: Pertains to risks associated with life insurance obligations, such as mortality, longevity, and morbidity risks, impacting the cost of insurance claims.
- *Non-Life Underwriting Risk*: Relates to risks in non-life insurance lines (e.g., property, casualty), including premium and reserve risks associated with the cost of claims and the adequacy of premiums and reserves.
- *Health Underwriting Risk*: Involves risks specific to health insurance, encompassing similar aspects to life and non-life risks but tailored to health-related insurance products.
- *Operational Risk*: Concerns losses stemming from inadequate or failed internal processes, people, systems, or external events.
- *Liquidity Risk*: The risk that the insurance company will not be able to meet its financial obligations as they fall due without incurring unacceptable losses.
- *Concentration Risk*: Arises from an undue concentration of exposures to a particular risk source, leading to a potentially significant loss.

Notably, even the methodologies deployed for estimating just the market risk for SCR are rather complex as different types of risks (stock risk, interest risk, spread risk, real estate risk, currency risk) have to be computed and aggregated. First these net risks have to be calculated and aggregated by a nonlinear function $f_{\text{aggregation}}(f_{\text{netrisk}}(w))$ for given portfolio weights w. The result is used to calculate the net market risk

$$f_{\text{market}}(x) = \sqrt{\max\left(x^T P_{\text{market}}(0)x, x^T P_{\text{market}}(1/2)x\right) + const^2}.$$

After adjusting the net market risk with constant risks $c_1,\ldots,c_5$ $f_{\text{constantrisks}}(x) = \sqrt{x^2 + c_3 x + c_4} + c_5$ we obtain the market risk part of the SCR:

$$f_{\text{SCRmarket}}(w) = f_{\text{constantrisks}}\left(f_{\text{market}}\left(f_{\text{aggregation}}\left(f_{\text{netrisk}}(\omega)\right)\right)\right).$$

Clearly, this function is not quadratic and provides extraordinary hurdles for the transformation to a quadratic function due to the presence of roots and maxima.

QML and ML offer a potent avenue for approximating such complex functions. The application of ML in this context involves generating a dataset from known portfolio weights to the corresponding SCR values. By learning from this data, QML algorithms can identify patterns and infer a mapping from portfolio weights to the SCR, essentially extracting the unknown SCR function from the known data. Classical ML techniques, particularly least squares regression models, have been utilized to approximate the SCR function by a quadratic function, facilitating its integration into the mean-variance analysis framework and enabling a QUBO formulation for portfolio optimization. The objective of using ML for SCR approximation is twofold. Firstly, it serves to simplify the SCR function into a quadratic form, which aligns with the requirements of QUBO models. Secondly, once the approximation model is trained, typically using techniques like back-propagation and evaluating its accuracy through metrics, it allows for the prediction of SCR values given new sets of portfolio weights. QML could further enhance this process by utilizing quantum algorithms for regression, potentially achieving more accurate approximations of the SCR function due to the quantum speedup.

The result is a quantum-ready QUBO formulation that incorporates a practical aspect of financial regulation, with only marginal training and validation error, thus, providing a compelling approximation of the SCR. This approach underlines the synergy between ML—quantum or classical—and financial regulation, heralding a new era where complex regulatory requirements like the SCR can be seamlessly incorporated into quantum finance frameworks.

2.3 THE ROLE OF QUANTUM COMPUTING IN SUSTAINABILITY

As we stand at the confluence of technological advancement and environmental urgency, it has never been more crucial to align our technological explorations with a strongly rooted commitment to fostering sustainability. In 1987, the United Nations Brundtland Commission defined sustainability as "meeting the needs of the present without compromising the ability of future generations to meet their own needs."[21] Today, the health of our planet hangs in the balance as we struggle with climate change, excessive greenhouse gas emissions, depletion of natural resources, biodiversity loss, and a myriad of other environmental challenges.

These pressing environmental concerns, underscored by the United Nations' Sustainable Development Goals, present a considerable risk to ecosystems worldwide but also a clear opportunity for transformative change toward a more sustainable future. In this context, the stakes are high for our species. The quality of our lives, the health of our societies, and the development of our economies over the coming decades depend heavily on how effectively we can address these persistent environmental challenges.

Quantum computing emerges as an exciting paradigm in this scenario. With its revolutionary features, it holds a unique potential to tackle some of the most significant and computationally demanding problems that currently impede progress in environmental sciences and sustainability. Quantum computers, unlike their classical counterparts, intentionally leverage the principles of quantum physics. Their power originates from their use of quantum bits, or qubits, which, unlike classical bits, can exist in multiple states simultaneously. This ability could lead us to an exponential increase in computational power, which can help in solving complex problems with extraordinary efficiency.

The potential impact of quantum computing on sustainability is multifaceted. It promises to accelerate the pursuit of Environmental, Social, and Governance (ESG) goals, which are becoming increasingly central to the agendas of organizations and governments worldwide. Firstly, quantum computing could potentially provide high-impact, innovative solutions aimed at accelerating progress toward sustainable development goals. It can tackle some of the most challenging computational tasks such as climate modeling, renewable energy optimization, efficient resource allocation, and many more. The increase in computational speed and enhanced problem-solving capabilities promised by quantum computing could lead to significant advancements in our journey toward sustainability. Some studies, like Nammouchi 2023,[22] provide a review of how quantum computing, and QML in particular, can help in addressing complex challenges in climate change and sustainability. This includes applications such as decarbonization, data forecasting, climate monitoring, and hazard prediction. Other works, like Ajagekar 2022,[23] delve deeper into how Quantum Artificial Intelligence can assist in predicting renewable energy production and optimizing energy systems. Additionally, Quantum Chemistry and quantum algorithms like the VQE can be used to design climate-friendly materials. These range from catalysts for water treatment to photovoltaic materials and electrocatalysts in energy storage devices.

Another promising aspect of quantum computing lies in its potential energy efficiency. Today's classical supercomputers, tackling computational tasks of high complexity, can consume vast amounts of energy and take years or even decades to reach a solution. In contrast, quantum computers, with their processing capabilities, could perform these tasks in drastically shorter timeframes, and with less hardware than what would be required if only classical computing were available, effectively reducing the resources needed to solve these tasks.

The role of quantum computing in sustainability represents a nascent yet exciting crossroads of technology and environmental stewardship. The wealth of opportunities it promises to accelerate our journey toward a sustainable future is vast. However, realizing this potential fully and responsibly necessitates a delicate balance between leveraging its strengths and mindfully addressing the potential risks and challenges linked to its development and deployment.

Quantum computing, like any transformative technology, must be developed and utilized thoughtfully and ethically. As we delve deeper into the world of quantum computing, this balanced perspective will guide us in harnessing its potential while staying true to our obligations toward sustainability.

In the following sections, we delve into the applications of quantum computing in decarbonization, optimized resource allocation, and forecasting weather phenomena. These prime examples will provide in-depth insight into how quantum computing could potentially act as a catalyst in humanity's efforts toward sustainability.

2.3.1 QUANTUM COMPUTING IN DECARBONIZATION

As we assert our commitment to achieving a sustainable future, the concept of decarbonization emerges as a key goal in this collective endeavor. Decarbonization refers to the process of lowering the emission of greenhouse gases, particularly carbon dioxide. It represents a fundamental strategy toward combating climate change and achieving sustainable development. The journey of decarbonization involves brave efforts to transition away from fossil fuels and carbon-intensive energy sources toward renewable and clean energy alternatives. It also encompasses the adoption of energy-efficient technologies and the development of sustainable practices across sectors, including manufacturing, transport, and agriculture.

On the environmental front, it can significantly mitigate climate change effects, lower air pollution, protect biodiversity, and conserve natural resources and the delicate balance of our ecosystems. Economically, it can generate new market opportunities, stimulate green growth, and enhance energy long-term security. Simultaneously, decarbonization can promote social equity by improving public health, creating new jobs, and fostering sustainable communities.

The road to decarbonization, however, is paved with considerable challenges. Key focus areas include enhancing energy efficiency, transitioning to renewable energy, developing cleaner fuels, and deploying carbon capture, storage, and utilization technologies. Each of these domains presents its own set of complex problems—be it technological constraints, economic viability, policy regulations, or social acceptance.

This is where quantum computing, as other emerging technologies, could play a pivotal role. With its immense computational power and ability to solve complex problems, quantum computing might emerge as a potent tool to propel decarbonization efforts. But why is quantum computing relevant in this context?

At its core, decarbonization is a problem of optimization. It involves optimizing energy use, resource allocation, and technological deployment to reduce carbon emissions, all while ensuring the least disruption to economic progress and social well-being. Quantum computing excels at solving optimization problems. It promises to handle large datasets and execute processes in a fraction of the time that classical computers would require, making it uniquely suited to advance decarbonization initiatives in the future.

QML has also shown great potential for decarbonization initiatives. In Cao 2023,[24] the authors use a linear-layer-enhanced Quantum Long Short-Term Memory (L-QLSTM) model to forecast carbon prices, an approach that could help identify opportunities where the transition to renewable alternatives is already economically advantageous.

Quantum simulations, another significant aspect of quantum computing, can help develop new materials that enhance energy efficiency and assist in carbon capture and storage. Analysis and optimization of these materials are computationally demanding tasks and typically beyond the reach of classical computers, but could one day be well within the capabilities of quantum computers.

In conclusion, quantum computing has the potential to be a significant catalyst in advancing decarbonization efforts. By accelerating solutions, enhancing efficiency, and providing deeper insights into complex problems, it may one day push the boundaries of what is achievable in our pursuit of a carbon-neutral future. As quantum technologies continue to evolve, their role in decarbonization is likely to expand, driving innovation and development in ways that bring us closer to our sustainability goals.

2.3.2 OPTIMIZED RESOURCE ALLOCATION USING QUANTUM COMPUTING

In an era defined by growing concerns about climate change, conserving resources, and sustainability, resource management has become more critical than ever. The need for optimized resource allocation, that is, using resources efficiently while minimizing waste, forms an essential pillar of sustainability.

Resource allocation involves distributing available resources in a manner that maximizes productivity while minimizing waste. On an organizational level, the resources in question could be anything from the workforce, production capacity, and facilities to finances. From a larger sustainability standpoint, this could extend to natural resources like water, land, and minerals, or renewable and non-renewable energy sources.

Effective resource allocation can have significant economic, social, and environmental impacts. Economically, it allows organizations to maximize their productivity and competitiveness. Socially, it generates jobs, supports communities, and drives sustainable economic growth. Environmentally, optimal resource usage can result in significant reductions in waste generation and carbon emissions, contribute to conservation efforts, and support climate change mitigation.

However, resource allocation is often a highly complex task. It generally involves balancing multiple variables and considerations such as availability, demand, cost, and environmental impact. Solving such multifaceted problems usually means dealing with a combinatorial explosion of possibilities that can be too computationally intensive for classical computers.

Quantum computing stands as a promising tool that could effectively address complex resource allocation challenges in the future. Its immense potential processing power, combined with the ability to explore multiple solutions at once, makes it particularly well-suited to handle optimization problems and enable better decision-making. Quantum computing has the potential to revolutionize how we approach, analyze, and solve resource allocation problems, ultimately contributing to a more sustainable approach to resource management. It represents a groundbreaking paradigm shift in our ability to optimize complex systems swiftly and efficiently.

Additionally, QML, where quantum computers are used to improve the efficiency and accuracy of ML models, could be leveraged for dynamic and adaptive resource allocation. ML can analyze vast amounts of data to identify complex patterns and trends, forecast future demand, and make real-time adjustments, which can significantly enhance resource allocation strategies. Quantum simulations could also aid in resource allocation. For example, they might be used to model and predict the behavior of complex systems such as energy grids, transport networks, or supply chains. Through these simulations, we can explore different scenarios, test strategies, and identify the most efficient and sustainable resource allocation solutions.

In conclusion, the advent of quantum computing could bring us closer to a new realm of opportunities for optimizing resource allocation toward a more sustainable future. While the full potential of this technology is yet to be realized, its capabilities in accelerating solutions, enhancing efficiency, and providing deeper insights into complex decision-making scenarios could be truly transformative in the future. As quantum technologies continue to evolve, their role in sustainable resource management is likely to broaden and deepen, fueling sustainable innovation and shaping a more resource-efficient future. The judicious and ethical use of quantum computing, integrated with a practical understanding of its potential and limitations, will be central to this journey toward optimized resource allocation and a sustainable future.

2.3.3 Forecasting Weather Phenomenon with Quantum Computing

Climate change and its associated impacts present one of the most pressing challenges of our time, with weather patterns and climate phenomena becoming increasingly erratic and extreme. Accurate weather forecasting and modeling of climate phenomena are thus of paramount importance in our journey toward a sustainable future and are crucial for mitigating the impact of climate change, managing resources efficiently, and safeguarding lives and livelihoods.

Weather forecasting involves predicting atmospheric conditions at a specific location over a period of time. It hinges upon the processing and interpretation of vast amounts of data from multiple sources, including weather satellites, ground observations, and ocean buoys, among others. The complexity increases manifold as we move from weather forecasting to climate modeling, which entails predicting long-term patterns of temperature, precipitation, wind, and other aspects of the Earth's climate system.

Weather forecasting and climate prediction are severely constrained by the computational limitations of classical computers. These tasks involve computations of enormous scale and proportion due to the sheer volume of data involved and the complexity of the Earth's atmosphere. Given these challenges, it's clear that we need powerful computational tools to enhance the accuracy and efficiency of weather forecasting and climate prediction.

Enter quantum computing. While the quantum computers required to even consider these challenges are still years or even decades away, their ability to hold, manipulate, and process vast amounts of data simultaneously could present a new avenue for advancing the field of weather forecasting and climate modeling in the future.

For instance, in the realm of weather forecasting, quantum computing could one day help predict severe weather events more accurately, thus providing crucial lead times for communities to safeguard against potential catastrophic events. Detailed insights into precipitation patterns, storm trajectories, and weather extremities could support preemptive action, reducing damage and saving lives.

When it comes to climate modeling, quantum computing could aid in extensively simulating and quantifying the impacts of various factors. These include greenhouse gas emissions, polar ice melts, and deforestation on long-term climate dynamics. Some studies have already begun exploring specific use cases. Take Senekane 2016,[25] for example, where the authors employ a Quantum Support Vector Machine algorithm and data from the Digital Technology Group (DTG) weather Station at the University of Cambridge to predict solar irradiation. Similar studies could guide policymaking and the development of strategies to combat climate change, thus contributing more effectively to sustainable development goals.

In conclusion, quantum computing presents revolutionary possibilities for improving weather forecasting and climate modeling, thereby enabling more informed decision-making in our fight against climate change. By leveraging the vast computational abilities of quantum computing, we can enhance our understanding of climate dynamics, devise efficient mitigation strategies, and move closer to a sustainable future. As we journey forward, sustainability should remain a guiding principle, aligning technological progress with a commitment toward an environmentally secure future.

2.3.4 FUTURE DIRECTIONS IN QUANTUM COMPUTING FOR SUSTAINABILITY

Looking ahead, the potential of quantum computing in environmental sciences and sustainability is vast and promising, as more and more use cases are identified.

As this field of technology continues to evolve and mature, its role in accelerating sustainable development and addressing climate change will become more pronounced. The potential of quantum computing hinges on its ability to tackle complex problems, from simulating intricate environmental systems to predicting climate dynamics with remarkable speed and accuracy.

For quantum computing to truly make an impact on sustainability, we need to address and overcome several technical and logistical challenges. These range from enhancing the stability and coherence of qubits, making quantum computers more reliable and robust—a crucial step toward ensuring their broader application in environmental sciences and other relevant fields, increasing the energy efficiency of quantum computers, and fine-tuning quantum algorithms for tackling optimization and other complex issues endemic to sustainability planning and management, but also to other areas.

From a societal perspective, achieving a "quantum-ready" status is not just about technical advancements. It requires building a quantum-literate workforce and fostering public awareness and understanding of quantum technologies. This education and awareness are critical to cultivating broad support for quantum technologies, addressing potential ethical and security concerns, and ensuring that the development and deployment of quantum computing are aligned with societal values and aspirations.

Moreover, collaborations play a critical role. Collaborative efforts among government, academia, and industry are necessary to pool resources, share expertise, and drive innovation in quantum computing for sustainability. Funding and governmental support can accelerate quantum research and development, while partnerships with industry can facilitate the practical application of quantum solutions in real-world sustainability challenges.

Lastly, it is crucial to keep sustainability at the forefront as we develop and deploy quantum technologies. Every step of the quantum journey, from research and development to commercialization and implementation, should be underpinned by a sustainability-focused ethos. This means consciously designing and selecting quantum technologies and applications that maximize positive environmental impact, minimize resource consumption, and contribute meaningfully to sustainability goals.

In conclusion, the future and potential of quantum computing for sustainability are vast and exciting, opening up unprecedented possibilities for accelerating our path to a sustainable future. As we venture further into this paradigm-shifting domain, it is essential to remember that the end goal is not just technological progress, but the creation of a more sustainable and resilient world. Quantum computing may represent a powerful tool in our arsenal for achieving this globe-embracing goal, bringing us a step closer to bridging the gap between our present challenges and future aspirations for a truly sustainable world.

2.4 CONCLUSION

Quantum computing, poised to revolutionize sectors such as energy and financial services, offers transformative solutions for complex optimization challenges and advanced analytical tasks. This chapter illustrated how quantum computing can significantly impact sectors such as energy and financial services by providing advanced solutions to complex optimization and analytical challenges. The ability of quantum computing to enhance energy forecasting, optimize energy production, and improve financial risk management underscores its transformative potential. Despite hurdles like high costs and integration challenges with classical systems, the strategic preparation and adoption of quantum technologies are essential for leveraging its capabilities. As we approach the quantum era, embracing these advancements will drive innovation, resilience, and sustainable progress across diverse industries.

REFERENCES

1. https://arxiv.org/abs/2106.10819
2. Kallrath, J., Pardalos, P. M., Rebennack, S., & Scheidt, M. (2009). In J. Kallrath, P. M. Pardalos, S. Rebennack, & M. Scheidt (Eds.), Energy Systems. Springer Berlin Heidelberg. https://doi.org/10.1007/978-3-540-88965-6
3. Padhy, N. P. (2004). Unit Commitment—A Bibliographical Survey. In IEEE Transactions on Power Systems (Vol. 19, Issue 2, pp. 1196–1205). Institute of Electrical and Electronics Engineers (IEEE). https://doi.org/10.1109/tpwrs.2003.821611
4. Depending on its type there are specific time constraints for power plants. When switched on, they need to run a minimum up time and similarly, when they are switched off, they need to keep in that state for a minimum down time.
5. Knueven, B., Ostrowski, J., & Watson, J.-P. (2020). On Mixed-Integer Programming Formulations for the Unit Commitment Problem. In INFORMS Journal on Computing. Institute for Operations Research and the Management Sciences (INFORMS). https://doi.org/10.1287/ijoc.2019.0944
6. https://power-grid-lib.github.io/
7. Halffmann, P., Holzer, P., Plociennik, K., & Trebing, M. (2023). A Quantum Computing Approach for the Unit Commitment Problem. In Lecture Notes in Operations Research (pp. 113–120). Springer International Publishing. https://doi.org/10.1007/978-3-031-24907-5_14
8. Lim, D., Doriguello, J. F., & Rebentrost, P. (2023). Quantum algorithm for robust optimization via stochastic-gradient online learning (Version 1). arXiv. https://doi.org/10.48550/ARXIV.2304.02262
9. Markowitz, H. (1952). Portfolio Selection. In The Journal of Finance (Vol. 7, Issue 1, p. 77). JSTOR. https://doi.org/10.2307/2975974
10. Markowitz, H. (1959). Portfolio Selection: Efficient Diversification of Investments. John Wiley & Sons.
11. Elton, E. J., Gruber, M. J., Brown, S. J., & Goetzmann, W. N. (2014, January 21). Modern Portfolio Theory and Investment Analysis. John Wiley & Sons.
12. See Note 8.
13. Best, M. J., & Fabozzi, F. J. (2021). Quantitative Portfolio Management: The Art of the Right Mix. John Wiley & Sons.
14. Korn, R., & Korn, E. (2000). Options Pricing and Portfolio Optimization: Modern Methods of Financial Mathematics (R. Korn, Trans.). American Mathematical Society.
15. Herman, D., Googin, C., Liu, X., Sun, Y., Galda, A., Safro, I., Pistoia, M., & Alexeev, Y. (2023). Quantum Computing for Finance. In Nature Reviews Physics (Vol. 5, Issue 8, pp. 450–465). Springer Science and Business Media LLC. https://doi.org/10.1038/s42254-023-00603-1
16. Rebentrost, P., & Lloyd, S. (2018). Quantum computational finance: quantum algorithm for portfolio optimization (Version 1). arXiv. https://doi.org/10.48550/ARXIV.1811.03975

17. Buonaiuto, G., Gargiulo, F., De Pietro, G., Esposito, M., & Pota, M. (2023). Best Practices for Portfolio Optimization by Quantum Computing, Experimented on Real Quantum Devices. In Scientific Reports (Vol. 13, Issue 1). Springer Science and Business Media LLC. https://doi.org/10.1038/s41598-023-45392-w

18. Egger, D. J., Gambella, C., Marecek, J., McFaddin, S., Mevissen, M., Raymond, R., Simonetto, A., Woerner, S., & Yndurain, E. (2020). Quantum Computing for Finance: State-of-the-Art and Future Prospects. In IEEE Transactions on Quantum Engineering (Vol. 1, pp. 1–24). Institute of Electrical and Electronics Engineers (IEEE). https://doi.org/10.1109/tqe.2020.3030314

19. https://www.eiopa.europa.eu/browse/regulation-and-policy/solvency-ii_en

20. Turkalj, I., Assadsolimani, M., Braun, M., Halffmann, P., Hegemann, N., Kerstan, S., Maciejewski, J., Sharma, S., & Zhou, Y. (2024). Quadratic Unconstrained Binary Optimization Approach for Incorporating Solvency Capital into Portfolio Optimization. In Risks (Vol. 12, Issue 2, p. 23). MDPI AG. https://doi.org/10.3390/risks12020023

21. Sustainability | United Nations: https://www.un.org/en/academic-impact/sustainability

22. Nammouchi, A., Kassler, A., & Theorachis, A. (2023). Quantum Machine Learning in Climate Change and Sustainability: A Review. https://doi.org/10.48550/arXiv.2310.09162

23. Ajagekar, A., & Fengqi, Y. (2022). Quantum Computing and Quantum Artificial Intelligence for Renewable and Sustainable Energy: A Emerging Prospect towards Climate Neutrality. In Renewable and Sustainable Energy Reviews (Vol. 165, pp. 112493). https://doi.org/10.1016/j.rser.2022.112493

24. Cao, Y., Xiyuan, Z., Xiang, F., Huan, Z., Wenxuan, L., & Junhua, Z. (2023). Linear-Layer-Enhanced Quantum Long Short-Term Memory for Carbon Price Forecasting. In Quantum Machine Intelligence (Vol. 5). https://doi.org/10.1007/s42484-023-00115-2

25. Senekane, M., & Taele, B. (2016). Prediction of Solar Irradiation Using Quantum Support Vector Machine Learning Algorithm. In Smart Grid and Renewable Energy (Vol. 07, pp. 293–301). https://doi.org/10.4236/sgre.2016.712022

3 The Role of Quantum Technologies in Driving Change in Business and Personal Domains

Wissam Steitie and Hanan Faour

3.1 INTRODUCTION

Quantum computing, a field at the intersection of computer science and quantum physics, stands as one of the most promising technological advancements of the 21st century. Its development marks a significant shift from classical computing paradigms, introducing new computational capabilities that hold massive potential for businesses and individuals alike. This chapter provides a comprehensive overview of quantum computing, tracing its historical development, explaining its fundamental principles, and discussing its potential applications and implications.

The concept of quantum computing can be traced back to the early 20th century with the advent of quantum mechanics. However, it was not until the 1980s that the idea of a quantum computer was seriously considered. Pioneers like Richard Feynman and David Deutsch proposed that a computer based on quantum principles could perform certain types of calculations much more efficiently than classical computers. Quantum mechanics, the underlying theory of quantum computing, departs significantly from the classical mechanics that govern macroscopic objects.

The journey from theoretical concepts to practical quantum computers involves significant scientific and engineering challenges. Early efforts in the field focused on proving the feasibility of quantum computing and addressing fundamental issues such as qubit stability and coherence. Recent advancements have seen the development of various types of quantum computers, including those based on superconducting circuits, trapped ions, and topological qubits.

Quantum computing holds promise for a wide range of applications, many of which are beyond the reach of classical computers. This includes complex problem-solving in fields such as cryptography, material science, pharmaceuticals, Artificial Intelligence (AI), and financial modelling. This section offers an overview of these applications, highlighting how quantum computing could revolutionise various industries. The impact of quantum computing on the business world is poised to be profound. Businesses stand to benefit from improved data analysis, enhanced security, and more efficient logistics and supply chain management. Quantum computing also has the potential to drive innovation in sectors like finance, where it can be

DOI: 10.1201/9781003537243-3

used for more complex and accurate modelling of markets. Beyond its commercial applications, quantum computing also has significant implications for individuals. This includes the development of advanced personal healthcare technologies, more immersive entertainment experiences, and more sophisticated personal computing capabilities.

This chapter explores the various dimensions of quantum computing and its ramifications for the commercial sector and individual use. The discussion extends to intricate technical concepts, practical business uses, individual benefits, prevailing challenges, and anticipations for the future, all aimed at enriching the reader's grasp of this transformative technology.

3.2   QUANTUM VS CLASSICAL COMPUTING

Classical computing is based on the binary system, where data is processed in bits that are either in a state of 0 or 1. Classical computers perform operations using logical gates, such as AND, OR, and XOR, which manipulate these bits to perform calculations and execute algorithms. While classical computers have driven technological advancements for decades, they have limitations in solving problems that require the processing of vast amounts of data or the execution of highly complex algorithms.

Quantum computing, by contrast, does not operate within the confines of binary logic. Its computational model is based on the principles of quantum mechanics, which allows for more complex and nuanced data representation and manipulation. The following are key differences highlighted in this comparative analysis:

- *Parallelism:* Quantum computers can leverage the principle of superposition to perform multiple calculations at once, offering a level of parallelism that classical computers cannot achieve.
- *Speed:* Certain algorithms that would take classical computers thousands of years to solve can potentially be processed by quantum computers in a fraction of the time, thanks to the unique properties of qubits.
- *Information Density:* Due to the multi-state nature of qubits, quantum computers can store and process information at a much higher density than classical computers, which can lead to more efficient use of energy and space.

However, quantum computing also faces significant challenges that are not present in classical computing. These include the following:

- *Error Rates:* Quantum systems are highly susceptible to errors due to decoherence and noise, which can affect the stability of qubits and the accuracy of quantum computations.
- *Temperature Requirements:* Maintaining qubits in a coherent state often requires extremely low temperatures, close to absolute zero, which can be challenging and expensive to achieve.
- *Algorithm Design:* Quantum algorithms are fundamentally different from classical ones, and designing algorithms that can fully utilise quantum parallelism remains a complex task.

The comparison between classical and quantum computing reveals a landscape where the two will likely coexist, complementing each other. Classical computing will continue to excel at tasks it is well-suited for, while quantum computing will open new frontiers in areas where classical systems struggle.

3.3 QUANTUM COMPUTING IN BUSINESS APPLICATIONS

Quantum computing is not simply a theoretical marvel, but it is rapidly becoming an operational technology with significant implications for various business sectors. The potential of quantum computing to solve complex optimisation problems, accelerate drug discovery, revolutionise financial modelling, and redefine cybersecurity presents a new frontier for business innovation and efficiency. This section explores current research and potential applications, including case studies where quantum computing has already begun to influence business practices. This section discusses current research, potential applications, and case studies where quantum computing is beginning to influence business practices.

3.3.1 LOGISTICS AND SUPPLY CHAIN OPTIMISATION

Logistics and supply chain management are critical components of modern commerce, often involving complex decision-making with numerous variables and constraints. Quantum computing presents a paradigm shift in how these problems are approached. Traditional methods, such as linear programming and heuristic algorithms, can be inefficient for global-scale logistics operations involving hundreds of variables. Quantum computing, however, can process vast data sets simultaneously and optimise routes and inventory levels in ways that were previously unimaginable.

Current research in quantum optimisation algorithms demonstrated their potential to significantly reduce processing times for complex logistics problems. Quantum algorithms can rapidly explore a multitude of possible combinations to find the most efficient solutions, considering factors such as delivery times, fuel consumption, traffic patterns, and resource availability. This optimisation can lead to substantial cost savings, reduced environmental impact, and enhanced service levels. Case studies from leading logistics companies that experimented with quantum computing algorithms suggest that this technology could reduce computational times from several hours to mere minutes, even for complex global supply chains.

3.3.2 PHARMACEUTICAL INDUSTRY

The pharmaceutical industry is set to benefit enormously from the application of quantum computing, particularly in drug discovery and development. The traditional drug discovery process is a costly and time-consuming endeavour, often taking over a decade to bring a new drug to market. Quantum computing has the potential to drastically shorten this timeline through more efficient molecular simulation and analysis.

Quantum algorithms enable the simulation of molecular and chemical interactions at unprecedented speeds and with greater accuracy. This capability is critical for identifying promising drug candidates and predicting their interactions with biological systems, thus streamlining the preclinical drug development phase. Personalised medicine, which tailors treatment to the individual genetic makeup of patients, could also see significant advancements through quantum computing. By analysing genetic information quickly, quantum computers could facilitate the design of customised therapies that are more effective and have fewer side effects. Several pharmaceutical companies are already investing in quantum computing to explore its potential in accelerating drug discovery, with some early successes reported in identifying new compounds for complex diseases.

3.3.3 FINANCIAL MODELLING

In finance, quantum computing offers the potential for more sophisticated modelling and risk analysis, allowing for more accurate predictions and strategies. Financial markets are complex, dynamic systems influenced by a multitude of interconnected factors. Quantum algorithms are particularly well-suited for modelling these systems because they can evaluate numerous market scenarios simultaneously.

Quantum-enhanced risk analysis could profoundly affect portfolio management, pricing of financial derivatives, and strategic planning. Banks and investment firms are beginning to explore quantum computing as a tool for stress testing and scenario analysis, which are essential for understanding potential vulnerabilities and exposures. While still in the early stages, research suggests that quantum computing could provide a competitive edge in financial services by enabling faster, more complex calculations that can adapt to rapidly changing market conditions.

3.3.4 CYBERSECURITY

Cybersecurity is a critical concern for businesses in the digital age. Quantum computing, with its ability to perform calculations at unprecedented speeds, poses both a threat and an opportunity in this domain. On the one hand, quantum computers could eventually break many of the cryptographic algorithms currently used to secure digital communications. On the other hand, quantum cryptography promises to create unbreakable encryption based on the laws of quantum physics.

Research into quantum-resistant encryption methods is rapidly advancing, aiming to develop new standards that can withstand the power of quantum computing. Quantum Key Distribution (QKD) is one such technology that uses the principles of quantum mechanics to secure data transmission, ensuring that any attempt at eavesdropping can be detected. Companies are beginning to incorporate quantum-resistant algorithms into their security strategies to protect against future threats. As quantum computing continues to evolve, it will be imperative for businesses to reassess their cybersecurity measures to safeguard their data and systems against quantum-enabled breaches.

3.3.5 METROLOGICAL APPLICATIONS

Quantum metrology, a rapidly developing field founded on the principles of quantum mechanics, is causing a paradigm shift in precision measurement capabilities. Quantum metrology exploits quantum mechanics phenomena, e.g., entanglement, superposition, and quantum discord, with the potential of overcoming the classical measurement limits defined by the standard quantum limit (the minimal uncertainty one can achieve from a classical measurement) and shot noise. Quantum metrology has already found applications and proof-of-concept demonstrations in optical and atomic clock measurements, bio-sensing, accelerometery, optical interferometry, and polarisation metrology. The development of atomic clocks, which leverage the exact transitions of atoms or ions to attain unmatched precision and stability, serves as an illustration of this revolution. These developments have extensive implications, underlying critical technologies such as navigation systems, telecommunications networks, and basic research initiatives.

In addition to its usage in timekeeping, quantum metrology is implemented in a wide range of disciplines via the advancement of quantum-enhanced sensors. By leveraging on quantum characteristics, these sensors are capable of quantifying physical quantities with unprecedented sensitivity, including gravitational forces, electric fields, and magnetic fields. Quantum-enhanced sensors hold the potential to revolutionise fields such as environmental monitoring, medical diagnostics, and geophysical exploration through the provision of measurement tasks with never-before-seen levels of accuracy and sensitivity.

Moreover, quantum metrology is catalysing advancements in imaging technologies, enabling the development of advanced imaging techniques with superior resolution and sensitivity. Quantum-enhanced imaging systems, such as quantum lidars and quantum-enhanced microscopes, offer enhanced capabilities for biomedical imaging, remote sensing, and security applications. The ongoing progress in quantum metrology is anticipated to bring about significant changes in various sectors, enhance our comprehension of fundamental physics, and establish a pathway for innovative breakthroughs and technological progress.

3.3.6 DEFENCE APPLICATIONS

Quantum technologies are poised to cause profound transformations within the defence sector, presenting novel capabilities across a spectrum of crucial domains, including secure communication, sensing, computing, and cryptography. These applications capitalise on the intrinsic properties of quantum mechanics to confront pressing challenges and fortify national security imperatives.

Quantum communication is among the top quantum defence applications, where quantum encryption methodologies provide communication channels invulnerable to adversarial eavesdropping and cyberattacks. QKD protocols, built on quantum principles like the uncertainty principle and entanglement, facilitate the exchange of cryptographic keys with unbreakable security, ensuring the confidentiality of sensitive military communications against interception and decryption by hostile entities.

Quantum sensing technologies promise to elevate situational awareness and threat detection capabilities in battlefield environments. By exploiting the tenets of superposition and entanglement, quantum sensors enable accurate measurements of magnetic fields, gravitational forces, and other environmental parameters, providing invaluable intelligence for military operations, surveillance endeavours, and reconnaissance missions. Additionally, quantum-enhanced imaging modalities offer augmented resolution and sensitivity, advancing target identification, surveillance efficacy, and cartographic accuracy, and enhancing military situational awareness within complex and dynamic operational setups.

Furthermore, the arrival of quantum computing is poised to revolutionise defence paradigms by facilitating swift simulation of complex systems, optimisation of logistical operations, and decryption of encrypted communications and data. Leveraging quantum bits (qubits), quantum computers orchestrate computations at exponentially accelerated rates compared to classical counterparts, offering strategic advantages in data analytics, cryptographic operations, and decision-making frameworks essential for defence agencies in navigating contemporary security landscapes.

3.3.7   RISK MODELLING APPLICATIONS

Quantum technologies offer novel approaches to risk assessment, portfolio optimisation, and financial modelling. The application of quantum principles to actuarial practices can lead to more accurate predictions, improved decision-making processes, and enhanced risk management strategies.

Risk modelling and analysis is one of the key areas where quantum computing could revolutionise actuarial science. Quantum computers, with their ability to process large volumes of data and perform complex calculations at unprecedented high speeds, offer the potential to develop more sophisticated risk models that account for a broader range of variables and interactions. This could result in more accurate assessments of insurance premiums, mortality rates, and investment risks, enabling actuaries to better anticipate and mitigate potential losses for financial institutions and insurance companies.

Quantum algorithms could also be used to optimise investment portfolios and asset allocation strategies. Quantum optimisation algorithms, such as quantum annealing and variational quantum algorithms, offer the potential to solve complex portfolio optimisation problems more efficiently, taking into account factors such as risk tolerance, return objectives, and market dynamics. By leveraging quantum computing capabilities, actuaries can develop more robust investment strategies that maximise returns while minimising risks, thereby enhancing the performance of investment portfolios and pension funds. Additionally, quantum cryptography promises enhanced security for actuarial data and transactions. QKD protocols provide secure communication channels that are immune to eavesdropping and hacking attempts, ensuring the confidentiality and integrity of sensitive actuarial information. This could significantly mitigate the risk of data breaches and cyberattacks, protecting the interests of critical infrastructure providers.

The integration of quantum technologies into actuarial practices has the potential to transform risk assessment, portfolio management, and data security in critical sectors. By employing the unique capabilities of quantum computing and cryptography, actuaries can develop more accurate models, optimise investment strategies, and ensure the security of sensitive data, ultimately leading to more efficient and resilient financial systems.

3.3.8 HUMAN RESOURCE MANAGEMENT

One area where quantum computing could have a significant impact on Human Resource Management (HRM) is in talent acquisition and recruitment processes. Quantum algorithms have the potential to analyse huge volumes of data from diverse sources, including resumes, social media profiles, and job performance metrics, to identify top candidates with greater accuracy and efficiency. By exploiting quantum computing capabilities, HR departments can develop more sophisticated candidate matching algorithms that take into account a broader range of factors, such as skills, experience, cultural fit, and growth potential, leading to more successful hires and reduced turnover rates.

Quantum-enhanced machine learning algorithms can transform training and development programmes within organisations. By analysing employee performance data and learning patterns, quantum algorithms can personalise training programmes to meet individual needs and preferences, leading to more effective skill development and knowledge retention. Additionally, quantum simulation techniques can be used to create virtual training environments that mimic real-world scenarios, providing employees with hands-on experience and practical skills that relate directly to their job roles.

The quantum technologies can enhance performance evaluation processes by providing more accurate and unbiased assessments of employee performance. Quantum algorithms can analyse diverse data sources, such as productivity metrics, feedback from colleagues, and customer satisfaction scores, to generate comprehensive performance evaluations that account for both quantitative and qualitative factors. By leveraging quantum computing capabilities, HR departments can develop fairer and more transparent performance evaluation systems that recognise and reward employees based on their contributions and achievements.

Additionally, quantum encryption and cybersecurity technologies can enhance data security and privacy in HRM systems, protecting sensitive employee information from unauthorised access and cyber threats. QKD protocols provide secure communication channels that are immune to eavesdropping and hacking attempts, ensuring the confidentiality and integrity of HR data, including payroll information, personal records, and performance evaluations.

3.4 IMPLICATIONS OF QUANTUM COMPUTING FOR INDIVIDUALS

Quantum computing, while often discussed in the context of large-scale industrial applications, also holds a wealth of potential for personal use. Its emergence is set to redefine the landscape of daily life, transforming the way individuals interact with technology, approach education, and manage their health. This section explores the promising personal applications of quantum computing, weaving together current research with speculative scenarios to offer a vision of how quantum computing could fundamentally alter individual experiences and capabilities.

3.4.1 QUANTUM COMPUTING IN DAILY LIFE

The arrival of quantum computing stands to revolutionise personal technology applications, most notably in AI, gaming, and Virtual Reality (VR). Quantum-enhanced AI could lead to the development of highly sophisticated personal assistants capable of understanding and predicting individual needs with unprecedented accuracy. This could mean more intuitive interfaces, adaptive learning systems, and even AI that anticipates user needs before they are explicitly stated.

In the field of gaming and VR, quantum computing could enable the creation of incredibly complex and realistic simulations. The enhanced computational power would allow for the rendering of highly detailed, interactive environments that respond to the user's every action and decision in real time, providing an immersive experience far surpassing current capabilities. Quantum computing could also revolutionise personal devices, making them more powerful and efficient. For instance, smartphones could become capable of performing complex tasks that currently require the resources of large data centres, such as real-time language translation and object recognition.

3.4.2 EDUCATIONAL TOOLS AND LEARNING METHODS

The impact of quantum computing on education could be profound, particularly in the fields of Science, Technology, Engineering, and Mathematics (STEM). Quantum computers could enable the development of new educational tools that simulate complex systems, such as quantum physics experiments or biological processes, which are currently abstract and difficult for students to comprehend.

These advanced simulations could facilitate experiential learning, where students can observe and manipulate quantum phenomena in virtual labs, leading to deeper understanding and retention. Furthermore, quantum computing could personalise education by quickly processing a student's performance data to tailor learning experiences to their individual learning style and pace, potentially transforming the educational system to be more efficient and effective.

3.4.3 HEALTH MONITORING AND DIAGNOSTICS

In healthcare, the potential applications of quantum computing are particularly transformative. Quantum computing could enhance the capabilities of health monitoring devices, enabling them to analyse vast amounts of data in real time. This would allow for early detection of potential health issues, long before symptoms present themselves, through the identification of subtle patterns in biometric data.

Additionally, in diagnostics, quantum computing could significantly accelerate the analysis of medical imaging, leading to quicker and more accurate diagnoses.

It could also contribute to the field of genomics, where it could be used to analyse genetic data to predict disease susceptibility and response to treatments, paving the way for personalised medicine on an unprecedented scale. Quantum computing could also aid in the development of new drugs by simulating the interactions of molecules with high precision, which would have direct benefits for individual health and wellness. This could lead to more effective treatments with fewer side effects, tailored to an individual's unique genetic makeup.

3.5 CHALLENGES AND ETHICAL CONSIDERATIONS IN QUANTUM COMPUTING

Quantum computing is poised to significantly advance technological capabilities, yet it encounters a host of significant challenges that go beyond the complexities of its development and widespread implementation. This section examines the broad spectrum of hurdles, ranging from technical constraints to ethical dilemmas, that need to be overcome to harness the full capabilities of quantum computing. Furthermore, it emphasises the critical importance of ethical and conscientious development and deployment practices to ensure that the benefits of this potent technology are accessible across the entirety of society. This section provides a critical analysis of the hurdles facing quantum computing, emphasising the need for responsible development and implementation.

3.5.1 TECHNICAL BARRIERS

Quantum computing technology is still in its nascent stage, and several technical hurdles must be overcome to achieve scalable, reliable, and efficient quantum computers. One of the most significant technical challenges is maintaining the stability of qubits. Quantum states are fragile, and external disturbances can easily cause decoherence, leading to the loss of quantum information. Moreover, quantum error correction is more challenging than in classical computing because measuring a quantum state can disturb it, thereby altering the information it holds. Developing error-correcting codes that can handle the unique properties of quantum data is critical for the practical use of quantum computers.

The current quantum computers with a modest number of qubits need to scale up to thousands, if not millions, of qubits to solve practical, large-scale problems. However, increasing the number of qubits while maintaining the quality and integrity of their interactions presents a significant engineering challenge. Additionally, quantum systems typically require extreme cooling to near absolute zero temperatures to maintain coherence. This demands sophisticated cryogenic technology and leads to high operational costs and complexity.

Quantum computing's potential to break conventional encryption algorithms poses a substantial threat to data security and privacy. Current public-key cryptographic systems, which secure everything from online transactions to confidential communications, could become vulnerable once sufficiently powerful quantum computers are developed. To mitigate these risks, the field of post-quantum cryptography is developing new algorithms that are believed to be secure against quantum attacks.

Transitioning to these new standards will be a significant shift for the global digital infrastructure. Beyond cryptography, quantum computing also raises concerns regarding the security of data storage and processing. The increased power of quantum computers necessitates a re-examination of data access protocols and security measures.

3.5.2 ETHICAL AND ACCESSIBILITY ISSUES

The ethical implications of quantum computing are as profound as the technical ones. Quantum computing has the potential to exacerbate existing inequalities and raise new ethical concerns. There is a risk that the benefits of quantum computing will be accessible only to a few, leading to increased inequality. Ensuring that this technology is developed and implemented in a way that offers broad societal benefits is crucial.

As with any powerful technology, there is potential for misuse. Quantum computing could be used in ways that harm individuals or societies, such as creating new types of weapons or enabling mass surveillance systems that infringe on privacy rights. Additionally, policymakers need a robust understanding of quantum computing to create regulations that balance innovation with societal protection. This includes considering how to handle intellectual property rights and the sharing of quantum technologies between nations and corporations.

3.6 QUANTUM COMPUTING ACROSS INDUSTRIES

Quantum computing is poised to have a wide-reaching impact across various industries, offering novel solutions and enhancing existing processes. This section details how quantum computing can be applied across different sectors, from finance and manufacturing to energy and healthcare.

Finance and Economics

- *Algorithmic Trading:* Quantum algorithms can process vast data sets much faster than classical computers, allowing for real-time market analysis and automated trading strategies that can adapt to changing market conditions almost instantaneously.
- *Risk Management:* Quantum computing can enhance risk assessment models by taking into account more variables and their interdependencies, providing a more comprehensive outlook on potential financial risks.
- *Portfolio Optimisation:* The ability to quickly calculate the optimal asset mix for investment portfolios can lead to significant gains for both institutional and individual investors.

Healthcare

- *Drug Discovery:* Quantum computers can model molecular interactions at an atomic level, which can reduce the time and cost associated with discovering new drugs.

- *Genetic Research:* By analysing genetic data at unprecedented speeds, quantum computing could lead to breakthroughs in understanding genetic diseases and the development of personalised medicine.
- *Diagnostics:* Advanced imaging techniques, powered by quantum computing, could improve the accuracy and speed of diagnostics.

Energy

- *Material Science:* Quantum computing can simulate the properties of materials at the atomic level, leading to the discovery of new materials for energy storage and generation.
- *Smart Grid Optimisation:* Quantum algorithms can optimise the distribution of energy across power grids, making them more efficient and reliable.
- *Renewable Energy:* Enhancing the design and location strategies for renewable energy sources such as wind farms and solar panels can be optimised using quantum computing.
- *Logistics:* Optimize complex processes, such as supply chain management and production scheduling, by rapidly analysing vast data sets for optimal solutions. This leads to increased efficiency, reduced operational costs, and enhanced adaptability to demand fluctuations and resource constraints.
- *Supply Chain Optimisation:* Quantum computing can solve complex logistics problems involving global supply chains, including inventory management, route optimisation, and demand forecasting.
- *Manufacturing Processes:* Quantum simulations can improve the design of manufacturing processes, leading to increased efficiency and reduced waste.
- *Quality Control:* Quantum sensors could enhance detection methods, allowing for more precise quality control in manufacturing.

Cybersecurity

- *Cryptography:* Quantum computing will necessitate the development of new cryptographic protocols to protect data against the enhanced computational power of quantum machines.
- *Network Security:* QKD can potentially offer a new level of security for transmitting information.

Transportation and Urban Planning

- *Traffic Optimisation:* Quantum algorithms can analyse traffic data to improve city traffic flow and reduce congestion.
- *Urban Development:* Quantum-assisted simulations can optimise the planning of utilities and services in growing urban environments.
- *Telecommunications:* Quantum technologies enable ultra-secure communication through quantum encryption and improve data transmission speeds via quantum networking. These advancements enhance the capacity and security of global communication systems.

- *Signal Processing:* Quantum computing could improve the efficiency of data transmission and error correction over vast distances.
- *Optical Networks:* Designing the next generation of optical networks could be enhanced through quantum simulations.

Agriculture

- *Crop Optimisation:* Quantum computing can model climate and soil data to improve crop yields and reduce the impact of pests and diseases.
- *Supply Chain Management:* Managing the agricultural supply chain from farm to table can be optimised for efficiency and waste reduction.

Other applications

- *Entertainment and Media:* Quantum technologies enhance data processing, enabling ultra-realistic simulations and improving content encryption for secure distribution. Quantum computing could also drive innovations in AI, offering users more immersive and personalized experiences.
- *Content Creation:* Quantum computing could drive new algorithms for CGI rendering and VR environments, enhancing the user experience.
- *Personalisation Algorithms:* Media platforms can use quantum computing to better understand user preferences and tailor content accordingly.

3.7   FUTURE PROSPECTS AND PREPARATIONS

This section explores the prospective developments in quantum computing over the next decade and provides strategic recommendations for businesses and individuals looking to adapt to and benefit from these changes. It draws on insights from earlier discussions, projecting how quantum computing might influence not only the technological domain but also societal structures in the years to come.

The future of quantum computing is full of possibilities, with expectations that it will bring about a new era of technological advancement. As quantum computing technology matures, we anticipate significant strides in its growth and adoption across various sectors. The coming decade may witness quantum computing moving beyond the research labs and into practical applications.

Quantum computing is expected to evolve rapidly in terms of both hardware and software. Advances in qubit coherence, error correction, and quantum algorithms will likely lead to more stable and powerful quantum computers. As these improvements materialise, we can expect to see the first wave of quantum applications in industries such as cryptography, pharmaceuticals, materials science, and complex system optimisation.

Different sectors may adopt quantum computing at varying paces. The financial sector, for instance, might be among the early adopters, using quantum computers for market analysis and risk management. The energy sector could leverage quantum simulations to discover new materials for better solar panels or more efficient batteries. In healthcare, quantum computing is poised to accelerate drug discovery and genetic research, potentially revolutionising personalised medicine.

Quantum computers will not replace classical computers but will instead complement them. Hybrid systems that leverage the strengths of both classical and quantum computing could become commonplace, with quantum processors handling specific tasks within a broader classical computing framework. Adapting to the quantum future will require strategic foresight and preparation, both for businesses and individuals. The following recommendations aim to position different stakeholders to take full advantage of quantum computing's capabilities:

1. *For Businesses:*
   a. *Invest in Quantum Skills:* Businesses should invest in training their workforce in quantum computing skills. This could involve partnerships with educational institutions or internal training programmes.
   b. *Develop Quantum-Ready Infrastructure:* Companies should begin assessing their IT infrastructure and data management systems to ensure they can integrate with quantum technologies when they become available.
   c. *Engage in Strategic Planning:* Organisations should incorporate quantum computing into their long-term strategic planning, considering how quantum technologies might disrupt or transform their industry.
2. *For Individuals:*
   a. *Quantum Literacy:* Individuals should seek to become quantum literate, understanding at least the basics of how quantum technologies work and their potential impact.
   b. *Career Development:* Professionals in fields likely to be affected by quantum computing should consider developing relevant skills that will be in demand, such as quantum algorithm development or quantum information theory.
   c. *Stay Informed:* Keeping abreast of developments in quantum computing will be crucial. Individuals can follow research publications, attend conferences, or participate in online forums dedicated to quantum computing.

3.8 CONCLUSION

As we have tackled the exploration of quantum computing in this chapter, it has become increasingly apparent that we stand on the edge of a new computational era. From the fundamental principles that govern quantum mechanics to the potential applications and inherent challenges, quantum computing promises to be as disruptive as it is promising, poised to reshape industries and personal lives alike. Quantum computing, at its core, is a testament to human ingenuity, harnessing the properties of quantum mechanics to solve problems that are currently difficult. The exploration of quantum computing's fundamentals has laid bare the complex, often counterintuitive, principles of superposition and entanglement, setting the stage for a new kind of problem-solving prowess. These principles grant quantum computers the potential to perform calculations at a speed and scale that surpasses the capabilities of even the most advanced classical computers.

The business applications of quantum computing are diverse and profound. From optimising logistics and supply chains to revolutionising drug discovery and reshaping financial modelling, the commercial implications are staggering. Quantum computing does not just offer incremental improvements but has the potential to redefine the very methodologies and strategies businesses employ, facilitating unprecedented efficiency and innovation.

For individuals, the implications of quantum computing are both intimate and far-reaching. The potential to transform daily life through advanced AI, immersive gaming, and VR, personalised education, and healthcare predicts a future where technology is not only a tool but an extension of human capability and experience. However, these advancements are not without their challenges. As individuals, the responsibility falls upon us to remain informed and adaptable to the seismic shifts that quantum computing will bring to the fabric of society.

The challenges and ethical considerations addressed highlight that the path to a quantum future is fraught with obstacles, both technical and moral. Issues such as qubit stability, error correction, and the need for quantum-resistant encryption are but a few of the technical hurdles that must be surmounted. Equally important are the ethical considerations, from ensuring equitable access to the technology to safeguarding privacy and security in a post-quantum world. These challenges necessitate a concerted, global effort in research, policy-making, and public discourse.

Looking ahead, strategic foresight is critical to the successful adoption of quantum technologies. The next decade will likely see quantum computing evolve from a growing technology to an integral component of the technological landscape, permeating various sectors and becoming a critical tool in addressing some of the most complex problems faced by humanity. Businesses and individuals must prepare for this future through education, infrastructure development, and strategic planning.

In conclusion, quantum computing is poised to redefine the capabilities of both enterprises and individuals. As we prepare to embrace this new technology, the dual threads of excitement and caution should guide our approach. The quantum future will be marked by incredible opportunities for those who are ready to harness its potential and navigate its complexities. The journey towards quantum maturity will require patience, investment, and a robust dialogue between technologists, ethicists, business leaders, and policymakers. It is a journey that promises not just evolutionary progress in computation but a revolutionary leap into the future of human potential.

BIBLIOGRAPHY

1. Nielsen, M. A., & Chuang, I. L. (2010). Quantum Computation and Quantum Information. Cambridge University Press.
2. Kaye, P., Laflamme, R., & Mosca, M. (2007). An Introduction to Quantum Computing. Oxford University Press.
3. Ladd, T. D., Jelezko, F., Laflamme, R., Nakamura, Y., Monroe, C., & O'Brien, J. L. (2010). Quantum computers. Nature, 464(7285), 45–53.
4. Harrow, A. W., Hassidim, A., & Lloyd, S. (2009). Quantum algorithm for linear systems of equations. Physical Review Letters, 103(15), 150502.
5. Farhi, E., Goldstone, J., & Gutmann, S. (2014). A Quantum Approximate Optimization Algorithm. arXiv:1411.4028.
6. Preskill, J. (2018). Quantum computing in the NISQ era and beyond. Quantum, 2, 79.
7. Gisin, N., Ribordy, G., Tittel, W., & Zbinden, H. (2002). Quantum cryptography. Reviews of Modern Physics, 74(1), 145.

8. Devitt, S. J., Munro, W. J., & Nemoto, K. (2013). Quantum error correction for beginners. Reports on Progress in Physics, 76(7), 076001.

9. Orús, R., Mugel, S., & Lizaso, E. (2019). Quantum computing for finance: Overview and prospects. Reviews in Physics, 4, 100028.

10. Cao, Y., Romero, J., Olson, J. P., Degroote, M., Johnson, P. D., & Aspuru-Guzik, A. (2018). Quantum chemistry in the age of quantum computing. Chemical Reviews, 119(19), 10856–10915.

11. Mosca, M. (2017). Cybersecurity in an era with quantum computers: Will we be ready? IEEE Security & Privacy, 15(5), 38–41.

12. Biamonte, J., Wittek, P., Pancotti, N., Rebentrost, P., Wiebe, N., & Lloyd, S. (2017). Quantum machine learning. Nature, 549(7671), 195–202.

13. Schuld, M., Sinayskiy, I., & Petruccione, F. (2015). An introduction to quantum machine learning. Contemporary Physics, 56(2), 172–185.

14. Tavani, H. T. (2007). Philosophical theories of privacy: Implications for an adequate online privacy policy. Metaphilosophy, 38(1), 1–22.

15. Yanofsky, N. S., & Mannucci, M. A. (2013). Quantum Computing for Computer Scientists. Cambridge University Press.

4 Fundamentals of Quantum Machine Learning, Applications, and Tools

Danish Vasan, Mohammad Hammoudeh,
and Abdulelah S Alghamdi

4.1 INTRODUCTION

Combining quantum computing and machine learning is a breakthrough point in computational science. Quantum physics, the foundational theory that governs particle behaviour at the quantum level, can improve machine learning, a branch of artificial intelligence that allows systems to uncover patterns and insights in data [1]. This chapter briefly discusses quantum computing and machine learning, providing insight into the benefits that motivate researchers and practitioners to merge these disparate domains.

Quantum computing uses quantum physics techniques to process information differently from classical computing. Quantum bits, or qubits, exist in several states simultaneously due to superposition [2]. This property allows quantum computers to study multiple solutions simultaneously, implying exponential acceleration in specialized tasks. Quantum gates, like traditional logic gates, use unitary transformations to manipulate qubits and construct quantum circuits that execute quantum algorithms. Quantum algorithms have the potential to accelerate optimization and data processing dramatically. The possibility of more successfully addressing computationally challenging problems fuels the drive to incorporate quantum computing into machine learning procedures.

Quantum Machine Learning (QML) identifies complex patterns and correlations in data through novel methodologies such as quantum feature mapping and entanglement [3]. These quantum-inspired techniques offer a chance to enhance the capabilities of machine learning models. Classical machine learning techniques, such as regression and decision trees, have proven tremendously beneficial in various applications [4]. These algorithms are based on sequential processing and classical bits, limiting their scalability as datasets grow and problems become more complex.

Multiple challenges and opportunities drive the application of quantum physics in machine learning. The quantum advantage arises because classical computers have limitations in solving complex issues. Quantum computers contain inherent parallelism, analysing multiple possibilities at once, and may solve problems that exceed conventional machines' computing power. The desire to acquire a quantum

 DOI: 10.1201/9781003537243-4

advantage motivates academics to investigate the relationship between quantum computing and machine learning.

4.2   QML LANDSCAPE

In this section, we look at the QML landscape, comparing classical machine learning approaches to their quantum counterparts and investigating quantum computing's critical role in advancing machine learning algorithms.

Classical machine learning includes numerous algorithms for extracting patterns and insights from data. These algorithms run on classical computers with classical bits. While conventional machine learning has had tremendous success in various disciplines, its scalability is constrained by the sequential structure of computation and the exponential growth of computational needs as dataset size and complexity increase.

QML provides a paradigm change from classical techniques, utilizing quantum mechanics principles to improve computational capabilities. QML algorithms take advantage of qubits' unique qualities, such as superposition and entanglement, to do parallel computations and explore numerous answers at the same time. This intrinsic parallelism can potentially provide exponential speedup for solving specific optimization issues, data processing activities, and pattern recognition tasks. The speedup achieved by quantum algorithms compared to their classical counterparts can be quantified using the concept of quantum advantage:

$$\text{Quantum Advantage} = \frac{\text{Time Complexity of Quantum Algorithm}}{\text{Time Complexity of Classical Algorithm}}$$

Quantum computing promises to accelerate some computer operations exponentially, improving the efficiency of machine learning systems. Grover's approach for unstructured search and the quantum phase estimation algorithm for eigenvalue estimation provide a quantum advantage by leveraging quantum parallelism and superposition. Quantum algorithms can potentially deliver exponential speedup for certain computer workloads, as expressed by the Quantum Speedup Factor (QSF):

$$QSF = \frac{\text{Quantum Complexity}}{\text{Classical Complexity}}$$

Because of their intrinsic parallelism, quantum computers perform exceptionally well at processing and analysing massive datasets. QML algorithms can use this parallelism to investigate many paths simultaneously, allowing for more effective pattern and insight extraction from large amounts of data. This capacity is especially useful in cases where complex data processing is a bottleneck in traditional machine learning. Because of their parallelism, quantum computers perform well in processing and analysing huge datasets. After processing N data points, the quantum state is represented by α_i, which encodes information about each data point x_i:

$$|\Psi_f\rangle = \sum_{i=1}^{N} \alpha_i |x_i\rangle$$

where α_i encodes information about each data point x_i. Quantum parallelism allows for the simultaneous exploration of multiple paths during computation, enabling more effective extraction of patterns and insights from vast amounts of data.

QML includes novel approaches like quantum feature mapping [5], which encodes classical data into quantum states. Quantum feature maps can detect complicated patterns and correlations in data that classical approaches may miss. This quantum-inspired approach to feature extraction and data representation opens up new opportunities for improving the performance of machine learning algorithms. In a quantum support vector machine (QSVM), the quantum kernel function ($QSVM$) determines the quantum kernel function $K(x_i, x_j)$, which is defined as follows:

$$K(x_i, x_j) = \langle \phi(x_i) | \phi(x_j) \rangle$$

where $\phi(x)$ is the quantum feature map. This methodology can reveal subtle patterns in data that traditional methods may ignore.

Beyond classical machine learning tasks, quantum computing allows for solving issues inspired by quantum physics. QML algorithms help analyse and optimize quantum-inspired problems in chemistry [6], materials science [7], and quantum simulation domains [8]. Machine learning algorithms that harness the power of quantum mechanics can unveil insights into quantum systems and phenomena, leading to dramatic advances in scientific research and engineering applications.

4.3   QUANTUM ENTANGLEMENT AND SUPERPOSITION IN QML

In this section, we look at two fundamental notions of quantum mechanics, entanglement and superposition, and explain their importance in QML.

4.3.1   ENTANGLEMENT AND ITS APPLICATION IN QML

Entanglement is a quantum physics phenomenon in which the states of two or more particles become correlated, such that the condition of one particle cannot be described independently of the state of the other particles, even when huge distances separate them [9]. This link is instantaneous, confounding traditional conceptions of locality and independence. Entanglement can be mathematically represented as the tensor product of quantum states. Assume two entangled qubits: $|\psi_1\rangle$ and $|\psi_2\rangle$. The joint state of entangled qubits can be expressed as follows:

$$|\Psi\rangle = |\psi_1\rangle \otimes |\psi_2\rangle$$

Entanglement is necessary in QML algorithms because it allows for generating highly linked quantum states. Entangled qubits in QML can encode complicated interactions and dependencies between data elements, resulting in more efficient information representation and processing. Quantum algorithms that use entanglement, such as Quantum Neural Networks (QNNs) and QSVMs, use these correlations to improve learning and classification tasks. We can represent this entangled state with a quantum circuit as follows:

$$\text{CNOT}|\psi_1\rangle|\psi_2\rangle = |\psi_1\rangle|\psi_1 \oplus \psi_2\rangle$$

where $\oplus$ denotes the *XOR* action. This entangled state can encode correlations between the input qubits, making it a useful representation for QML algorithms.

4.3.2 SUPERPOSITION'S IMPACT ON QUANTUM ALGORITHMS

Another essential component of quantum physics is superposition [10], which allows quantum systems to exist in more than one state simultaneously. Unlike classical systems, where bits may only be in one state (0 or 1), qubits in superposition can represent both 0 and 1 and other combinations of these states. Mathematically, superposition permits qubits to exist in a linear combination of states. Let $|\psi\rangle$ be a qubit in superposition; it may be expressed as follows:

$$|\psi\rangle = \alpha|0\rangle + \beta|1\rangle$$

where α and β are probability amplitudes that satisfy $|\alpha|^2 + |\beta|^2 = 1$.

Superposition is at the foundation of quantum algorithm power and efficiency. Quantum algorithms use superposition to investigate several solutions to a problem simultaneously, dramatically increasing computation performance for specific jobs. For example, Grover's search method uses superposition to search unsorted databases in quadratically fewer steps than conventional algorithms, resulting in a quantum speedup.

Superposition in the quantum circuit model allows for the simultaneous execution of many quantum operations. Quantum gates alter qubits in superposition, allowing for simultaneous exploration of different computational paths. Quantum circuits, made up of interconnected quantum gates, use superposition to perform complicated computations efficiently. For example, a Hadamard gate can create a superposition by changing the $|0\rangle$ state into an equal superposition of $|0\rangle$ and $|1\rangle$.

$$H|0\rangle = \frac{1}{\sqrt{2}}\left(|0\rangle + |1\rangle\right)$$

Superposition in QML allows several data points and computational routes to be processed simultaneously. Quantum algorithms can encode and process large volumes of data simultaneously, giving them a significant edge over traditional machine learning approaches. Superposition allows QML algorithms to explore huge solution spaces efficiently, improving learning, classification, and optimization capabilities.

4.4 QML ALGORITHMS

QML algorithms use quantum mechanics principles to accomplish data classification, regression, clustering, and optimization [11]. These algorithms use quantum features like superposition and entanglement to process and interpret data faster than classical algorithms. This section introduces some of the common QML algorithms.

QSVMs bring classical support vector machine techniques into the quantum domain [12]. In QSVMs, quantum kernels are used to implicitly translate input data into high-dimensional feature spaces, from which classification boundaries are established. The decision boundary maximizes the margin between classes while minimizing classification error. Additionally, QSVMs use a quantum feature map ($\phi(x)$) to transform input data points into quantum states. The quantum kernel function ($K(x_i, x_j)$) computes the inner product of quantum feature maps representing input data points:

$$K(x_i, x_j) = \langle \phi(x_i), | \phi(x_j) \rangle$$

This inner product measures the similarity of data points in the quantum feature space. QSVMs train quantum circuits to optimize classification boundaries by increasing class margins.

QNNs are variations on classical neural networks that use quantum operations for data processing and training [13]. QNNs comprise layers of quantum gates that use quantum computing to transform input data into output predictions. These networks may represent complex nonlinear functions and perform classification, regression, and generative modelling tasks.

A single layer of a QNN can be expressed mathematically as follows:

$$|\psi_{out}\rangle = U_L \cdot U_{L-1} \cdot \ldots \cdot U_1 |\psi_{in}\rangle$$

where U_i represents the layer's quantum gates, and ψ_{in} and ψ_{out} are the layer's input and output states, respectively. QNNs are trained with optimization techniques like gradient descent to reduce a loss function and increase prediction accuracy.

Quantum optimization algorithms, such as the Quantum Approximate Optimization Algorithm (QAOA) and the Variational Quantum Eigensolver (VQE), seek to solve optimization problems with quantum computers efficiently [14]. Mathematically, these techniques entail building variational quantum circuits with classical parameters (θ). The variational circuit calculates the anticipated value of an objective function, such as a cost or energy function, for the quantum state output:

$$\langle \psi(\theta) | H | \psi(\theta) \rangle$$

The classical parameters (θ) are modified iteratively to reduce or maximize the objective function, resulting in optimal solutions.

4.5 CHALLENGES AND LIMITATIONS

Implementing QML presents several obstacles, most of which originate from the fundamental features of quantum systems and existing constraints in quantum computer technology [15]. This section reviews some of the significant challenges facing QML.

The first challenge is related to error correction. Quantum systems are highly susceptible to mistakes caused by decoherence, noise, and other external influences. Error correction is critical for accurate quantum computation, particularly in QML, where algorithms rely on delicate quantum states. Current error correction approaches, such as surface and quantum error correcting codes, are still in their early phases and are insufficiently mature to meet the issues of quantum noise fully.

Decoherence, another challenge facing QML, is the loss of coherence in quantum systems, which destroys quantum superpositions and the entanglement required for quantum computation. Decoherence periods in present quantum hardware are relatively short, limiting the depth and complexity of quantum algorithms that may be implemented before significant mistakes occur. Mitigating decoherence necessitates advances in error correction and improvements in qubit coherence times via improved hardware and environmental control.

Current quantum hardware has constraints on qubit connection, coherence times, gate fidelities, and number of qubits. These constraints limit the size and complexity of quantum circuits that can be built, impacting the scalability and performance of QML algorithms. To overcome these hardware limitations, qubit technology requires developing more stable and coherent qubits and scalable systems with enhanced connectivity.

Creating QML algorithms that leverage the potential of quantum processing while reducing the impacts of noise and mistakes is difficult. Quantum algorithms frequently necessitate approaches that differ from classical machine learning, and developing practical quantum circuits for specific applications is still an active area of research. Translating conventional machine learning methods to their quantum counterparts is not always easy and may necessitate significant changes to account for quantum features.

Similarly, it is not easy to convert classical data into a quantum representation that can be processed using quantum technology. Quantum data encoding techniques must ensure data integrity while remaining compatible with quantum algorithms. Also, obtaining meaningful information from quantum states at the output step and converting it to classical data creates difficulties. Creating effective encoding and decoding techniques specialized for QML applications is critical for improving the performance of quantum algorithms.

Quantum algorithms frequently require enormous computational resources, such as a large number of qubits, precise control over quantum gates, and low error rates. As a result, implementing QML algorithms on existing quantum technology may be resource-intensive and computationally expensive. Optimizing resource consumption and creating efficient qubit allocation and gate synthesis approaches are critical for effective QML implementations.

Addressing these issues necessitates a multidisciplinary approach that includes advances in quantum hardware, error correction techniques, algorithmic design, and theoretical knowledge of quantum computation. While progress has been achieved in recent years, significant research efforts are still required to overcome these constraints and fulfil QML's full potential.

4.6   QML APPLICATIONS

QML has the potential for a wide range of applications across multiple areas. While still in its early phases, research in this sector is moving quickly, paving the path for novel approaches to complicated challenges. QML has several present and potential applications, including drug discovery [16] and molecular modelling [17]. Quantum computers can mimic molecular systems with extraordinary accuracy, allowing for more efficient drug discovery and development. QML algorithms can evaluate complex molecular structures, predict molecular properties, and create new medications with desired properties, resulting in faster and more cost-effective drug development processes.

QML can be used to improve standard optimization techniques. Hybrid quantum-classical optimization techniques combine classical and quantum computation strengths to solve complicated optimization problems more effectively, enhancing logistics, scheduling, and resource allocation performance [18]. Quantum optimization techniques can tackle complex optimization problems faster than traditional algorithms. QML approaches can optimize financial portfolios, logistics networks, supply chains, and resource allocation challenges, resulting in better decision-making and resource usage. QML algorithms have applications in financial modelling, risk assessment, and forecasting. It may evaluate market data, find trends and patterns, and anticipate more accurately, allowing for more educated investment decisions and risk management measures.

QML algorithms can perform pattern recognition, data categorization, and clustering tasks. This enables it to handle vast and complicated datasets more effectively than traditional methods, increasing accuracy and scalability in image recognition, natural language processing, and anomaly detection. For instance, QML has the potential to transform healthcare through personalized medication and predictive analytics. QML algorithms can use genomic data, medical imaging, and clinical records to diagnose diseases, predict treatment outcomes, and tailor treatment plans to individual patients, resulting in more effective and personalized healthcare solutions.

QML has important applications in secure communications and cryptography [19]. It helps improve the security of communication networks and cryptographic protocols. Quantum algorithms can create secure quantum key distribution protocols, quantum-resistant encryption methods, and authentication processes immune to quantum attacks, protecting the confidentiality and integrity of sensitive data.

In quantum physics, QML can improve our understanding of quantum systems and phenomena. QML algorithms may evaluate experimental data, find patterns, and extract valuable insights from quantum experiments, thereby advancing quantum physics research and enabling the discovery of new materials and phenomena.

Overall, QML has enormous potential to address complex real-world challenges across multiple disciplines, opening up new avenues for creativity and discovery. As quantum technology progresses, the number of applications for QML is projected to grow, fuelling additional research and development in this intriguing subject.

4.7   QML TOOLS AND FRAMEWORKS

Several existing tools and frameworks provide essential resources for researchers, developers, and enthusiasts interested in exploring QML algorithms and applications [20]. They offer various functionalities for constructing, simulating, and executing quantum circuits and integrating quantum computations with classical machine learning. As the field of QML continues to evolve, these tools are expected to advance further, driving innovation and discovery at the intersection of quantum computing and machine learning. This section reviews the features and limitations of the standard QML tools and frameworks.

4.7.1   PENNYLANE

PennyLane,[1] developed by Xanadu, is an open-source QML library designed to bridge the gap between quantum computing and machine learning. It integrates seamlessly with popular machine learning frameworks like TensorFlow and PyTorch, allowing users to construct and optimize quantum circuits using automatic differentiation. Table 4.1 summarizes PennyLane's features and differences.

The following example demonstrates the construction of a simple quantum circuit using PennyLane. It defines a quantum circuit that applies single-qubit rotations (RX and RY gates) to a qubit and measures the expectation value of the Pauli-Z operator.

```
1 import pennylane as qml
2 from pennylane import numpy as np
3 from sklearn.datasets import make_classification
4 from sklearn.model_selection import train_test_split
5
6 # Generate a dummy dataset
7 X, y = make_classification (n_samples =100, n_features =2, n_classes =2, random_state
      = 42)
8
9 # Split the dataset into training and testing sets
10 X_train, X_test, y_train, y_test = train_test_split (X, y, test_size =0.2,
      random state =42)
```

```
1 # Define a PennyLane quantum function
2 dev = qml.device (" default . qubit", wires=2)
3
```

TABLE 4.1

PennyLane Features and Differences

Features	Differences
• Supports various quantum simulators and hardware platforms.	• Focuses on bridging quantum computing and machine learning.
• Facilitates training of quantum circuits with classical optimization techniques.	• Strong emphasis on differentiable programming for quantum circuits.
• Provides a user-friendly interface for QML model development.	
• Rich ecosystem of tutorials and documentation.	

```
4 @qml.qnode (dev)
5 def circuit (params, x):
6   qml.RX(params [0], wires=0)
7   qml.RY(params [1], wires=1)
8   qml.CNOT(wires=[0, 1])
9   return qml. expval (qml.PauliZ (0) @ qml.PauliZ (1))
```

```
1 # Define a cost function
2 def cost (params, x, y):
3   predictions = [circuit (params, x_i) for x_i in x]
4   return np.mean ((predictions – y) ** 2)
```

```
1 # Initialize random parameters
2 params = np.random.rand (2)
3
4 # Optimize the parameters using gradient descent
5 opt = qml.GradientDescentOptimizer (0.1)
6 for i in range (100):
7     params = opt.step (lambda v: cost (v, X_train, y_train), params)
```

```
1 # Evaluate the model
2 predictions = [np.sign (circuit (params, x)) for x in X_test]
3 accuracy = np.mean(predictions == y_test)
4 print (" PennyLane accuracy :", accuracy)
```

4.7.2   Qiskit Machine Learning

Qiskit,[2] an open-source quantum computing framework developed by IBM, includes a module dedicated to QML. Qiskit machine learning provides tools and algorithms for quantum-enhanced machine learning tasks, such as data encoding, feature map design, and quantum classification. Table 4.2 summarizes Qiskt's machine learning features.

The following example showcases using Qiskit machine learning to generate and evaluate quantum kernel matrices for a given dataset. It demonstrates how to create a quantum kernel using a quantum feature map, assess the kernel matrices, and use them for classification tasks.

```
1 from qiskit_machine_learning . datasets import breast_cancer
2 from sklearn.  model_selection import train_test_split
3 from qiskit_machine_learning . algorithms import QSVC
4
5 # Load the dummy dataset
```

TABLE 4.2

Qiskit Machine Learning Features and Differences

Features	Differences
• Integration with IBM Quantum Experience for real quantum hardware access.	• Developed by IBM, offering integration with IBM Quantum Experience.
• Implementation of quantum algorithms for classification, regression, and clustering.	• Provides a wide range of quantum algorithms out-of-the-box.
• Support for hybrid classical-QML models.	

```
6 X, y = breast_cancer (training_size =100, test_size =30, n=2, plot_data=False)
7
8 # Split the dataset into training and testing sets
9 X_train, X_test, y_train, y_test = train_test_split (X, y, test_size =0.2,
       random_state=42)
```

```
1 # Train a QSVC model
2 qsvc = QSVC(quantum_instance=' qasm_simulator')
3 qsvc. fit (X_train, y_train)
```

```
1 # Evaluate the model
2 accuracy = qsvc. score (X_test, y_test)
3 print (" Qiskit Machine Learning accuracy : ",  accuracy)
```

4.7.3 TENSORFLOW QUANTUM

TensorFlow Quantum (TFQ)[3] is a Google-developed open-source library that integrates quantum computing with TensorFlow, Google's machine learning framework. TFQ enables the construction and training of QML models, allowing researchers to experiment with hybrid quantum-classical algorithms. Table 4.3 summarizes TensorFlow's quantum features.

The following example illustrates the construction of a hybrid quantum-classical machine learning model using TFQ. It defines a quantum circuit, combines it with a classical neural network model, and trains the combined model using TensorFlow's optimization capabilities.

```
1 import tensorflow as tf
2 import tensorflow_quantum as tfq
3 import cirq
4 from sklearn . datasets import make_classification
5 from sklearn . model_selection import train_test_split
6
7 # Generate a dummy dataset
8 X, y = make_classification (n_samples=100, n_features=2, n_classes=2, random_state
       =42)
9
10 # Split the dataset into training and testing sets
```

TABLE 4.3

TensorFlow Quantum Features and Differences

Features	Differences
• Seamless integration of quantum circuits with TensorFlow.	• Developed by Google, leveraging TensorFlow for quantum machine learning.
• Support for quantum data preprocessing and circuit generation.	• Integrates with Google's quantum simulators and hardware through Cirq.
• Training and optimization of QML models with classical and quantum datasets.	
• Access to Google's quantum simulators and hardware.	

```
11 X_train, X_test, y_train, y_test = train_test_split(X, y, test_size=0.2,
       random_state=42)
```

```
1 # Define a quantum circuit
2 qubit = cirq . GridQubit (0, 0)
3 circuit = cirq . Circuit (cirq.X(qubit))
4
5 #Convert the quantum circuit to TensorFlow Quantum circuit
6 tfq_circuit = tfq . convert_to_tensor ([circuit])
```

```
1 # Define a classical input data
2 inputs = tf . keras . Input (shape=(), dtype=tf . dtypes . string)
3
4 #Define a quantum data layer
5 quantum_layer = tfq . layers.PQC(circuit=tfq_circuit, operators=[cirq . Z(qubit)])
6
7 # Build the quantum model
8 outputs = quantum_layer (inputs)
9 model = tf . keras . Model (inputs=inputs, outputs=outputs)
10
11 # Compile and train the model
12 model . compile (optimizer='adam', loss='mse')
13 model . fit (X_train, y_train, epochs=10, verbose=0)
```

```
1 # Evaluate the model
2 accuracy = model . evaluate (X_test, y_test, verbose=0)
3 print ("TensorFlow Quantuma ccuracy :", 1 - accuracy)
```

4.7.4 Cirq

Cirq,[4] developed by Google, is an open-source framework for quantum computing that provides tools for constructing, simulating, and executing quantum circuits. While not specifically tailored for machine learning, Cirq can be used in conjunction with other libraries to develop QML algorithms. Table 4.4 summarizes Cirq's quantum features.

This example demonstrates the construction and simulation of a simple quantum circuit using Cirq. It defines a quantum circuit that applies a Hadamard gate to a qubit and measures the resulting state multiple times to obtain measurement outcomes.

TABLE 4.4

Cirq: Quantum Features and Differences

Quantum Features	Differences
• Platform-agnostic API for quantum circuit construction and manipulation.	• Primarily focuses on low-level quantum circuit construction and simulation.
• Simulators for debugging and testing quantum circuits.	• Provides flexibility for custom quantum algorithms and protocols.
• Integration with Google's quantum hardware.	

```
1 import cirq
2 from sklearn . datasets import make_classification
3 from sklearn . model_selection import train_test_split
4 from sklearn . metrics import accuracy_score
5
6 # Generate a dummy dataset
7 X, y = make_classification (n_samples=100, n_features=2, n_classes=2, random_state
      =42)
8
9 # Split the dataset into training and testing sets
10 X_train, X_test, y_train, y_test = train_test_split (X, y, test_size =0.2,
        random_state =42)
```

```
1 # Define a simple quantum circuit
2 qubits = cirq . LineQubit . range (2)
3 circuit = cirq . Circuit (cirq . H(qubits [0]), cirq.CNOT(qubits [0], qubits [1]))
4
5 # Simulate the quantum circuit
6 simulator = cirq . Simulator ( )
7 result = simulator . simulate (circuit)
```

```
1 # Define a classical classifier
2 def classify (data) :
3      return [0 if x [0] > 0 else 1 for x in data]
4
5 # Classify the test data
6 predictions = classify (X_test)
```

```
1 # Calculate accuracy
2 accuracy = accuracy_score (y_test, predictions)
3 print ("Cirq accuracy :", accuracy)
```

4.7.5 RIGETTI FOREST SDK (PYQUIL)

Rigetti Forest SDK,[5] with its pyQuil library,[6] offers tools and utilities for program-ming and executing quantum algorithms on Rigetti's quantum processors and simulators. While not exclusively focused on machine learning, pyQuil provides functionalities for quantum circuit construction and execution. Table 4.5 summa-rizes RIGETTI's FOREST SDK features.

The provided example showcases the construction and execution of a simple quantum circuit using pyQuil. It defines a quantum circuit that prepares an entangled state using a Hadamard gate and a controlled-NOT gate and measures the resulting state to obtain measurement outcomes.

```
1 from pyquil import Program, get_qc
2 from pyquil . gates import *
3 from sklearn . datasets import make_classification
4 from sklearn . model_selection import train_test_split
5 from sklearn . metrics import accuracy_score
6
7 # Generate a dummy dataset
8 X, y = make_classification (n_samples=100, n_features=2, n_classes=2, random_state
      =42)
```

TABLE 4.5

Rigetti Forest SDK (pyQuil) Features and Differences

Features	Differences
• Access to Rigetti's quantum processors and cloud-based simulators.	• Offers access to Rigetti's quantum processors and cloud-based simulators.
• Programming quantum circuits using Quil.	• Utilizes Quil, Rigetti's quantum instruction language, for programming quantum circuits.
• Visualization and debugging tools for quantum circuits.	• Provides visualization and debugging tools for quantum circuits.
• Integration with classical ML frameworks.	

```
9
10 # Split the dataset into training and testing sets
11 X_train, X_test, y_train, y_test = train_test_split (X, y, test_size =0.2,
        random_state=42)
```

```
1 # Define a simple quantum program
2 p = Program ( )
3 p += H(0)
4 p += CNOT(0,1)
5
6 # Compile the program for execution on a quantum device
7 qc = get_qc ('9q–square–qvm')
8 executable = qc . compile (p)
9
10 # Run the compiled program on the quantum device
11 result = qc . run (executable)
```

```
1 # Define a classical classifier
2 def classify (data):
3     return [0 if x[0] > 0 else 1 for x in data]
4
5 # Classify the test data
6 predictions = classify (X_test)
```

```
1 # Calculate accuracy
2 accuracy = accuracy_score (y_test, predictions)
3 print ("Rigetti Forest SDK (PyQuil) accuracy :", accuracy)
```

4.8   FUTURE PERSPECTIVES

As quantum computing technology progresses, we expect more examples of quantum advantage in machine learning applications. Quantum algorithms have the potential to outperform classical algorithms in specific domains, leading to important breakthroughs in areas such as optimization, cryptography, and data analysis.

Classical algorithms based on quantum principles, such as quantum-inspired optimization algorithms and quantum-inspired sampling methods, will be further investigated. These algorithms use insights from quantum computing to increase the efficiency and performance of classical machine learning approaches, resulting in practical solutions for large-scale optimization and data analysis challenges. Hybrid quantum-classical machine learning models are likely to become more widespread. These models combine the advantages of conventional and quantum computing, utilizing quantum resources for certain tasks while employing classical preprocessing, postprocessing, and optimization techniques. Creating efficient methods for merging quantum and classical components will be a major priority.

With the introduction of large-scale quantum computers, there is rising concern about the security of traditional machine learning methods against quantum attacks. Quantum-safe machine learning techniques seek to create secure algorithms and protocols in the face of quantum adversaries. The goal of this research is to provide cryptographic primitives, safe protocols, and robust machine learning models that are resistant to quantum attacks. QNNs show promise in addressing challenging machine learning tasks using quantum resources. Research in this domain focuses on developing efficient training algorithms for QNNs, exploring new architectures that exploit quantum properties such as entanglement and superposition, and investigating applications in image recognition, natural language processing, and reinforcement learning.

Quantum data science is expected to become a new interdisciplinary area. It seeks to address the distinct challenges and opportunities presented by quantum data, which includes data generated by quantum devices, data processing with quantum algorithms, and data characterizing quantum systems. This topic investigates novel data representation, storage, and processing strategies designed for quantum applications.

Creating comprehensive QML frameworks and libraries is expected to speed up research and development. These frameworks include tools for creating, simulating, and running QML algorithms and interfaces for incorporating quantum computing into traditional machine learning pipelines. Continued collaboration among scholars, engineers, and industry stakeholders will drive the evolution of these frameworks. The experimental validation of QML algorithms, frameworks and libraries using cutting-edge quantum hardware is critical for determining their viability and scalability. Collaborations between quantum computing researchers and machine learning practitioners will help to construct and test quantum algorithms on quantum processors, providing insights into their real-world performance and limitations. To this end, education and training activities will develop quantum-literate people with expertise in computers and machine learning. Universities, research institutes, and business partners are providing specialized courses, workshops, and certifications to help prepare the next generation of QML researchers and practitioners.

Finally, as QML technology advances, it is critical to consider its ethical, legal, and societal ramifications. This includes considerations for data privacy, algorithmic bias, security risks, and the appropriate deployment of QML systems. Interdisciplinary collaboration among ethicists, policymakers, and stakeholders is critical in defining rules and frameworks to ensure the ethical and equitable use of QML technology.

4.9 CONCLUSION

Finally, QML is at the front line of research and innovation, potentially revolutionizing how we approach complicated computational jobs. This chapter looked at the fundamental principles of quantum computing and machine learning, the intersection of these fields, and essential concepts, techniques, and tools in QML. From studying the unique features of qubits to examining quantum algorithms such as QSVM and QNN, we looked into QML's theoretical basis and practical applications. We also discussed quantum acceleration, the role of quantum entanglement and superposition, and the state of QML frameworks and tools.

Looking forward, the future of QML seems promising. As quantum computing technology progresses, we expect breakthroughs in quantum algorithms, hybrid quantum-classical approaches, and quantum-inspired machine learning methods. With the creation of quantum-safe machine learning protocols, the validation of quantum algorithms on real hardware, and the training of quantum-literate professionals, we are on the verge of a new era in computational science and AI. However, as we move forward on this frontier, we must keep ethical considerations, societal implications, and appropriate QML technology deployment in mind. We can use the transformative power of quantum computing to address some of the world's most pressing concerns by encouraging interdisciplinary collaboration, promoting transparency, and adhering to ethical principles.

NOTES

1. https://pennylane.ai
2. https://qiskit.org/documentation/machine-learning/index.html
3. https://www.tensorflow.org/quantum
4. https://quantumai.google/cirq
5. https://www.rigetti.com/forest
6. https://pyquil-docs.rigetti.com/en/stable/

REFERENCES

1. Maria Schuld, and Francesco Petruccione. *Machine learning with quantum computers.* Springer, 2021.
2. S Harini, R Dharshini, R Praveen, A Abirami, S Lakshmanaprakash, and Amit Kumar Tyagi. Qubits, quantum bits, and quantum computing: The future of computer security system. In *Automated Secure Computing for Next-Generation Systems*, 385–402, 2024.
3. Linshu Chen, Tao Li, Yuxiang Chen, Xiaoyan Chen, Marcin Wozniak, Neal Xiong, and Wei Liang. Design and analysis of quantum machine learning: A survey. *Connection Science*, 36(1):2312121, 2024.
4. Tariq M Khan, and Antonio Robles-Kelly. Machine learning: Quantum vs classical. *IEEE Access*, 8:219275–219294, 2020.
5. Vojtěch Havlíček, Antonio D Córcoles, Kristan Temme, Aram W Harrow, Abhinav Kandala, Jerry M Chow, and Jay M Gambetta. Supervised learning with quantum-enhanced feature spaces. *Nature*, 567(7747):209–212, 2019.

6. Benjamin P Lanyon, James D Whitfield, Geoff G Gillett, Michael E Goggin, Marcelo P Almeida, Ivan Kassal, Jacob D Biamonte, Masoud Mohseni, Ben J Powell, and Marco Barbieri, et al. Towards quantum chemistry on a quantum computer. *Nature Chemistry*, 2(2):106–111, 2010.

7. Andreas Bayerstadler, Guillaume Becquin, Julia Binder, Thierry Botter, Hans Ehm, Thomas Ehmer, Marvin Erdmann, Norbert Gaus, Philipp Harbach, and Maximilian Hess, et al. Industry quantum computing applications. *EPJ Quantum Technology*, 8(1):25, 2021.

8. Wen Lin Tan, Patrick Becker, F Liu, G Pagano, KS Collins, A De, L Feng, HB Kaplan, A Kyprianidis, and R Lundgren, et al. Domain-wall confinement and dynamics in a quantum simulator. *Nature Physics*, 17(6):742–747, 2021.

9. Ryszard Horodecki, Paweł Horodecki, Michał Horodecki, and Karol Horodecki. Quantum entanglement. *Reviews of Modern Physics*, 81(2):865, 2009.

10. Laszlo Gyongyosi, and Sandor Imre. A survey on quantum computing technology. *Computer Science Review*, 31:51–71, 2019.

11. Maiyuren Srikumar, Charles D Hill, and Lloyd CL Hollenberg. Clustering and enhanced classification using a hybrid quantum autoencoder. *Quantum Science and Technology*, 7(1):015020, 2021.

12. Gian Gentinetta, Arne Thomsen, David Sutter, and Stefan Woerner. The complexity of quantum support vector machines. *Quantum*, 8:1225, 2024.

13. Sanjay Gupta, and RKP Zia. Quantum neural networks. *Journal of Computer and System Sciences*, 63(3):355–383, 2001.

14. Edward Farhi, Jeffrey Goldstone, and Sam Gutmann. A quantum approximate optimization algorithm. *arXiv preprint arXiv:1411.4028*, 2014.

15. Sau Lan Wu, and Shinjae Yoo. Challenges and opportunities in quantum machine learning for high-energy physics. *Nature Reviews Physics*, 4(3):143–144, 2022.

16. Stefano Mensa, Emre Sahin, Francesco Tacchino, Panagiotis Kl Barkoutsos, and Ivano Tavernelli. Quantum machine learning framework for virtual screening in drug discovery: A prospective quantum advantage. *Machine Learning: Science and Technology*, 4(1):015023, 2023.

17. Felix A Faber, Anders S Christensen, Bing Huang, and O Anatole Von Lilienfeld. Alchemical and structural distribution based representation for universal quantum machine learning. *The Journal of Chemical Physics*, 148(24), 2018.

18. Akshay Ajagekar, Travis Humble, and Fengqi You. Quantum computing based hybrid solution strategies for large-scale discrete-continuous optimization problems. *Computers & Chemical Engineering*, 132:106630, 2020.

19. Syed Junaid Nawaz, Shree Krishna Sharma, Shurjeel Wyne, Mohammad N Patwary, and Md Asaduzzaman. Quantum machine learning for 6G communication networks: State-of-the-art and vision for the future. *IEEE Access*, 7:46317–46350, 2019.

20. Prateek Singh, Ritangshu Dasgupta, Anushka Singh, Harsh Pandey, Vikas Hassija, Vinay Chamola, and Biplab Sikdar. A survey on available tools and technologies enabling quantum computing. *IEEE Access*, 2024.

5 Quantum Optimization, Machine Learning, Annealing, and Neural Networks

Pascal Halffmann and Shivam Sharma

5.1 INTRODUCTION

This chapter explores the innovative application of quantum computing methods to optimization problems, particularly through variational quantum algorithms and Quantum Annealing (QA) lenses. As classical optimization faces the limits of computational speed and efficiency in tackling complex and large-scale problems, quantum computing emerges as a potent alternative, offering breakthroughs in speed and novel problem-solving strategies. The chapter delves into the principles of quantum optimization, highlighting variational algorithms like the Quantum Approximate Optimization Algorithm (QAOA) and the Variational Quantum Eigensolver (VQE), which represent hybrid approaches blending quantum and classical computing techniques. Furthermore, it examines QA, a method inspired by physical annealing processes, which uniquely exploits quantum tunnelling and superposition to navigate the complex landscapes of optimization problems efficiently. Alongside optimization, the chapter introduces the promising arena of Quantum Machine Learning (QML), where quantum algorithms are poised to revolutionize machine learning models by accelerating training processes and enhancing model capabilities. This intersection of quantum computing with traditional optimization and machine learning offers a new paradigm for addressing some of the most challenging problems in science and engineering today.

The chapter is structured to first tackle quantum optimization by introducing the general concept of mathematical optimization and presenting the most prominent quantum algorithms for solving optimization problems such as variational quantum algorithms. We highlight details in applying these algorithms such as the appropriate modelling of optimization problems and suitable application areas in practice. Later we introduce QA and its classical counterpart, simulated annealing. We show how QA is used in both optimization and machine learning and give insights into QA hardware. At last, we motivate the introduction of QML by classical machine learning and we give an overview of different QML methods such as quantum neural networks that are suitable for different use cases, e.g., classification or clustering. Each

DOI: 10.1201/9781003537243-5

section of this chapter is accompanied by a concluding outlook and a discussion of existing challenges.

5.2 QUANTUM OPTIMIZATION

5.2.1 Introduction to Optimization

Optimization is a cornerstone of decision-making in both everyday life and sophisticated scientific and business applications. It involves finding the best solution from a set of available alternatives based on specific criteria. Optimization applies to various domains, from simple task scheduling in our daily routines to complex problems like route planning, financial portfolio management, and machine learning model training.

At its core, optimization deals with making choices that yield the highest benefit or the lowest cost. The solutions are not always apparent or intuitive, especially as the complexity of the decision environment increases. This is where optimization techniques come in, utilizing mathematical models to systematically explore possible options and identify the optimal choice under given constraints. The optimization process typically involves defining an objective function, which needs to be maximized or minimized. For instance, a business might want to maximize its profit (the objective) by determining the optimal mix of products to produce. This objective function is subject to constraints, which are limitations or requirements that the solution must satisfy. Continuing the previous example, constraints could include the availability of raw materials, production capacity, or market demand.

The history of optimization traces back centuries, with its roots deeply embedded in mathematics, engineering, and economics. The formal study of optimization began in the 17th century with mathematicians such as Fermat and Lagrange. However, it was in the 20th century that optimization truly blossomed, driven by the need to solve complex problems arising from the industrial revolution, wartime logistics, and the burgeoning field of operations research. In recent decades, the field of optimization has continued to evolve rapidly, and the advent of powerful computers and advanced algorithms has made it possible to tackle increasingly complex problems across various disciplines.

Optimization methods are roughly categorized into three types, including linear optimization, where the objective function and constraints are linear equations; nonlinear optimization, which deals with nonlinear relationships; and discrete optimization, focusing on problems where the decision variables are discrete, such as scheduling and routing problems. Each of these categories has its specific methodologies and algorithms designed to efficiently navigate the solution space.

Understanding optimization and its applications allows individuals and organizations to make informed, rational decisions that lead to optimal outcomes. As the complexity of our world increases, the importance of optimization in making sense of vast choices and constraints cannot be overstated. It is a field that combines analytical rigor with practical applications, offering tools and techniques to tackle challenges ranging from the mundane to the highly complex. For those embarking on a journey into the world of optimization, three standout resources are

"Convex Optimization" by S. Boyd and L. Vandenberghe [1]; "Introduction to Linear Optimization" by D. Bertsimas and J. N. Tsitsiklis [2]; and "A gentle introduction to optimization" by B. Guenin, J. Könemann, and L. Tuncel [3]. These books, authored by luminaries in the field, offer clear, comprehensive introductions to convex and linear optimization, respectively, ideal for both beginners and practitioners.

For educational purposes we introduce the Maximum Weighted Independent set (MWIS) problem that will guide us as an example through this section. This is a fundamental question in graph theory and combinatorial optimization, where the goal is to select a set of vertices in a graph (given by a set of vertices and a set of edges connecting vertices) such that no two vertices are adjacent, meaning there is no edge between these, and the sum of the weights of the selected vertices is maximized. Each vertex in the graph has a weight, representing its value or importance. The practical relevance of the MWIS problem spans several domains, including scheduling, resource allocation, and network design, where conflicts or compatibility issues must be resolved efficiently.

Let us denote the following:

- $G = (V, E)$ as the graph with vertices V and edges E.
- w_i as the weight of vertex $i \in V$.
- x_i as a binary variable where $x_i = 1$ if vertex i is included in the independent set and 0 otherwise.

We can formulate the MWIS as follows:

Objective: Maximize $\sum_{i \in V} w_i \cdot x_i$
Subject to: $x_i + x_j \leq 1$ for every edge $(i, j) \in E$

$$x_i \in \{0, 1\} \text{ for all } i \in V$$

An example can be found in Figure 5.1. In this context, the **objective** is to maximize the total weight of the selected set of vertices. The **constraint** is that no two

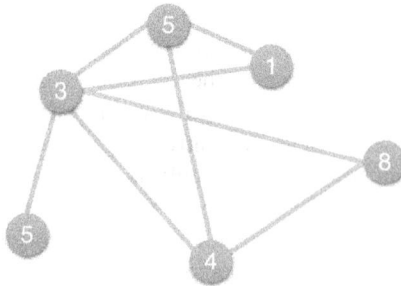

FIGURE 5.1 Example graph for the maximum weighted independent set problem with vertex weights. The independent set with the maximal weight of 18 is indicated by red vertices.

vertices in the set can be directly connected by an edge in the graph, ensuring the set is independent. The **variables** in this problem are binary indicators associated with each vertex, representing whether a vertex is included (1) or not included (0) in the independent set.

Replace this with: It is important to note that the MWIS problem is NP-hard, meaning that there is no known polynomial-time algorithm to solve all instances of the problem efficiently. In computational complexity theory, NP-hardness indicates that a problem is at least as hard as the hardest problems in NP (nondeterministic polynomial time). This suggests that the problem cannot be solved in polynomial time unless $P = NP$, and thus cannot be solved quickly for large instances. This complexity has significant implications for practical applications, often requiring the use of approximation algorithms or heuristic methods to find solutions that are good enough within a reasonable amount of time, especially for large or complex graphs.

5.2.2 QUANTUM OPTIMIZATION ALGORITHMS

The NP-hardness of problems like MWIS problem serves as a compelling motivation for exploring the potential of quantum computing in optimization. Traditional computational methods struggle with the exponential increase in complexity associated with NP-hard problems, leading to prohibitive solving times for large-scale instances. Quantum computing, with its principles rooted in quantum mechanics, offers a paradigm shift in computational capability. Quantum algorithms, such as Shor's algorithm for factoring and Grover's algorithm for search, demonstrate the potential for significant speed improvements over their classical counterparts. This potential may extend to optimization problems, where quantum computing could theoretically explore vast solution spaces more efficiently, potentially turning intractable problems into solvable ones within practical time frames.

Moreover, the increasing complexity and uncertainty of real-world problems provide a second strong motivation for integrating quantum computing into optimization. Modern challenges often involve robust, multi-objective, or online optimization to navigate uncertainties and achieve high performance in decision-making. For example, in supply chain management, optimizing for cost, reliability, and speed simultaneously under uncertain demand and supply conditions requires sophisticated multi-objective approaches. Quantum computing's ability to handle superposition and entanglement could enable more effective exploration of multiple objectives and scenarios simultaneously, offering solutions that are more robust and adaptable to changing conditions.

In essence, the intersection of quantum computing with optimization represents a frontier with the potential to revolutionize how we tackle complex, uncertain problems across industries. By harnessing quantum technologies, we could achieve unprecedented computational efficiencies, making it possible to address real-world challenges with greater precision, adaptability, and scale than ever before. This promising synergy between quantum computing and optimization opens up new avenues for advancing decision-making processes, significantly enhancing performance in a world characterized by complexity and rapid change.

One of the hallmark approaches in quantum optimization is the Quantum Approximate Optimization Algorithm (QAOA) [4], designed to tackle combinatorial optimization challenges by approximating the best solution through a series of quantum operations. Similarly, Quantum Annealing (QA) utilizes the natural evolution of quantum states to minimize energy functions, effectively finding the lowest points in a complex landscape of solutions which correspond to optimal or near-optimal solutions.

Moreover, hybrid quantum-classical algorithms like the Variational Quantum Eigensolver (VQE) represent a pragmatic approach to optimization, leveraging quantum resources for specific computational tasks while relying on classical systems for others. This synergy allows for the practical application of quantum optimization within the current era of Noisy Intermediate-scale Quantum (NISQ) computers.

The exploration of quantum optimization algorithms is not just an academic endeavour but a practical pursuit aimed at solving real-world problems that are beyond the reach of classical computing. From logistics and finance to drug discovery and materials science, the potential applications are vast and varied. As quantum hardware continues to evolve, the development and refinement of quantum optimization algorithms will play a crucial role in unlocking new possibilities across industries, heralding a new era of computational capability and efficiency.

In the following, we will introduce the most important quantum optimization algorithms that are available right now. We focus on variational algorithms like QAOA and VQE, and Grover Adaptive Search (GAS). Further, we dive into the peripherals of these algorithms and provide a guide on how to apply these to optimization problems. A summary of the current performance of these algorithms is given and we highlight success stories in practical applications. We close with an outlook on quantum optimization and the challenges that remain. We refer to two notable publications from last year that all provide a compelling introduction and overview of quantum optimization: there is an extensive overview given by Abbas et al. in the IBM optimization workgroup, and Au-Yeung et al. who investigate the whole optimization procedure from modelling to benchmarking. These publications have served as a foundation for this chapter.

5.2.2.1 Variational Algorithms

Variational algorithms represent a novel class of hybrid quantum-classical algorithms designed to tackle optimization and other computational problems within the capabilities of NISQ devices. These algorithms leverage the strengths of both quantum and classical computing: they use a quantum computer to evaluate the cost function and explore the solution space, while a classical optimizer adjusts the parameters of the quantum system to minimize this cost function. The "variational" aspect of these algorithms stems from their iterative process of variational principle application, where the quantum system is guided toward an optimal or near-optimal solution through successive adjustments based on classical feedback. This approach makes variational algorithms particularly suitable for solving problems that can be framed in terms of finding the ground state of a Hamiltonian, such as in quantum chemistry and complex optimization tasks. By bridging the gap between current quantum capabilities and the requirements of solving real-world problems, variational algorithms are at the forefront of practical quantum computing research and applications.

5.2.2.1.1 Variational Quantum Eigensolver

The VQE is an algorithm tailored for solving eigenvalue and optimization problems, particularly finding the ground state energy of molecular systems in quantum chemistry. At its core, VQE operates by exploiting the quantum hardware to evaluate the properties of quantum states and employing classical computing resources to iteratively refine these states toward the desired solution. The algorithm's essence lies in its ability to find the ground state energy, E_0, of a Hamiltonian, H, which describes a quantum system. Mathematically, this problem is formulated as finding the minimum eigenvalue of H, given by

$$E_0 = \min_{\psi} \langle \psi | H | \psi \rangle$$

where $|\psi\rangle$ is a quantum state produced by the ansatz circuit, and $\langle \psi | H | \psi \rangle$ represents the expectation value of H for the state $|\psi\rangle$.

VQE consists of two main components: a quantum circuit with parametrized gates, known as the ansatz, and a classical optimizer. The ansatz is designed to generate quantum states that approximate the system's ground state, with its parameters being adjustable knobs that the classical optimizer tunes. The ansatz is a parametrized quantum circuit, $U(\theta)$, designed to prepare the quantum state:

$$|\psi(\theta)\rangle = U(\theta)|\phi_0\rangle,$$

where $|\phi_0\rangle$ is an initial state (often chosen to be the ground state of a reference Hamiltonian for simplicity) and θ represents the set of parameters controlling the quantum gates in the circuit. The goal is to optimize θ to minimize the expectation value of H:

$$E(\theta) = \langle \psi(\theta) | H | \psi(\theta) \rangle.$$

The choice of ansatz is crucial, as it needs to balance expressibility—its capacity to represent complex quantum states—and trainability, to avoid the pitfalls of barren plateaus where gradients vanish, making optimization intractable.

The workflow of VQE begins with the initialization of the ansatz parameters. The quantum circuit then prepares a quantum state by applying the parametrized gates to an initial state, usually the quantum system's ground state for a simple reference Hamiltonian. This state is measured to evaluate the expectation value of the Hamiltonian representing the problem of interest. Essentially, this step involves calculating the energy of the quantum state with respect to the problem's Hamiltonian, a process that quantum mechanics uniquely facilitates through its probabilistic nature and the principle of superposition.

These measurements are relayed to the classical optimizer, which analyzes the energy computed by the quantum circuit. Based on this analysis, the optimizer adjusts the parameters of the ansatz with the aim of minimizing the energy, thus steering the quantum state closer to the system's true ground state. This iterative process between the quantum state preparation and measurement, followed by classical optimization, continues until the energy converges to a minimum value, which ideally corresponds to the lowest eigenvalue of the Hamiltonian.

The optimization process is iterative, involving the following steps:

1. Prepare the quantum state $| \psi(\theta) \rangle$ using the ansatz circuit, $U(\theta)$.
2. Measure the expectation value $E(\theta)$ of the Hamiltonian H for the state $| \psi(\theta) \rangle$.
3. Optimize the parameters θ using a classical optimizer to minimize $E(\theta)$.
4. Repeat steps 1–3 until $E(\theta)$ converges to a minimum value, ideally close to E_0.

Figure 5.2 provides an overview of the functioning of VQE. The VQE algorithm was first introduced by Peruzzo et al. [5]. This seminal work laid the groundwork for using parametrized quantum circuits in conjunction with classical optimization to solve eigenvalue problems, illustrating the potential of hybrid quantum-classical algorithms for the era of NISQ technology. Since then, many variants of VQE have been proposed, including other measurements (e.g., the solution with the best objective function in the current iteration) such

- *Adaptive VQE (AVQE):* Adjusts the structure of the ansatz during the optimization process, adding or removing gates based on the current solution's needs to improve expressibility and efficiency.
- *q-UCCSD VQE*: Uses a quantum version of the Unitary Coupled Cluster singles and Doubles (UCCSD) ansatz, which is particularly suited for quantum chemistry problems, offering a more accurate description of electronic structures.

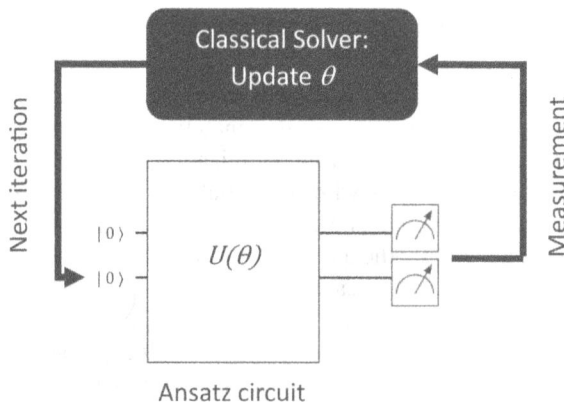

FIGURE 5.2 Schematic overview on VQE. The ansatz circuit is executed on the quantum hardware. The outcome is used to improve the parameters that are used for the next iteration.

The performance of VQE depends on the choice of the ansatz, the Hamiltonian complexity, and the classical optimizer's efficiency. While an explicit quantum speedup over classical algorithms has not been universally demonstrated due to these dependencies, VQE shows promising results in quantum chemistry and material science, where classical methods struggle with the exponential growth of the Hilbert space. VQE's hybrid approach effectively leverages NISQ devices to address problems previously out of reach, offering potential computational advantages in specific instances.

One of the VQE's remarkable features is its robustness against quantum noise, making it exceptionally well-suited for execution on NISQ devices, which are characterized by their relatively high error rates and limited qubit coherence times. This resilience stems from the algorithm's variational principle, which inherently seeks the lowest energy state that is theoretically attainable given the ansatz and the quantum hardware's constraints.

Overall, VQE represents a significant advance in quantum computing, demonstrating a practical approach to leveraging current quantum technologies for solving complex scientific problems. Its hybrid nature, combining quantum state evaluation with classical optimization, not only mitigates the limitations of NISQ devices but also paves the way for tackling a broader array of problems that were previously beyond reach, heralding a new era in computational science.

5.2.2.2 Quantum Approximate Optimization Algorithm and Quantum Alternating Operator Ansatz

The QAOA is a hybrid quantum-classical algorithm introduced by Farhi et al. [6] and designed for solving combinatorial optimization problems. It was initially proposed as a technique to leverage quantum computing's power to find approximate solutions to optimization problems that are classically challenging, bridging the gap between current quantum capabilities and the demands of real-world problems.

QAOA operates by encoding the optimization problem into a cost Hamiltonian, HCHC, whose ground state corresponds to the optimal solution of the problem. The algorithm then uses a combination of quantum state evolution and classical optimization to approximate this ground state and is closely connected to VQE. The structure is less variable as in VQE which comes with the advantage of fewer parameters that have to be optimized by classical solvers.

The process involves two main steps:

1. *Quantum State Preparation:* QAOA prepares a quantum state by applying a sequence of unitary transformations, governed by H_C and a mixer Hamiltonian H_M, to an initial state (often chosen to be a superposition of all possible states). These transformations are parameterized by angles $\vec{\gamma}$ and $\vec{\beta}$, which are optimized to minimize the expectation value of H_C.
2. *Classical Optimization:* The expectation value of H_C, given the current parameters, is measured and used as feedback for a classical optimization algorithm, which adjusts angles $\vec{\gamma}$ and $\vec{\beta}$ to find the minimum possible expectation value. For the classical optimizer heuristics and gradient-based algorithms are applied.

The QAOA circuit is characterized by its depth p, indicating the number of times the unitary transformations are applied. For a given p, the QAOA circuit is

$$U\left(\vec{\beta},\vec{\gamma}\right) = \prod_{k=1}^{p} e^{-i\beta_k H_M} e^{-i\gamma_k H_C}.$$

The goal is to optimize the parameters $\vec{\gamma}$ and $\vec{\beta}$ to minimize:

$$\langle \psi(\vec{\beta},\vec{\gamma}) | H_C | \psi(\vec{\beta},\vec{\gamma}) \rangle.$$

where $| \psi\left(\vec{\beta},\vec{\gamma}\right) \rangle = U\left(\vec{\beta},\vec{\gamma}\right) | s \rangle$ *and* $| s \rangle$ is the initial state.

The Quantum Alternating Operator Ansatz by Hadfield et al. [7] extends the QAOA framework by generalizing the concept of the mixer Hamiltonian used in the original QAOA. Instead of using a single, standard mixer that applies uniform transitions across all states, the Quantum Alternating Operator Ansatz allows for the use of problem-specific mixers and phase separators. This approach enables the encoding of problem constraints directly into the quantum circuit, ensuring that the quantum evolution respects these constraints and focuses the search on feasible solution spaces.

The enhanced ansatz can be represented as a sequence of alternating operators:

$$U\left(\vec{\beta},\vec{\gamma}\right) = \prod_{k=1}^{p} U_M\left(\beta_k\right) U_P\left(\gamma_k\right),$$

where $U_P\left(\gamma_k\right)$ is the phase separation operator (generalizing $e^{-i\gamma_k H_C}$ in QAOA), applied to incorporate the objective function, and $U_M\left(\beta_k\right)$ represents the mixer, which is now tailored to preserve the feasibility of solutions with respect to the problem's constraints. An overview on QAOA is given in Figure 5.3.

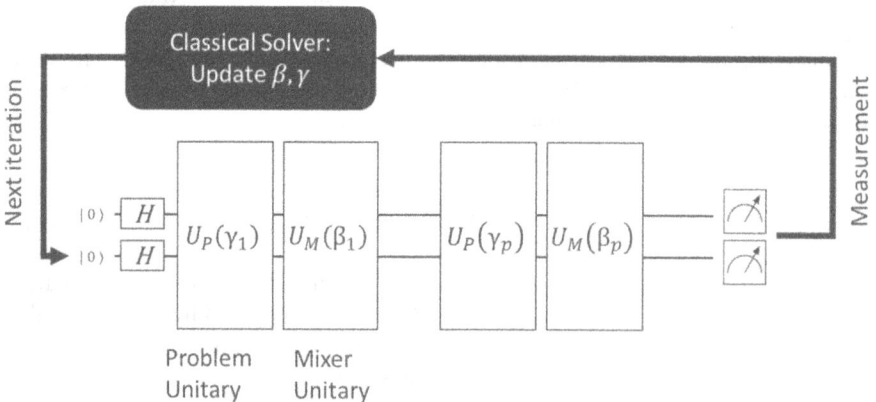

FIGURE 5.3 Overview on QAOA: After getting the qubits in superposition using Hadamard gates, we alternately apply problem and mixer unitaries. The measured states are used to optimize the parameters via a classical solver and utilize these for the next iteration.

The original QAOA has inspired several variants aimed at addressing its limitations and enhancing its application to different types of optimization problems. These include the following:

- *Adaptive QAOA:* It adjusts the circuit depth pp and the form of the ansatz dynamically based on the problem and intermediate results.
- *Warm-Start QAOA:* It initializes the quantum circuit with a classical approximation to the solution, potentially reducing the quantum resources required for convergence.
- *QAOA with Local Mixers:* It employs mixers that act on subsets of qubits to navigate the solution space more effectively, particularly useful for problems with locality in their constraints.

The performance of QAOA and its variants is highly problem-dependent, with empirical results showing promise for certain combinatorial optimization challenges. The effectiveness of QAOA is influenced by factors such as the choice of ansatz, circuit depth, and the capability to fine-tune the parameters, due to the current NISQ devices the circuit depth p is one. While quantum performance over classical algorithms has been theoretically proposed for $p \to \infty$, practical demonstrations remain an active area of research, largely contingent on advancements in quantum hardware and algorithmic refinements. Remark that QAOA has a close connection to QA, in the next section.

The enhanced flexibility of the Quantum Alternating Operator Ansatz and other variants broadens the applicability of QAOA to a wider range of problems, including those with complex constraints and large solution spaces. However, QAOA is the most used and investigated quantum algorithm on gate-based quantum computers. As quantum computing technology matures, continued exploration and benchmarking of these variants against classical algorithms will be crucial for understanding their potential and limitations in solving real-world optimization problems.

5.2.2.3 Grover Adaptive Search

To set the stage, let's recall that Grover's algorithm [8] achieves a quadratic speedup for searching through an unsorted database. The beauty of Grover's algorithm lies in its ability to amplify the amplitude of the target state (or states) through a series of quantum operations, making it increasingly likely to measure the solution upon observation of the quantum system. Specifically, it can find a target item in an unsorted database of n items in $O\left(\sqrt{n}\right)$ steps, a marked improvement over the classical approach, which requires $O(n)$.

GAS [9, 10] extends these principles to tackle optimization problems. GAS iteratively applies Grover's algorithm, adjusting its parameters based on the results of previous iterations to hone in on the optimal solution. This adaptiveness allows GAS to efficiently explore the solution space of optimization problems, significantly reducing the number of evaluations needed to find the optimum or near-optimum solutions. The adaptive aspect of GAS is particularly useful for problems where the solution space is not well-defined or where the optimization landscape is complex and filled with local optima. By intelligently guiding the search process, GAS minimizes the computational resources required to achieve high-quality solutions.

In principle GAS works as follows to minimize a function $f(x)$, $x \in \mathbb{B}^n$:

1. Find an initial solution x_{init} and set a threshold $T = f(x_{init})$. Set a bound on the maximum amount of amplitude amplification repetitions to $m = 1$.
2. While optimality has not been reached or maximum iterations are reached:
   a. Use Grover's Algorithm with an oracle that marks all states $x \in \mathbb{B}^n$ with $f(x) < T$ and random number of repetitions between 1 and m. Denote the output by x_{out}.
   b. If $f(x_{out}) < T$, set $T = f(x_{init})$ and $m = 1$. Otherwise increase m.

The solution with the best objective function value is returned. It can be shown that also GAS has an expected quadratic speedup against the worst-case performance of finding the optimal solution with its exponential in the number of variables.

Let us highlight the key ingredient of GAS, the adoption of Grover's algorithm. The oracle plays a pivotal role by marking states that satisfy certain criteria, similar to Grover's original algorithm where the oracle marks the sought-after item in a database. However, for optimization tasks, the oracle's task is to evaluate and mark states based on how well they meet the objective function's criteria. This typically involves additional quantum registers:

- One register that can encode the value $f(x) - T$ for each x is brought into superposition over all values and entangled with the original qubit register for encoding the variables x. The so-called A operator acts on the original n-qubit register and the ancillary m-qubit register, where m is the encoding length for the objective function value:

$$A_T |0\rangle_n |0\rangle_m = \frac{1}{\sqrt{2^n}} \sum_{x=0}^{2^n-1} |x\rangle_n |f(x) - T\rangle_m.$$

   In general, one uses a so-called quantum adder or the Quantum Fourier Transform (QFT). We refer to Ref. [10] for the details.
- The second ancillary qubit register is used for the oracle. It catches the sign of the other ancillary register $|z\rangle_m$ and the oracle uses this to flag states with negative values:

$$O|x\rangle_n |z\rangle_m = sign(z)|x\rangle_n |z\rangle_m.$$

A schematic overview is given in Figure 5.4. While GAS is rather intriguing from a theoretical point of view, it is seen as rather impractical, as it faces the same drawbacks as the original Grover's algorithm: the circuit depth is besides minimalistic toy examples so long that its execution is longer than the coherence time ensuring the stability of the quantum state.

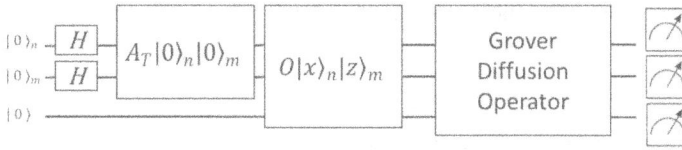

FIGURE 5.4 Overview of Grover Adaptive Search.

5.2.2.4 Other Approaches

Several lesser known approaches and numerous variants of the aforementioned algorithms exist in the literature. While QA is covered later in this chapter, we highlight two intriguing approaches to quantum optimization in the following.

5.2.2.4.1 Quantum Walks

Quantum walks represent a quantum mechanical analogue of classical random walks, serving as a foundational concept in quantum computing with applications in algorithm design, including solving optimization problems. There are two main types of quantum walks: discrete and continuous. Both types exhibit quantum properties such as superposition and interference, which enable them to explore a problem space more efficiently than their classical counterparts. Discrete quantum walks involve a walker that can move in superposition, meaning it simultaneously explores multiple paths or states. The walker's movement is determined by a coin flip operation, which, unlike a classical random coin, can put the walker in a superposition of moving left or right. This process is coupled with a shift operator that moves the walker through the graph or lattice, leading to a complex interference pattern that dictates the probability distribution of the walker's position. Continuous quantum walks do not rely on an external coin flip to determine their evolution. Instead, the walker moves continuously on the graph, with the evolution governed by the Schrödinger equation using the adjacency matrix of the graph as the Hamiltonian. This type allows for continuous evolution and exploration of the graph structure.

Quantum walks can be harnessed for solving optimization problems by exploiting their ability to rapidly explore and evaluate a vast solution space through quantum superposition and interference. For example, this has been applied to portfolio optimization by Slate et al. [11]. The efficiency of quantum walks in traversing a graph or network makes them particularly suitable for optimization problems that can be represented as finding particular nodes or paths within a graph, such as finding the shortest path or the maximum cut. The optimization problem is mapped onto a graph or network, where the solution corresponds to finding a specific node or configuration of nodes that minimizes or maximizes an objective function. The quantum walk is initialized in a superposition of states corresponding to potential solutions, allowing the system to explore multiple paths simultaneously. The quantum walk evolves according to the rules of discrete or continuous quantum walks, exploring the solution space through quantum superposition and interference. The constructive and destructive interference patterns generated by the quantum walk guide it toward regions of the solution space that are more likely to contain the optimal solution. By measuring the state of the quantum walk after a certain period, one can collapse the superposition to a particular state, which corresponds to a candidate solution to the optimization problem.

5.2.2.4.2 Quantum Interior Point Methods

The quantum interior point method is an advanced concept that combines quantum computing techniques with classical optimization algorithms, specifically interior point methods, which are a class of algorithms widely used for solving linear and nonlinear optimization problems. While simplex methods traverse the boundary of the feasible region, these methods iteratively improve a candidate solution by moving through the interior of the feasible region, guided by gradients or approximations of the objective function and constraints. They are particularly noted for their polynomial-time complexity for certain classes of problems, such as linear problems, making them an efficient choice for large-scale optimization tasks.

The quantum interior point method, such as the one by Kerenidis and Prakash [12], seeks to harness the computational advantages of quantum computing, such as quantum parallelism and amplitude amplification, to improve the efficiency of interior point methods. The idea is to leverage quantum algorithms to perform some of the computationally intensive tasks involved in interior point methods, such as solving systems of linear equations (for which quantum algorithms like the Harrow–Hassidim–Lloyd [HHL] algorithm can offer exponential speedups in certain conditions) or matrix inversion.

5.2.3   APPLICATION OF QUANTUM OPTIMIZATION ALGORITHMS

5.2.3.1   QUBO Formulations

Most quantum optimization algorithms like QAOA or QA require the transformation of the optimization problem into a quantum mechanical system in order to solve the problem. Typically, one transforms the optimization problem into an Ising model Hamiltonian, which can be expressed as:

$$H = -\sum_{i<j} J_{i,j} \cdot s_i \cdot s_j - \sum_i h_i \cdot s_i,$$

where s_i represents the spin of the i-th particle (taking values of +1 or -1), $J_{i,j}$ denotes the interaction strength between spins i and j, and h_i is the external magnetic field applied to spin i.

The Ising Hamiltonian has a close resemblance with the quadratic unconstrained binary optimization (QUBO) problem:

$$\min_{x \in \mathbb{B}} x^T Q x.$$

Indeed, for binary variables the linear part of the Ising Hamiltonian can be identified as the diagonal of the matrix Q. Further, the transformation from binary variables to spins can be realized by:

$$s_i = 2x_i - 1.$$

By translating an optimization problem into a QUBO problem, it can then be mapped onto an Ising model, making it suitable for QA. There exists a generic transformation to QUBOs suitable for most combinatorial and other optimization problems that have non-binary variables and constraints:

1. Transform inequality to equality constraints by introducing additional so-called slack variables $s \geq 0$:

$$Ax \leq b \Rightarrow Ax + s = b.$$

2. Transform equality constraints to quadratic penalty terms in the objective function and introduce a penalty factor p:

$$\min_{x \in X} f(x) \text{ with } Ax + s = b \Rightarrow \min_{x \in X} f(x) + p \cdot (Ax + s - b)^2.$$

3. Transform non-binary variables by substituting them with a binary encoding:

$$\min_{x \in X} f(x) + p \cdot (Ax + s - b)^2 \Rightarrow \min_{x \in X} f(x) + p \cdot (Ax + encod(s) - b)^2.$$

While this is versatile approach that works in many cases, it has its drawback. Take the MWIS introduced earlier and its constraints of the form $x_i + x_j \leq 1$ for every edge. We have to introduce a binary variable s and obtain the penalty term

$$(x_i + x_j + s - 1)^2,$$

to the objective function. Thus, we need for every edge $(i, j) \in E$ a slack variable. As each quadratic term in the QUBO's objective function requires a connection between the qubits corresponding to the variables, we need an all-to-all connectivity of the qubits. Due to the number of variables, this quickly exceeds what is available in current NISQ devices. Furthermore, the right choice of the penalty factor is difficult to assess.

For specific problems better QUBO and thus Ising Hamiltonian formulations exist; see Refs. [13–15]. For MWIS, we could use the formulation:

$$x_i \cdot x_j.$$

In previous chapters, we provide a QUBO-efficient formulation of the unit commitment problem. Furthermore, there exist better encodings of non-binary variables such as a phase encoding of continuous variables [16]. In the wake of nonlinear and nonquadratic objective functions and constraints, one could reside to use machine learning techniques to approximate the objectives and constraint with quadratic expressions, as a portfolio optimization problem.

5.2.3.2 Hardware and Benchmarking

Embedding and transpiling quantum algorithms onto physical quantum hardware are crucial steps in the quantum computing workflow, involving the adaptation of high-level algorithmic descriptions to the constraints and architecture of specific quantum devices. Embedding refers to the mapping of a quantum algorithm's logical qubits and their interactions (as defined by the algorithm's quantum gates or the problem's interaction) onto the physical qubits and connections available on the quantum processor in the case of QA. Transpiling, on the other hand, involves translating and optimizing a quantum algorithm's gate sequence into a form compatible with the target quantum processor's native gate set and connectivity constraints. It includes optimizing the circuit for fewer gates and depth to mitigate errors and adapting the algorithm to the specific topology of the quantum processor, ensuring that gates involving multiple qubits can be executed given the direct couplings between physical qubits. Both embedding and transpiling introduce the qubit routing problem, where logical qubits involved in multi-qubit gates must be "routed" through the quantum processor's topology to positions where the necessary direct interactions are physically available. This routing must be done efficiently to minimize the introduction of additional operations that could increase the computation's error rate. The challenges associated with embedding, transpiling, and qubit routing stem from the limited connectivity between qubits, the native gate limitations of quantum hardware, and the inherent noise in current quantum systems. These challenges require sophisticated algorithms to find optimal or near-optimal solutions that can significantly impact the practicality and efficiency of executing quantum algorithms on real hardware. Advances in quantum compiler design, error mitigation techniques, and hardware architecture are critical for overcoming these challenges and fully realizing the potential of quantum computing.

For quantum optimization algorithms to achieve their full potential, effective quantum error correction is indispensable. These algorithms, which promise to tackle complex optimization problems more efficiently than classical algorithms, are particularly sensitive to errors due to the intricate quantum states they manipulate, including superpositions and entanglements across multiple qubits. Errors arising from decoherence, operational imperfections, and environmental noise can disrupt the quantum algorithm's process, leading to incorrect solutions or significantly reduced advantages over classical approaches. Implementing quantum error correction allows a quantum optimization algorithm to maintain the coherence and fidelity of its quantum states throughout the computation, thereby preserving the algorithm's integrity and performance. However, the overhead associated with error correction—requiring additional qubits and quantum gates—poses a challenge, especially for near-term quantum devices with limited qubit counts and connectivity. Advances in error correction codes tailored for optimization tasks, such as low-overhead schemes and codes optimized for specific hardware architectures, are critical for enabling quantum optimization algorithms to operate reliably on scalable quantum computing platforms. These developments will be key to unlocking the practical applications of quantum optimization in fields ranging from logistics and finance to materials science and machine learning.

Benchmarking quantum algorithms, especially those designed for optimization tasks, is crucial for assessing their performance, scalability, and practical applicability compared to classical optimization algorithms. The process involves a systematic comparison using well-defined problems, metrics, and conditions under which the algorithms operate. Typical benchmarking problems could be the well-used port-folio optimization problem, max cut, or the introduced MWIS problem. Several key metrics are used to evaluate and compare the performance of quantum opti-mization algorithms against classical counterparts like solution quality and run-ning time.

Gurobi is a state-of-the-art classical optimization solver known for its efficiency in solving a wide range of linear and nonlinear optimization problems and thus an ideal candidate to benchmark quantum algorithms against. Currently, most quantum optimization algorithms, particularly those implementable on NISQ-era, are con-sistently outperformed by Gurobi and similar classical solvers on a broad range of practical optimization problems. This is due in part to limitations in current quantum hardware, such as qubit count, error rates, and connectivity, as well as the overhead associated with quantum error correction and problem embedding. However, there are specific instances and problem classes where quantum optimization algorithms have shown promising results, especially in terms of solution quality and the demon-stration of quantum speedup under idealized conditions or simulations. For example, QA and QAOA have exhibited potential advantages in solving certain combinatorial optimization problems and quantum chemistry tasks where the structure of the prob-lem aligns well with quantum hardware capabilities.

5.2.3.3 Application Areas

Quantum optimization, leveraging the principles of quantum mechanics to solve complex optimization problems, stands at the forefront of the transformative poten-tial of quantum computing. This field promises to revolutionize a broad spectrum of industries by offering solutions that are either intractable or exceedingly time-consuming for classical computers. Here are some key application areas where quan-tum optimization is poised to make significant impacts:

- *Logistics and Supply Chain Optimization:* Quantum optimization can drastically improve logistics and supply chain management by optimizing routes, reducing delivery times, and minimizing costs. For instance, the traveling salesman problem, a classic optimization challenge, can poten-tially be solved more efficiently with quantum algorithms, leading to opti-mized routing for delivery vehicles, thus enhancing operational efficiency and sustainability in logistics networks.
- *Financial Modelling:* In finance, quantum optimization offers the ability to solve complex portfolio optimization problems, risk assessment, and pric-ing derivatives more accurately and swiftly. By navigating the vast solution spaces of financial models, quantum algorithms can help identify optimal investment strategies and manage risk more effectively, giving financial institutions a competitive edge.
- *Energy Sector:* In the energy sector, quantum optimization can be used to design more efficient renewable energy systems, optimize grid distribution, and manage resources effectively. For example, additional material in this book highlights how quantum optimization solves the unit commitment problem that provides an optimal plan for power plant dispatch and load.

- *Drug Discovery and Material Science:* The field of drug discovery and material science can benefit from quantum optimization by accelerating the identification of molecular structures with desired properties. Quantum algorithms can optimize the arrangement of molecules for drug compounds or new materials, potentially reducing the development time and cost for new medicines and materials with advanced features.
- *Machine Learning and Artificial Intelligence (AI):* Quantum optimization algorithms can enhance machine learning and AI by efficiently solving problems related to clustering, classification, feature selection, and neural network training. The capability of quantum computing to handle high-dimensional data and explore complex optimization landscapes can lead to more powerful AI models and innovative machine learning techniques.
- *Telecommunications:* Quantum optimization has applications in telecommunications for optimizing network configurations, enhancing bandwidth allocation, and improving the robustness of communication systems. This can lead to more efficient data transmission, reduced latency, and enhanced security measures against eavesdropping through quantum encryption techniques.

As quantum computing technology matures and becomes more accessible, the application areas of quantum optimization are expected to expand further, unlocking new efficiencies and capabilities across diverse fields.

5.2.4 OUTLOOK AND CHALLENGES

This chapter on quantum optimization delves into the intersection of quantum computing and optimization techniques, showcasing how quantum principles can be harnessed to address complex optimization problems that challenge classical computing approaches. It introduces foundational concepts in optimization, emphasizing its ubiquitous nature across various domains and the evolution of optimization methods, from early mathematical formulations to sophisticated algorithms powered by computational advances. The discussion transitions to quantum optimization algorithms, highlighting QAOA and VQE, which represent quantum computing's potential to revolutionize optimization tasks through superior efficiency and novel computational capabilities.

Despite the promising advancements in quantum optimization, the chapter acknowledges the current landscape where classical optimization, exemplified by solvers like Gurobi, often outperforms quantum methods for a broad spectrum of practical problems. This reality underscores the necessity to further develop and enhance quantum algorithms, possibly by integrating strategies from classical optimization such as branch-and-bound or Benders Decomposition, to bridge the performance gap.

Moreover, it can be suggested that quantum optimization should concentrate on areas where classical methods face significant challenges, such as robust and multi-objective optimization. These domains, scarcely explored by quantum algorithms to date, offer fertile ground for demonstrating quantum computing's unique advantages.

As we stand at the precipice of a new era in computational science, the potential of quantum optimization shines as a beacon of innovation, promising to unlock solutions to some of the most complex and pressing optimization challenges that have long eluded classical computing. The journey thus far has laid a solid foundation, with quantum algorithms like QAOA and VQE illustrating the profound capabilities of quantum mechanics to redefine what's possible in optimization. While the current landscape acknowledges the superiority of classical optimization in many areas, the relentless pace of advancements in quantum computing heralds a future where quantum algorithms not only complement but also enhance classical methods, especially in domains where classical approaches stumble.

The path forward is one of collaboration and exploration, drawing upon the rich heritage of classical optimization while forging new frontiers with quantum technologies. By embracing the challenges and focusing on application areas ripe for breakthroughs, the quantum computing community is poised to deliver on the transformative promise of quantum optimization. The synergy between quantum and classical optimization strategies, alongside continued innovation in quantum hardware and algorithm design, will undoubtedly lead to groundbreaking advancements across science, engineering, finance, and beyond. In this light, the future of quantum optimization is not just promising; it is radiant with potential, beckoning us toward a horizon brimming with possibilities yet to be discovered and achievements yet to be realized.

5.3 QUANTUM ANNEALING

5.3.1 QUANTUM ANNEALING OVERVIEW

Algorithms, the heartbeats of computational systems, often draw their inspiration from the intricate and diverse phenomena observed in the natural world. This cross-pollination of ideas from the physical, biological, chemical, and social sciences into the realm of computing not only exemplifies the interdisciplinary nature of technological advancement but also highlights humanity's enduring quest to mirror the efficiency, resilience, and elegance of nature's processes in solving complex problems. Among the myriad examples of this inspiration, the principles governing physical processes have proven particularly fruitful, giving rise to algorithms that leverage the fundamental laws and behaviours observed in the material universe. Annealing stands as a prime exemplar of this category, embodying a computational technique that mirrors the physical process of annealing found in metallurgy. This process, where a material is heated to a high temperature and then cooled slowly to remove defects and improve its structure, serves as a metaphor for a sophisticated optimization algorithm. QA, by harnessing the peculiar and counterintuitive principles of quantum mechanics, extends this metaphor into the quantum domain. It offers a novel approach to solving optimization problems by navigating the complex energy landscapes of these problems more efficiently than classical methods can, especially for certain classes of problems. This section delves into the fascinating interplay between quantum physics and computational algorithms, exploring how QA leverages phenomena such as superposition and quantum tunnelling to offer groundbreaking solutions to some of the most challenging problems in optimization and machine learning.

5.3.1.1 Simulated Annealing

Before we dive into QA, we first introduce its classical counterpart: Simulated Annealing (SA). SA is a probabilistic technique for approximating the global optimum of a given function. This is particularly effective for solving optimization problems where the search space is large and the global optimum is hidden among numerous local optima. The essence of SA lies in its analogy to the metallurgical practice of annealing. Starting at a high temperature, the material is allowed to cool slowly so that its structure reaches a state of minimum energy, thereby achieving stability. Translated into the computational domain, this process involves an exploration of the solution space that starts broadly, allowing for significant jumps to escape local minima, and gradually becomes more refined, focusing on exploring the vicinity of the current solution to find the global minimum.

The concept of SA was first introduced in the context of optimization in a seminal paper by S. Kirkpatrick, C. D. Gelatt, and M. P. Vecchi [17]. This work laid the foundational principles of SA, drawing an analogy between the annealing process in metallurgy and the challenge of optimization in computational mathematics. For a more recent review of SA, we recommend the "Handbook of Metaheuristics" [18].

The SA algorithm can be summarized in the following steps:

- *Initialization:* Start with an initial solution and an initial temperature high enough to allow for extensive search.
- *Iteration:* At each step, a new solution is generated by making a small random change to the current solution.
- *Evaluation and Acceptance:* The change in the cost function, ΔE, due to the new solution is calculated. If the new solution is better (lower cost for minimization problems), it is accepted as the current solution. If the new solution is worse, it is accepted with a probability that decreases with the cost increase and the temperature, typically $P\left(e^{-\frac{\Delta E}{T}}\right)$, where T is the current temperature.
- *Cooling:* The temperature is gradually decreased according to a cooling schedule, which determines the rate at which the temperature is lowered.
- *Termination:* The process is repeated until the system has cooled down to a predefined final temperature or other stopping criteria are met, such as a maximum number of iterations or a minimum improvement threshold.

See Figure 5.5 for a graphical overview. The performance of SA critically depends on the cooling schedule—the rate at which the temperature is decreased. A slow cooling schedule allows the algorithm more time to explore the solution space, increasing the chances of finding the global optimum but at the cost of computational time. Conversely, a fast cooling schedule results in quicker convergence but risks missing the global optimum.

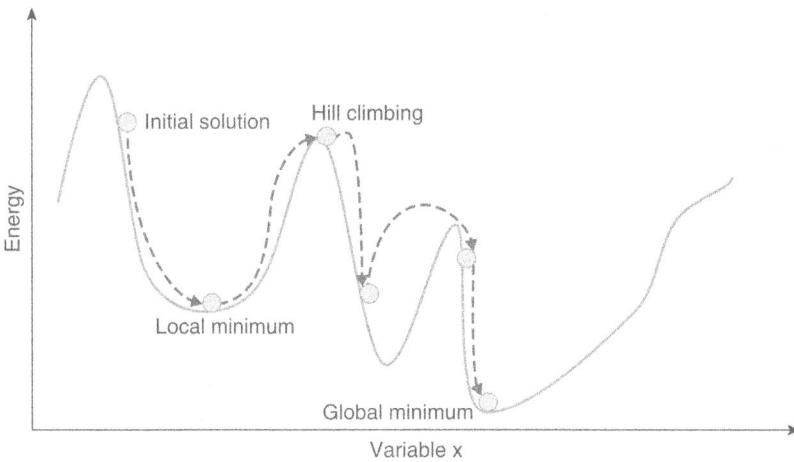

FIGURE 5.5 Simulated annealing: Starting with an initial solution the algorithm improves until a local minimum is reached. Other algorithms would stop there, but simulated annealing allows worsening the objective function so the solution can "climb" the hill toward a local maximum and then get to the next local minimum. This is repeated until eventually the global minimum is found or the temperature is cooled down completely.

Another key factor influencing performance is the choice of the mechanism for generating new solutions. This mechanism should ensure a sufficient exploration of the solution space while also allowing the algorithm to exploit the most promising regions of this space.

Variants of the SA algorithm often involve modifications to the cooling schedule, acceptance criteria, or solution generation mechanism. For example, adaptive SA attempts to adjust the cooling rate based on the progress of the search, improving efficiency. SA has been successfully applied to a wide range of problems, particularly those for which the solution space is discrete, and the number of potential solutions is exponentially large. Such problems include the MWIS problem introduced in the previous section, the traveling salesman problem, scheduling, allocation problems, and various design and configuration problems in engineering. Its flexibility and simplicity make it a powerful tool for these complex optimization tasks. Remark that for a successful application the necessary ingredient initialization, building new solutions, and cooling schedule have to be adjusted to the specific problem. Thus, the versatility comes with the price of optimizing the algorithm to the specific problem.

In summary, SA offers a robust and versatile approach to finding global optima in complex optimization problems. Its performance and effectiveness can be influenced by several factors, including the cooling schedule and the method for generating new solutions. While it may not always guarantee finding the absolute global optimum, its ability to navigate large, complex solution spaces efficiently makes it a valuable tool for a broad range of applications.

While this sounds too good to be true, SA has indeed several inherent drawbacks that can limit its effectiveness and efficiency, particularly for complex or high-dimensional problem spaces. First, the convergence speed of SA can be relatively slow, especially as the size and complexity of the search space increase due in part to the algorithm's reliance on a gradually decreasing temperature. While the algorithm is designed to probabilistically accept worse solutions to avoid being trapped in local optima, its success in escaping these traps heavily depends on the cooling schedule and temperature decrement strategy. For problems characterized by a rugged energy landscape with numerous local minima, SA may struggle to find the global minimum within a reasonable timeframe. The performance of SA is highly sensitive to its parameters, such as the initial temperature, cooling rate, and termination condition. Optimal parameter settings can vary widely across different problems, requiring extensive experimentation and making the algorithm less straightforward to apply universally. Finally, scalability is a concern. As the size and complexity of the optimization problem grow, the computational resources required by SA to find an optimal or near-optimal solution can increase significantly, limiting its applicability to very large or complex problem domains. These drawbacks motivate the exploration and development of alternative optimization techniques, such as QA, which seeks to leverage quantum mechanical phenomena to overcome some of the limitations faced by classical methods like SA.

5.3.1.2 Quantum Annealing

QA emerges as a cutting-edge optimization technique, drawing upon the principles of quantum mechanics to transcend the limitations inherent in classical optimization methods like SA. By exploiting quantum phenomena such as superposition, entanglement, and especially quantum tunnelling, QA offers a novel approach to navigating the complex landscapes of optimization problems. Unlike SA, which may struggle with slow convergence and difficulty escaping local minima due to its reliance on a metaphorical cooling process, QA harnesses quantum tunnelling to move through potential barriers directly, rather than over them. This ability significantly enhances the algorithm's efficiency in finding global optima, even in the presence of numerous local minima. Furthermore, quantum superposition enables a form of parallel computation, allowing QA to explore multiple states simultaneously, thereby addressing the scalability and convergence speed issues faced by SA. While QA operates under a different set of parameters, such as the annealing schedule, it is notably less burdened by the extensive parameter tuning that SA requires, offering a more robust solution pathway across various problem types. As such, QA not only opens new horizons for solving optimization problems but also showcases the potential of quantum computing to tackle challenges that have long hindered classical computational approaches.

QA, first introduced by Kadowaki and Nishimori [19], operates by exploiting quantum mechanical phenomena to find the minimum energy state of a system, which corresponds to the optimal solution of an optimization problem. At its core, QA begins with a quantum system whose qubits are prepared in a superposition of all possible states, representing the entire search space simultaneously. The system then undergoes an annealing process, where the initial Hamiltonian, governing the system's behaviour, is gradually evolved into a final Hamiltonian that encodes the problem to be solved.

One of the key quantum phenomena leveraged by QA is quantum tunnelling. Quantum tunnelling allows particles to pass through energy barriers, not by overcoming them with sufficient energy as in classical physics but by exploiting the probabilistic nature of quantum mechanics to "tunnel" through barriers directly, as shown in Figure 5.6. This phenomenon is crucial for QA because it enables the system to escape local minima that would trap classical optimization methods. One of the earliest references to tunnelling comes from Gamow [20]. In essence, quantum

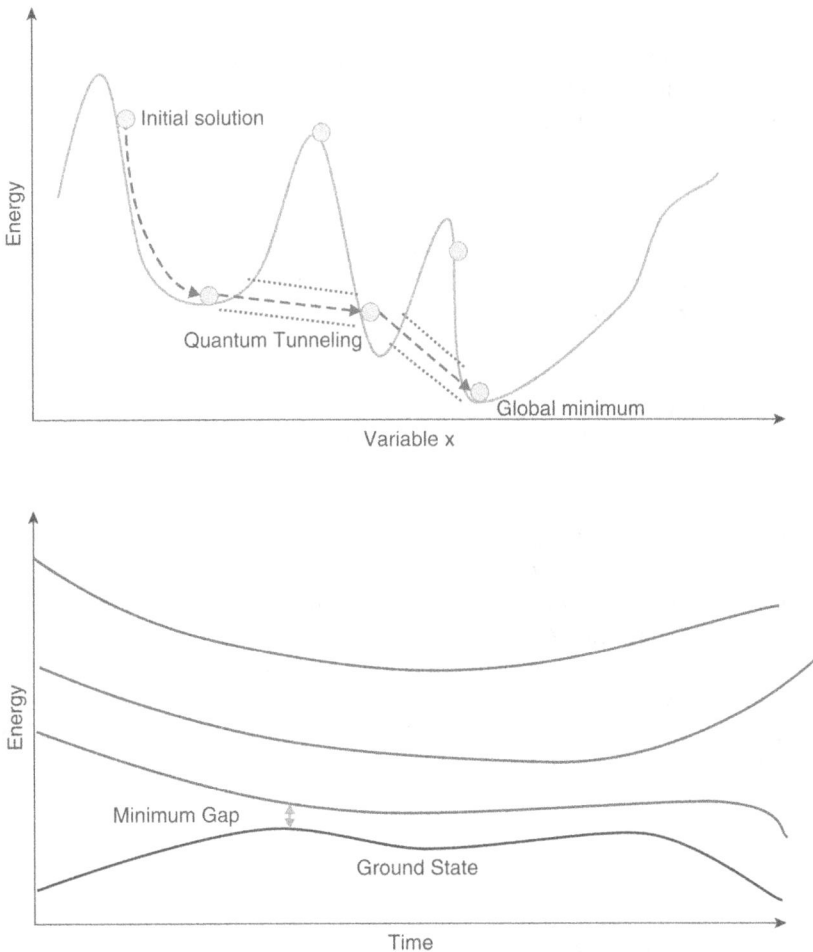

FIGURE 5.6 A visualization of quantum annealing. Above: Via quantum tunnelling, the solution can improve without "climbing over the hill" and increase the objective function value again. Below: The adiabatic theorem ensures that during the transition over time, the composite Hamiltonian stays in the ground state. Remark that there is a minimum non-zero gap between the ground state and the next state, which makes it possible for a real quantum device to "jump" to the next state due to noise.

tunnelling accelerates the search for the global minimum by allowing the system to explore the solution space more efficiently.

The mathematical framework of QA can be described through the time-dependent Hamiltonian:

$$H(t) = A(t) H_{init} + B(t) H_{prob},$$

where $H(t)$ represents the Hamiltonian of the system at time t, H_{init} is the initial Hamiltonian that prepares the system in a superposition of all possible states, and H_{prob} *** is the problem Hamiltonian that encodes the optimization problem. The functions $A(t)$ and $B(t)$ control the annealing schedule, where $A(t)$ decreases and $B(t)$ increases over time. Initially, $A(t)$ is large enough to dominate the system's behaviour, ensuring the qubits are in a superposition state. As time progresses, $B(t)$ becomes dominant, gradually transitioning the system toward the state that minimizes H_{prob}.

But how do we obtain the state that minimizes the problem Hamiltonian with this process? The key lies in the adiabatic theorem by Born and Fock [21] that provides the theoretical foundation for the gradual evolution of quantum systems and their ability to maintain their state relative to the ground state of a changing Hamiltonian, under certain conditions. The theorem states that a quantum system can remain in its instantaneous ground state if the Hamiltonian that governs its dynamics changes sufficiently slowly. This principle ensures that if the system starts in the ground state of an initial Hamiltonian, it will end in the ground state of a final Hamiltonian, provided that the evolution between these Hamiltonians is carried out slowly enough, and there are no crossings between the ground state energy level and the excited states.

Mathematically, the adiabatic theorem applies to a Hamiltonian $H(t)$ that varies with time t, where t ranges from 0 to T, with T being the total time over which the Hamiltonian changes. If $|\psi_0(t)\rangle$ represents the ground state of $H(t)$ at any time t, and the system starts in $|\psi_0(0)\rangle$, the theorem asserts that the system will be in $|\psi_0(T)\rangle$ at time T, assuming the change in $H(t)$ is adiabatic.

The condition for adiabatic evolution is often related to the gap between the ground state energy and the first excited state energy, denoted as ΔE. The change in the Hamiltonian must be slow compared to the inverse square of this energy gap, i.e.,

$$\left| \frac{dH}{dt} \right| \ll \frac{(\Delta E)^2}{\hbar},$$

where $\hbar$ is the reduced Planck constant. This ensures that transitions to excited states due to the Hamiltonian's time dependence are highly improbable, as shown in Figure 5.6.

The adiabatic theorem underpins the concept of Adiabatic Quantum Computation (AQC) [22], where a problem is encoded in the final Hamiltonian's ground state. By starting with a simple Hamiltonian whose ground state is easy to prepare and then slowly evolving to the problem Hamiltonian, the system remains in its ground state, encoding the solution to the problem. In QA, the adiabatic theorem one starts with a quantum system in a simple initial state and gradually evolves the system's Hamiltonian to encode an optimization problem. If the evolution is adiabatic and this can be ensured by a proper choice of the schedule quantified with $A(t)$ and $B(t)$, the system's final state will correspond to the problem's optimal solution or a close approximation. Usually, $A(t)$ and $B(t)$ describe a convex combination of the two Hamiltonians meaning $A(t) = \frac{T-t}{T}$ and $B(t) = \frac{t}{T}$ and the schedule is given by the annealing time, the total time T.

QA's reliance on quantum tunnelling and superposition offers a fundamentally different approach to optimization, in comparison to classical and other quantum algorithms. Its ability to explore the solution space more comprehensively and escape local minima more effectively positions QA as a powerful tool for tackling complex optimization challenges across various fields.

5.3.1.3 Relation between Quantum Annealing and QAOA

In its original version, QAOA consists of the problem Hamiltonian and the mixer Hamiltonian, where the latter mimics the initial Hamiltonian H_{init} in QA. However, the question arises of how we can incorporate the time dependency and the evolvement from one Hamiltonian to another. The solution is the Trotter–Suzuki formula [23, 24]. It is a crucial mathematical tool in quantum computing and physics and provides a method to approximate the exponential of the sum of two non-commuting operators, which is essential for simulating the time evolution of quantum systems, especially in contexts where the Hamiltonian of the system is composed of several parts that do not commute.

Consider a quantum system governed by a Hamiltonian H that is a sum of two parts, $H = A + B$, where A and B are operators that do not commute (i.e., $AB \neq BA$). The evolution of the system over time tt is described by the unitary operator $U(t) = e^{-iHt}$. However, directly computing $e^{-i(A+B)t}$ is not straightforward due to the non-commutation of A and B.

The Trotter–Suzuki formula provides a way to approximate this evolution by breaking it down into a sequence of smaller steps, each of which involves evolutions under A and B separately. The simplest form of this approximation, known as the Trotter formula, is given by:

$$e^{-i(A+B)t} \approx \left(e^{-\frac{iAt}{n}} e^{-\frac{iBt}{n}} \right)^n,$$

for a large n. This formula says that instead of directly computing the evolution under the combined Hamiltonian $A + B$, one can approximate this evolution by alternating between short evolutions under A and B, repeated n times. As n becomes larger, this approximation becomes more accurate.

In the context of QA and AQC, this formula enables the digital simulation of continuous quantum processes by discretizing the Hamiltonian evolution into a series of manageable steps n, which are the layers of QAOA. For $n \to \infty$ QAOA becomes QA.

5.3.2 QUANTUM ANNEALING FOR QUANTUM OPTIMIZATION AND QUANTUM MACHINE LEARNING

5.3.2.1 Quantum Optimization

Using QA to solve optimization problems is straightforward in principle: one simply needs to formulate the optimization problem as the problem Hamiltonian H_{prob}. A common approach is to use the Ising model Hamiltonian, due to its direct correspondence with QUBO problems. The Ising Hamiltonian can be expressed as:

$$H = -\sum_{i<j} J_{i,j} \cdot s_i \cdot s_j - \sum_i h_i \cdot s_i,$$

where s_i represents the spin of the i-th particle (taking values of $+1$ or -1), $J_{i,j}$ denotes the interaction strength between spins i and j, and h_i is the external magnetic field applied to spin i. This model captures the essence of many optimization problems, where the goal is to find the configuration of spins (s_i) that minimizes the system's energy (the Hamiltonian H).

By translating an optimization problem into a QUBO problem, it can then be mapped onto an Ising model, making it suitable for QA. This mapping leverages the natural ability of QA to find the ground state of a given Hamiltonian, which corresponds to the optimal solution of the original optimization problem.

5.3.2.2 Quantum Machine Learning

In the realm of Quantum Machine Learning (QML), QA can be utilized to optimize the parameters of quantum models or to find the optimal solution in algorithms that rely on optimization, such as clustering, classification, and feature selection. By formulating the learning task as an optimization problem, it can be mapped onto a Hamiltonian that QA is designed to minimize. This is particularly relevant for training quantum neural networks, where the goal is to minimize a cost function that measures the difference between the predicted outputs and the actual data. The ability of QA to efficiently explore the solution space and exploit quantum tunnelling to escape local minima enables it to potentially find better solutions faster than classical optimization methods as the learning task is often hard to optimize due to its nonlinear shape.

For example, for the task of feature selection, one can utilize QA as follows: given a data set $D = \{(z^i, y^i)\}_{i \in [N]}$ with n-dimensional features $z^i \in X \subseteq \mathbb{R}^n$ and class labels $y^i \in Y \subseteq [N] = \{1,...,N\}$., find a subset S of these n features such that the reduced data set leads to comparable performance as the original data, given a task such as classification. If one calculates the importance I_i of each feature i and the redundancy $R_{i,j}$ between two features i and j for every pair of features using knowledge or an approximation of the joint probability mass function of features and labels, one can state the feature selection problem as follows:

$$\min_{x \in \mathbb{B}} -\alpha \sum_{i=1}^n I_i \cdot x_i + (1-\alpha) \sum_{i,j=1}^n R_{i,j} \cdot x_i \cdot x_j,$$

where x_i are binary variables that have a value of 1 if feature i is in the subset S and 0 otherwise. This is not just an optimization problem but a QUBO and, thus, QA can be applied straightforwardly.

5.3.2.3 Quantum Annealing Hardware

The application of QA in practice is marked by the development of specialized QA hardware, designed to implement QA algorithms on a physical system. Among the companies pioneering this technology, D-Wave Systems stands out as a leader, having developed the first commercially available QA but also quantum computers in general, although considering QA as quantum computers is challenged. D-Wave's QA hardware is engineered around a lattice of superconducting qubits that embody the quantum bits of information. The core of D-Wave's technology is the superconducting flux qubit, which operates at temperatures close to absolute zero. At these cryogenic temperatures, electrical current flows without resistance in the superconducting loops, allowing the qubits to exhibit quantum mechanical properties. These qubits are arranged in a structure known as the Chimera graph, facilitating the encoding of optimization problems into the hardware. The interaction between qubits in this graph, essential for representing the problem's cost function, is mediated by devices called couplers, which control how the state of one qubit influences the state of another, thus encoding the optimization problem's structure.

D-Wave's offerings have evolved over the years, with each generation of their QA increasing in the number of qubits and the complexity of problems it can solve. As of the last update, the D-Wave Advantage system boasts over 5,000 qubits, representing a significant leap in their QA capabilities. This advancement not only increases the size of the problems that can be addressed but also improves the precision and flexibility in mapping real-world optimization problems onto the annealer.

Besides D-Wave, there exist a few other QA, mainly as a built-in feature in universal, gate-based quantum computers such as Rigetti. For example, Pasqal's neutral atom platform features an analogue mode that basically is a QA. Furthermore, there are classical computers such as the digital annealer by Fujitsu or Toshiba's Simulated Bifurcation Machine that are inspired by QA and try to mimic its behaviour.

5.3.2.4 Outlook and Challenges

The performance of QA as an optimization technique presents a nuanced landscape, with theoretical assessments of its speedup over classical solvers varying widely. From a theoretical standpoint, the anticipated performance of QA compared to classical algorithms ranges from no performance gain to quadratic and even possible exponential performance improvements for certain types of optimization problems. The annealing time, T, is a critical parameter in QA, influencing the algorithm's effectiveness and efficiency. It is generally hoped that, even as problem sizes increase, the required annealing time scales in a manner that does not grow exponentially, thereby maintaining the practicality of QA for larger and more complex problems. As of now, QA is the best quantum optimization algorithm available, with a significant advantage in performance against other approaches such as QAOA or VQE.

There have been notable successes in applying QA to real-world problems. Two such instances include the following:

1. *Scheduling Problems in Health Care:* QA has been utilized to find schedules for nurses and physicians in clinics during the Covid-19 crisis [25]. Complex problems with several constraints could be solved to (near-) optimality.
2. *Supply Chain Logistics:* QA has been applied as part of a hybrid algorithm to multi-truck vehicle routing for supply chain logistics using around 2,500 binary variables [26].

Despite these successes, when directly compared to state-of-the-art classical solvers like CPLEX or Gurobi, QA often finds itself at a disadvantage. This is predominantly due to the overhead associated with mapping the optimization problem onto the physical qubit arrangement, such as the Chimera graph used in D-Wave systems. The embedding process, which is NP-hard itself, can introduce significant delays, sometimes taking seconds to complete, whereas the actual annealing process might only last microseconds. This discrepancy highlights a key bottleneck in the current implementation of QA.

Looking forward, the field of QA faces several challenges and opportunities. Enhancing the efficiency of the embedding process, increasing the connectivity and number of qubits, and reducing noise in quantum systems are critical areas of focus. Moreover, theoretical advancements are needed to better understand and predict the scenarios under which QA provides a significant advantage over classical methods. As QA hardware and algorithms continue to evolve, so too will its applications, potentially unlocking new solutions to problems that are currently intractable or inefficiently solved by classical computing methods. The ongoing development of hybrid quantum-classical approaches presents a promising avenue for leveraging QA in solving complex optimization problems.

5.4   CONCLUSION

This chapter studied the potential of quantum computing in the field of optimization and machine learning. By exploring variational quantum algorithms and QA, we highlighted how these quantum approaches can redefine classical optimization paradigms. The QAOA and the VQE illustrate the blend of quantum and classical techniques to address combinatorial and eigenvalue problems efficiently.

QA, with its foundation in quantum tunnelling and superposition, provides a novel mechanism for navigating the complex landscapes of optimization problems, contrasting traditional methods like SA. Its applications extend beyond optimization, offering intriguing possibilities in QML where speed and model capabilities are enhanced. While QML stands at the intersection of quantum computing and traditional machine learning, presenting opportunities to accelerate training processes and improve model performance. This fusion is set to revolutionize fields ranging from classification to clustering, leveraging the inherent advantages of quantum computation.

In this chapter, we demonstrate the significance of quantum computing in addressing the limitations of classical optimization, especially in dealing with NP-hard problems. As quantum hardware continues to evolve, the synergy between quantum algorithms and optimization techniques is expected to unlock unprecedented computational efficiencies, tackling real-world challenges with greater precision and adaptability.

This chapter gives the foundations for a deeper understanding of how quantum technologies can be harnessed to enhance optimization and machine learning, paving the way for future advancements in science and engineering. The continuous development and refinement of quantum algorithms will be crucial in transforming complex, computationally intensive problems into solvable tasks, marking the advent of a new computational era.

REFERENCES

1. Boyd, S. P., & Vandenberghe, L. (2004). Convex Optimization. Cambridge, UK: Cambridge University Press.
2. Bertsimas, D., & Tsitsiklis, J. N. (1997). Introduction to Linear Optimization (Vol. 6, pp. 479–530). Belmont, MA: Athena Scientific.
3. Guenin, B., Könemann, J., & Tuncel, L. (2014). A Gentle Introduction to Optimization. Cambridge, UK: Cambridge University Press.
4. Abbas, A., Ambainis, A., Augustino, B., Bärtschi, A., Buhrman, H., Coffrin, C., Cortiana, G., Dunjko, V., Egger, D. J., Elmegreen, B. G., Franco, N., Fratini, F., Fuller, B., Gacon, J., Gonciulea, C., Gribling, S., Gupta, S., Hadfield, S., Heese, R., …, & Zoufal, C. (2023). Quantum Optimization: Potential, Challenges, and the Path Forward (Version 1). arXiv. https://doi.org/10.48550/ARXIV.2312.02279
5. Peruzzo, A., McClean, J., Shadbolt, P., Yung, M.-H., Zhou, X.-Q., Love, P. J., Aspuru-Guzik, A., & O'Brien, J. L. (2014). A Variational Eigenvalue Solver On a Photonic Quantum Processor. In Nature Communications (Vol. 5, Issue 1). Springer Science and Business Media LLC. https://doi.org/10.1038/ncomms5213
6. Farhi, E., Goldstone, J., & Gutmann, S. (2014). A Quantum Approximate Optimization Algorithm (Version 1). arXiv. https://doi.org/10.48550/ARXIV.1411.4028
7. Hadfield, S., Wang, Z., O'Gorman, B., Rieffel, E., Venturelli, D., & Biswas, R. (2019). From the Quantum Approximate Optimization Algorithm to a Quantum Alternating Operator Ansatz. In Algorithms (Vol. 12, Issue 2, p. 34). MDPI AG. https://doi.org/10.3390/a12020034
8. Grover, L. K. (1996). A fast quantum mechanical algorithm for database search. In Proceedings of the twenty-eighth annual ACM symposium on theory of computing – STOC '96. the twenty-eighth annual ACM symposium. ACM Press. https://doi.org/10.1145/237814.237866
9. Dürr, C., & Hoyer, P. (1996). A Quantum Algorithm for Finding the Minimum (Version 2). arXiv. https://doi.org/10.48550/ARXIV.QUANT-PH/9607014
10. Gilliam, A., Woerner, S., & Gonciulea, C. (2021). Grover Adaptive Search for Constrained Polynomial Binary Optimization. In Quantum (Vol. 5, p. 428). Verein zur Forderung des Open Access Publizierens in den Quantenwissenschaften. https://doi.org/10.22331/q-2021-04-08-428
11. Slate, N., Matwiejew, E., Marsh, S., & Wang, J. B. (2021). Quantum Walk-Based Portfolio Optimisation. In Quantum (Vol. 5, p. 513). Verein zur Forderung des Open Access Publizierens in den Quantenwissenschaften. https://doi.org/10.22331/q-2021-07-28-513

12. Kerenidis, I., & Prakash, A. (2020). A Quantum Interior Point Method for LPs and SDPs. In ACM Transactions on Quantum Computing (Vol. 1, Issue 1, pp. 1–32). Association for Computing Machinery (ACM). https://doi.org/10.1145/3406306

13. Au-Yeung, R., Chancellor, N., & Halffmann, P. (2023). NP-Hard but No Longer Hard to Solve? Using Quantum Computing to Tackle Optimization Problems. In Frontiers in Quantum Science and Technology (Vol. 2). Frontiers Media SA. https://doi.org/10.3389/frqst.2023.1128576

14. Lucas, A. (2014). Ising Formulations of Many NP Problems. In Frontiers in Physics (Vol. 2). Frontiers Media SA. https://doi.org/10.3389/fphy.2014.00005

15. Glover, F., Kochenberger, G., & Du, Y. (2018). A Tutorial on Formulating and Using QUBO Models (Version 6). arXiv. https://doi.org/10.48550/ARXIV.1811.11538

16. Bermejo, P., & Orus, R. (2022). Variational Quantum Continuous Optimization: A Cornerstone of Quantum Mathematical Analysis (Version 1). arXiv. https://doi.org/10.48550/ARXIV.2210.03136

17. Kirkpatrick, S., Gelatt, C. D., Jr., & Vecchi, M. P. (1983). Optimization by Simulated Annealing. In Science (Vol. 220, Issue 4598, pp. 671–680). American Association for the Advancement of Science (AAAS). https://doi.org/10.1126/science.220.4598.671

18. Gendreau, M., & Potvin, J. Y. (Eds.) (2010). Handbook of Metaheuristics (Vol. 2, p. 9). New York: Springer.

19. Kadowaki, T., & Nishimori, H. (1998). Quantum Annealing in the Transverse Ising Model. In Physical Review E (Vol. 58, Issue 5, pp. 5355–5363). American Physical Society (APS). https://doi.org/10.1103/physreve.58.5355

20. Gamow, G. (1928). Zur Quantentheorie des Atomkernes. In Zeitschrift für Physik (Vol. 51, Issues 3–4, pp. 204–212). Springer Science and Business Media LLC. https://doi.org/10.1007/bf01343196

21. Born, M., & Fock, V. (1928). Beweis des Adiabatensatzes. In Zeitschrift für Physik (Vol. 51, Issues 3–4, pp. 165–180). Springer Science and Business Media LLC. https://doi.org/10.1007/bf01343193

22. Farhi, E., Goldstone, J., Gutmann, S., & Sipser, M. (2000). Quantum Computation by Adiabatic Evolution (Version 1). arXiv. https://doi.org/10.48550/ARXIV.QUANT-PH/0001106

23. Trotter, H. F. (1959). On the Product of Semi-Groups of Operators. In Proceedings of the American Mathematical Society (Vol. 10, Issue 4, pp. 545–551). American Mathematical Society (AMS). https://doi.org/10.1090/s0002-9939-1959-0108732-6

24. Suzuki, M. (1976). Generalized Trotter's Formula and Systematic Approximants of Exponential Operators and Inner Derivations with Applications to Many-Body Problems. In Communications in Mathematical Physics (Vol. 51, Issue 2, pp. 183–190). Springer Science and Business Media LLC. https://doi.org/10.1007/bf01609348

25. Sadhu, A., Zaman, S., Das, K., Banerjee, A., & Khan, F. S. (2020). Quantum Annealing for Solving a Nurse-Physician Scheduling Problem in Covid-19 Clinics. Unpublished. https://doi.org/10.13140/RG.2.2.22952.80648

26. Weinberg, S. J., Sanches, F., Ide, T., Kamiya, K., & Correll, R. (2023). Supply Chain Logistics with Quantum and Classical Annealing Algorithms. In Scientific Reports (Vol. 13, Issue 1). Springer Science and Business Media LLC. https://doi.org/10.1038/s41598-023-31765-8

6 Hybrid Quantum-Classical Computing Architectures

Rafael Martín-Cuevas and Guzmán Calleja

6.1 INTRODUCTION

Hybrid quantum-classical computing architectures represent a pivotal evolution in computational technology, blending the strengths of quantum computing with the robustness of classical computing paradigms. At the core of this integration lies the recognition of the unique capabilities and limitations of both quantum and classical computing models. While many players within the global quantum ecosystem have already demonstrated the promise of quantum computing through pilot projects and Proofs-of-Concept (PoCs) aimed to prove theoretical quantum supremacy, the need for the integration and industrialization of these prototypes is emerging, along with the necessity for hybrid software architectures, to prepare the industry for a practical quantum advantage or quantum utility phase.

In designing and implementing hybrid quantum-classical computing architectures, principles from traditional software engineering and software architecture play a crucial role. Concepts such as modularity, scalability, usability, and interoperability provide a framework for organizing and integrating quantum and classical components within a unified architecture. Additionally, techniques for error correction, fault-tolerance, and algorithm optimization are essential for ensuring the reliability and efficiency of hybrid systems. Moreover, a solid understanding of quantum computing principles, algorithms, and programing languages is imperative for developers and architects working on hybrid quantum-classical computing projects. While traditional software engineering skills remain relevant, familiarity with quantum concepts such as qubits, quantum gates, quantum algorithms, and quantum error correction is essential for leveraging the full potential of hybrid architectures.

It is important to note that despite the transformative potential of quantum computing, it is unlikely to replace classical computing in the foreseeable future. Instead, the integration of quantum computing with classical technologies opens up new avenues for innovation and problem-solving, enabling organizations to tackle complex computational challenges more effectively by leveraging the best of both computing paradigms.

In the following sections, we delve deeper into the benefits of hybrid computing, explore the design principles guiding architecture development, discuss approaches and frameworks for implementation, address integration challenges, and speculate on the future trends shaping the evolution of hybrid quantum-classical computing

DOI: 10.1201/9781003537243-6

architectures. Through this exploration, we aim to provide insights and guidance for organizations seeking to harness the transformative power of quantum technologies within their computational ecosystems.

6.2   BENEFITS AND A NEED FOR HYBRID COMPUTING

As discussed earlier, while quantum computing offers unparalleled potential for processing vast amounts of data and solving complex problems in parallel, it is still in its infancy and faces inherent limitations, such as error rates, qubit coherence times, and scalability challenges. Conversely, classical computing provides stability, reliability, and a mature ecosystem of tools and algorithms for general-purpose computation. Hybrid quantum-classical computing architectures represent a strategic approach to harnessing the combined strengths of quantum computing and classical computing paradigms.

The need for hybrid computing arises from several factors:

- *Alignment with Business Needs:* Many PoCs in quantum computing have been developed without direct integration into organizational business processes. As these PoCs demonstrate feasibility and performance, there is a pressing need to integrate them into classical enterprise architectures, considering existing hardware and software features. This alignment ensures that quantum solutions are tailored to address specific business challenges effectively.
- *Leveraging Current and Future Quantum Hardware:* Hybridizing quantum technologies with classical ones facilitates a smoother transition to quantum adoption. With the landscape of quantum hardware rapidly evolving, organizations must assess new quantum hardware and leverage the best features of both quantum and classical systems, ensuring that the quantum algorithms developed today will remain operative and functional with minimal changes as new quantum computers become available. However, due to the lack of standardization in algorithms and methods across different quantum computing hardware, it is crucial to design future-proof architecture layers that maintain compatibility with emerging quantum processing units.
- *Making Quantum Tech Widely Accessible:* Quantum computing complexities must be isolated and simplified to enable developers with classical skillsets and legacy IT processes to leverage quantum capabilities effectively. Democratizing the usage of quantum computing entails empowering classical developers with tools and frameworks, and go-to interfaces and application layers, that abstract the intricacies of quantum technology, enabling them to integrate quantum solutions seamlessly into existing and future workflows without requiring in-depth knowledge of the underlying quantum mechanics.

In essence, hybrid quantum-classical computing architectures offer a pragmatic approach to unlocking the transformative potential of quantum technologies while mitigating the challenges associated with the adoption of these emerging technologies. By aligning quantum solutions with business objectives, leveraging the strengths of both quantum and classical computing, and simplifying and democratizing access to quantum capabilities, organizations can drive innovation and gain a competitive edge in an increasingly digital and data-driven landscape.

6.3 DESIGN PRINCIPLES GUIDING THE DESIGN OF HYBRID ARCHITECTURES

Design principles are fundamental guidelines that inform the creation and implementation of software architectures. They provide a structured approach to crafting systems that are robust, scalable, and adaptable to evolving requirements. In the context of hybrid quantum-classical computing architectures, design principles play a crucial role in guiding software architects and developers to integrate quantum and classical computing technologies seamlessly. Any hybrid quantum-classical computing architecture will need to observe the following design principles, as keystones of its definition:

1. *Openness and Flexibility:* Hybrid architectures should be designed with openness and flexibility in mind, leveraging open-source technologies where possible, and implementing clean and clear interfaces between their internal components and any current and future external systems, allowing for easy integration of quantum and classical components. This openness facilitates interoperability and ensures that architectures can evolve to accommodate future advancements in both forms of computing.

2. *Scalability:* Architectures must be scalable to support increasing computational demands, both in terms of the number of users and the complexity of the workloads being executed, in order to remain effective for organizations of any size. By designing architectures that can seamlessly integrate additional quantum and classical computing resources, organizations can adapt to evolving workload requirements and harness the full potential of quantum technologies.

3. *Hardware-Agnosticity:* Hybrid architectures should be hardware-agnostic, allowing organizations to deploy computing resources across different cloud environments or on-premise resources, with minimal adaptations depending on the underlying classical infrastructure. This agnosticism ensures flexibility in resource allocation and enables organizations to leverage the strengths of various hardware providers without being locked into a single vendor. Conversely, this property, common in classical applications, should now be extended to quantum-classical architectures that should be compatible with multiple quantum backends, supporting complex interactions transparently for the classical layers. The design should accommodate different quantum processing units and simulators, ensuring flexibility and futureproofing (where possible) against advancements in quantum hardware.

4. *Distribution and Fault-Tolerance:* Hybrid architectures should incorporate fault-tolerant mechanisms to mitigate the impact of errors inherent in quantum computing systems, through techniques like quantum error suppression (through control signals right next to the quantum hardware), mitigation (analyzing the results from an ensemble of quantum circuits), and correction (encoding single qubit values – called logical qubits – across multiple physical qubits), as well as the distribution of computing workloads across multiple backends, ensuring availability to the end users even if some of the underlying systems fail. Even though many of these solutions will already be integrated within the solutions offered by many quantum computing hardware vendors, software architectures working on the development of industrialization architectures need to ensure that these aspects have been considered.

5. *Compatibility with Traditional Architecture Patterns:* Architectures should be designed to seamlessly integrate with traditional and widely used architectures and design patterns. This compatibility facilitates the adoption of hybrid quantum-classical computing within existing IT ecosystems, enabling organizations to leverage quantum technologies without disrupting existing workflows and with minimal impact on the business and existing infrastructures, thereby enhancing the maintainability of the applications.

6. *Integration of Traditional Systems and Technologies:* Hybrid architectures that leverage quantum resources should seamlessly integrate with traditional databases, authentication and authorization systems, visualization and user interface layers, and other components, ensuring continuity and compatibility with established enterprise IT infrastructures and well-known technologies, as well as continued applicability of the software stack.

By adhering to these design principles, software architects can craft effective hybrid quantum-classical computing architectures, enabling organizations to harness the transformative power of quantum technologies while maintaining compatibility with existing classical computing environments. Through thoughtful design and implementation, organizations can embark on a journey toward realizing the full potential of hybrid quantum-classical computing in driving innovation and competitive advantage.

6.4 PROPOSED APPROACHES FOR HYBRID COMPUTING ARCHITECTURES

The design of hybrid quantum-classical computing architectures can draw many insights from the traditional disciplines of software engineering and software architecture, provided that software architects also acquire a foundational understanding of the concepts behind quantum computing, as well as its potential, application areas, and limitations. Some of the existing frameworks that are commonly used in enterprise environments to design advanced architectures – like TOGAF, Zachman, COBIT, and ITIL, briefly described below, and others – can also assist in the development of these hybrid architectures, as many of the proposed principles remain pertinent.

- *The Open Group Architecture Framework (TOGAF)*, developed by The Open Group in 1995, is a prominent enterprise architecture framework that assists businesses in defining their goals and aligning them with architectural objectives focused on enterprise software development. It offers a systematic approach to organizing the development process, minimizing errors, and aligning IT with business units to deliver quality results. Its structure consists of fundamental content and extended guidance, which provide businesses with a modular and scalable framework. The latest version, TOGAF 10, brings a stronger focus to agile methods and introduces a more streamlined structure, making it easier for businesses across industries to adopt and implement. Additionally, it provides certification and training programs that are globally recognized and beneficial for enterprise architects.
- The Zachman Framework is a fundamental structure that provides various perspectives on how an enterprise and its IT systems are interrelated. It's an enterprise ontology that offers a means of classifying and managing the intricate structure and components of an organization's architecture. Unlike traditional software process approaches, which are organized around system development phases, the Zachman Framework focuses on the perspectives of different stakeholders involved in systems development. It operates around a two-dimensional, 36-cell matrix that depicts different viewpoint perspectives of stakeholders (rows) and the interrogatives or descriptive artifacts from specific viewpoints (columns). The versatility of this framework lies in its compatibility with other frameworks like UML, BPMN, and ERD, delivering predictable and repeatable results by leveraging the structures provided by the Zachman Framework. This unique model serves as an effective tool for managing business change and for facilitating smoother transitions within complex business environments.
- *The Control Objectives for Information and Related Technology (COBIT)* Framework is a comprehensive IT governance tool developed by the Information Systems Audit and Control Association (ISACA). It supports organizations by offering control measures surrounding IT applications, allowing businesses to improve value realization from IT decisions while mitigating potential risks. In essence, it is a roadmap for developing, managing, and improving IT governance practices. By leveraging COBIT, businesses can bridge the gap between business and IT issues, offering better risk management, compliance, and process coordination. The latest iteration – COBIT 2019 – is designed to update with technological advances facing businesses, focusing on areas such as cloud computing and security. COBIT 2019 also includes dedicated concepts for small and medium-sized businesses (SMBs) apart from the enterprise-level governance structure extending its principles of accessibility. It aims to ensure IT investment

prioritization aligns with business objectives and helps organizations achieve them without incurring undue IT risk.

- ITIL (Information Technology Infrastructure Library), is a widely recognized framework for IT service management centered on delivering value to customers. It was first developed in the UK during the 1980s with the latest update, ITIL 2011, to further aid industries in providing IT services with quality and efficiency. ITIL's concepts can be grouped into services, service assets, service management, utility, warranty, value, processes, functions, roles, and capabilities. It features a structure of five stages: service strategy, service design, service transition, service operation, and continual service improvement – each crucial in the life cycle of the service. ITIL's growing demand worldwide is due to its major benefits, such as improved product delivery, enhanced customer satisfaction, better risk management, increased understanding between IT and business, improved service management to accommodate changes, and improved cost management due to resource optimization. Additionally, ITIL offers a five-tier certification structure that imparts knowledge on all elements of the ITIL service life cycle and validates expertise in the field. The adoption of ITIL across companies worldwide, coupled with its link to ISO/IEC 20000 norms, indicates a high demand for ITIL-certified professionals. This certification is a significant credential for IT project managers who are purposed to boost their competency levels.

While these frameworks can provide the common tools to design hybrid computing architectures, some studies already provide a comprehensive classification of the software layers into which the components of a hybrid computing architecture could be structured. The following classification proposes a way to organize the quantum-classical computing stack into seven layers – and, though it is focused on the gate model of quantum computing, its ideas could be adapted for more application-oriented architectures like those based on quantum annealers:

- *LAYER 1 – The Physical Layer:* This bottom-most layer encompasses the material fundamentals of quantum computing. It includes the actual physical qubits such as superconducting qubits and neutral-atom qubits. The connectivity among these qubits, hardware-native quantum gates, and readout or measurement processes form the core operational elements at this level. Functions like qubit integration and decoding are also part of this layer, effectively encapsulating the physical quantum system. This layer serves as the foundation upon which the entire quantum-classical hybrid system is built.
- *LAYER 2 – The Control Layer:* This layer is responsible for hardware characterization and optimization, pulse and timing calibration, and stabilization processes. This layer should also try to minimize the impact of quantum errors by applying control signals directly next to the quantum hardware (quantum error suppression) and by analyzing results after executing ensembles of quantum circuits (quantum error mitigation). This layer

makes the quantum hardware accessible to the rest of the stack, setting up the interaction between the quantum system and classical operations.

- *LAYER 3 – The Hardware-Aware Compilation Layer:* At this stage, several steps take place to translate hardware-agnostic (logical) circuits into hardware-aware operations that can be submitted for execution. First, the optimization of logical circuits and decomposition of complex qubit gates into simpler one-qubit and two-qubit gates occur. Then, this layer handles logical-to-physical compilation, therefore enabling quantum error correction by mapping single qubit values (logical qubits) across several physical qubits of the underlying hardware. It also then translates standard one-qubit and two-qubit gates into basis gates and performs physical circuit optimization by then translating those basis gates into hardware operations that depend on the qubit architecture of the underlying quantum computer. Furthermore, this layer provides the interface for quantum simulators that operate on classical systems, when applicable, offering an alternative to the quantum developer by enabling the execution of those same logical quantum circuits into quantum simulators that run on classical systems, and skipping those steps of the compilation process described above that are no longer necessary, therefore replacing the previous two layers of the quantum stack (physical and control layer).

- *LAYER 4 – The Quantum Orchestration Layer:* This layer manages the selection and utilization of underlying quantum computers from multiple vendors and qubit architectures, as well as quantum simulators. It handles system access, user quotas (particularly useful when sharing a limited number of quantum resources among a large user base), execution of one or several quantum computers and simulators (also enabling benchmarking capabilities), and fault tolerance in case of system failure or maintenance. For variational quantum algorithms requiring iterative execution of parameterized quantum circuits, whose parameters are slightly updated after every execution, this layer ensures minimal latency by tying the classical optimizer closely with the quantum system on which each iteration is executed.

- *LAYER 5 – The Quantum Computing Framework Layer:* This layer offers software coding capabilities for quantum computing. Offering high-level, hardware-agnostic circuit models and multi-qubit quantum gates, it paves the way for quantum developers to implement algorithms. This layer can also provide auxiliary software tools, libraries, and software development kits (SDKs or, when focused particularly on quantum computing, QDKs) along with commonly used quantum subroutines to develop more intricate quantum algorithms.

- *LAYER 6 – The Quantum Algorithm Layer:* Stepping up, this layer enables the implementation of high-level, business/application-oriented quantum algorithms, by harnessing high-level cross-application quantum algorithms from the previous layer as well as domain-specific business requirements and data processing capabilities that tailor the behavior of the underlying quantum algorithm to a particular business application. This layer, being the first to incorporate business logic, allows the five previous layers to maintain application-agnosticism to ensure the widespread applicability of quantum computing across different organizations.

- *LAYER 7 – The Quantum Application Layer:* Finally, the topmost layer spotlights the integration of quantum algorithms into hosted software applications within classical environments. Through this layer, a quantum solution meets business logic and intertwines with other tech domains through Quantum-as-a-Service (QaaS) aspects like storage, visualization, data input/output, API, and authentication and authorization, maximizing its potential. This layer serves as the final gateway to turn quantum power into real-world applications.

This seven-layer approach enables businesses and individuals to maintain a structured and reusable approach to leverage quantum computing capabilities while ensuring basic principles of software architecture such as modularity, maintainability, and separation of concerns. This paves the way for the development of more complex quantum-powered applications.

Additionally, enterprise architects must also consider other aspects associated with these execution capabilities that complement them, like the implementation of development architectures and methodologies that enable the continuous development and integration of quantum-powered algorithms and applications. Operations architectures that monitor the performance of the execution architecture and capture data can lay the foundation for future improvements.

6.5   MAIN CHALLENGES

While hybrid quantum-classical computing architectures can bring unprecedented computing capabilities and a promise to transform industries, it is important to recognize the difficulties associated with their adoption and implementation. The quantum field is still evolving, with several complications that need to be addressed to leverage its full potential.

- *Lack of Standardization:* The quantum computing ecosystem is still maturing with diverse approaches. As a result, there is a lack of standardization in terms of involved systems, processes, and interfaces, creating interoperability barriers and obstructing widespread adoption.
- *Multiple Quantum Paradigms:* There are several quantum computing paradigms and hardware types, including superconducting qubits, topological qubits, and trapped ions, among many others. The coexistence of these approaches, and the uncertainty around which qubit architecture will offer the best performance in the long term, causes confusion and hinders the development of universal solution strategies.
- *Lack of Service-Level Agreements (SLAs):* Presently, major hardware vendors do not provide robust SLAs. Issues like poor response times, long latencies, and frequent downtimes can disrupt consistency and application availability, making this technology unreliable for critical operations in the short term.

- *Scarcity of Experts:* Quantum computing requires a high level of expertise. There is a paucity of professionals with a quantum computing background who combine the appropriate foundations from physics, mathematics and computer science with a deep understanding of quantum computing technology in particular. This skills gap is and will remain a significant bottleneck for the widespread adoption of this technology, offering exciting and competitive career opportunities for those willing to go through quantum computing training plans.
- *Classical Architecture Diversity:* The diversity of current classical architectures presents compatibility challenges when integrating quantum solutions. Designing hybrid systems that work seamlessly across all platforms is complex.
- *Limited Performance and High Error Rates:* Current quantum computing hardware suffers from limited performance and high error rates. These systems are often unstable, requiring frequent corrections and recalibrations, undermining their efficacy and applicability in productive environments.
- *Quick Evolution of the Infrastructures:* The rapid evolution of quantum computing infrastructures, software libraries, and application interfaces requires organizations to continually update their quantum algorithms and applications, necessitating significant time and financial investment, and limiting the reliability of these solutions.
- *Persistence and Processing Flows:* Quantum states are not as easily persisted as in classical computing. The complex processing flows need detailed consideration, and the development of new solutions, to ensure accurate and reliable quantum operations.
- *Integration with Classical Infrastructure:* Merging these new quantum architectures with existing classical infrastructures is a colossal task. The integration needs to be smooth to prevent disruptions in the ongoing operations, as covered throughout this chapter.

While the challenges are evident, the transformative potential of hybrid quantum-classical computing architectures is undeniable. As the field matures and technological advancements are made, there is optimism that these challenges can be addressed effectively. The current stage is reminiscent of the early days of classical computing, pointing toward a long, yet promising journey ahead. This exciting era of quantum computing will usher in revolutionary applications across various domains, justifying the efforts to overcome these hurdles.

6.6 CONCLUSION AND FUTURE TRENDS

Through this chapter, we have sought to unpack the intricacies of hybrid quantum-classical computing architectures, elucidate their need and potential benefits, the design principles that could guide their design and development, a proposed multi-layered design, and outline the challenges that their adoption currently poses. As we close, we cast our gaze forward, envisioning the future trends that will shape this dynamic field.

Future work in hybrid quantum-classical computing architectures promises to be shaped by remarkable innovation and breakthroughs. Advancements in – and a broader understanding of – quantum technologies will ensure more robust and reliable systems. We anticipate greater progress around standardization within the quantum computing ecosystem, which will significantly aid integration efforts and improve operability.

The coexistence of multiple quantum paradigms, while currently presenting a challenge, foreshadows a future where organizations can leverage the strengths of different paradigms to optimally solve complex problems. Surely, this suggests that more adaptable and flexible hybrid systems are on the horizon.

Mirroring advancements in standardizing and improving quantum architectures, we expect classical architectures to become more accommodating of quantum technologies. The diversity of classical architectures, currently a hurdle, may thus transform into an advantage, providing ample ground for customization and optimization.

The integration of quantum and classical architectures poses a significant engineering challenge. However, the benefits gained from successful integration, such as solving problems that are currently unsolvable or improving computational efficiency, make it a worthwhile endeavor. As such, we expect future trends to focus heavily on achieving this integration as smoothly as possible.

In conclusion, the journey toward practical and widespread use of hybrid quantum-classical computing is fraught with complexities and challenges. However, the promise and transformative potential of quantum technologies makes for an engaging, rewarding journey.

7 Quantum Data Centers and Quantum Cloud

Abdelkader Laouid, Mostefa Kara, and Khaled Chait

7.1 INTRODUCTION

Quantum Data Centers (QDCs) promise a new era in computing, outperforming classical computers across various dimensions, such as speed, storage, feasibility, cost, and energy consumption [1]. While traditional computers are the backbone of digital technology, their performance is bound by classical physics, limiting their speed and communication capabilities [2]. QDC technology exploits the principles of quantum mechanics and promises exponential speedups for certain computations, potentially solving problems intractable for classical computers [1]. In digital representation, QDCs introduce quantum memory concepts like Quantum Random Access Memory (QRAM), offering efficient data retrieval methods that could surpass classical storage solutions [3, 4].

Currently, the feasibility of QDCs faces many challenges due to the need for ultra-low temperatures and error correction techniques, aspects less critical for traditional computers [5]. The initial investment for QDC infrastructure surpasses that of classical computers, reflecting the demand for cutting-edge technology and specialized operating conditions. However, the operational energy consumption of QDCs could be lower in the long run, as quantum processes allow for more energy-efficient computations at a fundamental level [5].

QDC is perceived as an enabler of quantum cloud computing and Quantum as a Service (QaaS). Therefore, this chapter is set to illustrate QDC first before diving into the discussion of QaaS in Chapter 8.

7.2 THE TRANSFORMATIVE POWER OF QDCS

In the rapidly evolving landscape of quantum technologies, QDCs emerge as a revolutionary paradigm poised to harness the full spectrum of quantum mechanics, quantum computing, communication, and quantum sensing. These advanced systems promise to transcend classical computing's limitations, addressing data-intensive challenges previously deemed impossible. This section provides an overview of the QDC concept, illustrated in Figure 7.1, which covers the core components, applications, and transformative implications of QDCs, heralding a new epoch in computational science and technology.

As we investigate the Noisy Intermediate-scale Quantum (NISQ) era, marked by rapid advancements in quantum technology, the ambition for large-scale,

DOI: 10.1201/9781003537243-7

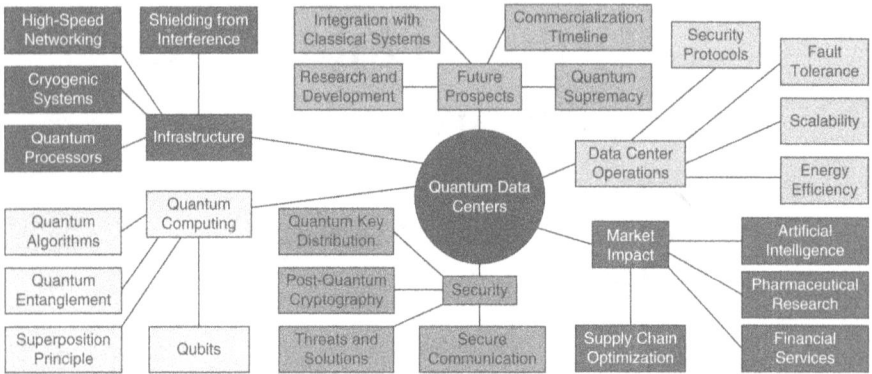

FIGURE 7.1   QDCs' fields.

fault-tolerant quantum devices becomes progressively attainable. QDCs, by bridging quantum technologies with classical data analytics and machine learning, redefine problem-solving across a multitude of domains [6]. Their counterparts in classical computing demonstrate a shift toward quantum-integrated data-processing solutions.

7.2.1   FUNDAMENTAL CONCEPTS IN QDCs

QDCs leverage principles of quantum mechanics to enhance computing, communication, and sensing capabilities, where QRAM and Quantum Networks (QN) are central to their operation. Here, we outline the mathematical definitions and foundational properties that underpin these technologies. Qubits, superposition, and entanglement emerge as fundamental operations in quantum computation.

7.2.1.1   Qubit

A qubit is the quantum analog of a classical bit. Unlike a bit, which can be in a state of 0 or 1, a qubit can be in a superposition of both states. This is mathematically represented as

$$|\psi\rangle = \alpha|0\rangle + \beta|1\rangle,$$

where $|0\rangle$ and $|1\rangle$ are the basis states; α and β are complex coefficients satisfying:

$$|\alpha|^2 + |\beta|^2 = 1.$$

7.2.1.1   Superposition – Uncertainty

A qubit can exist in a superposition of states, allowing it to represent both 0 and 1 simultaneously:

$$|\psi\rangle = \frac{1}{\sqrt{2}}\left(|0\rangle + |1\rangle\right).$$

7.2.1.2 Entanglement

Entanglement is a quantum phenomenon where qubits become interconnected, and the state of one cannot be described without the state of the other, regardless of the distance separating them. An example of an entangled state of two qubits is the Bell state:

$$\left|\Phi^{+}\right\rangle = \frac{1}{\sqrt{2}}\left(\left|00\right\rangle + \left|11\right\rangle\right)$$

The mathematical formalism of QDCs highlights the quantum mechanical principles enabling their advanced capabilities. Through superposition and entanglement, QDCs achieve superior data processing and communication, laying the groundwork for future technological advancements.

7.2.1.3 Quantum Data Manipulation

Quantum gates manipulate qubit states, functioning as the quantum equivalent of classical logic gates. For instance, the Hadamard gate (H) applied to a qubit in state $\left|0\right\rangle$ creates a superposition state:

$$H\left|0\right\rangle = \frac{1}{\sqrt{2}}\left(\left|0\right\rangle + \left|1\right\rangle\right)$$

7.2.1.4 Quantum Data Transfer – Quantum Teleportation

Quantum teleportation transfers qubit states between two locations without moving the physical qubit itself, using entanglement and classical communication. The basic protocol involves three main steps: entanglement creation, Bell-state measurement, and qubit-state reconstruction.

7.2.1.4.1 Quantum States and Entanglement

A qubit, the basic unit of quantum information, can be in a superposition of states, represented as $\left|\psi\right\rangle = \alpha\left|0\right\rangle + \beta\left|1\right\rangle$, where α and β are complex numbers, and $\left|0\right\rangle$ and $\left|1\right\rangle$ are the basis states.

Entangled states are quantum states of two or more qubits where the state of one qubit instantaneously affects the state of the other, regardless of the distance separating them. A common example is the Bell state:

$$\left|\Phi^{+}\right\rangle = \frac{1}{\sqrt{2}}\left(\left|00\right\rangle + \left|11\right\rangle\right)$$

7.2.1.4.2 Quantum Teleportation Protocol

The protocol involves three qubits: the one to be teleported (qubit 1), and an entangled pair shared between the sender (Alice) and the receiver (Bob) (qubits 2 and 3, respectively).

1. *Preparation:* Alice and Bob share an entangled pair of qubits in state $\left|\Phi^{+}\right\rangle$.
2. *Bell-State Measurement:* Alice performs a Bell-state measurement on the qubit she wishes to teleport and her part of the entangled pair.

3. *Classical Communication:* Alice sends the result of her measurement to Bob via a classical communication channel.
4. *Quantum State Reconstruction:* Using the information received from Alice, Bob applies a corresponding quantum gate (*I, X, Z,* or *XZ*) to his qubit, completing the teleportation process.

The initial state of the three qubits can be represented as

$$|\psi\rangle_{123} = |\psi\rangle_1 \otimes |\Phi^+\rangle_{23} = \left(\alpha|0\rangle_1 + \beta|1\rangle_1\right) \otimes \frac{1}{\sqrt{2}}\left(|00\rangle_{23} + |11\rangle_{23}\right)$$

After the Bell-state measurement, depending on the outcome, Bob applies the appropriate operation to his qubit. The teleportation of the quantum state |ψ⟩ is achieved without physically sending the qubit from Alice to Bob [7].

Quantum teleportation showcases the peculiarities of quantum mechanics, notably entanglement, to achieve instant transfer of quantum information. This protocol is foundational for quantum computing and quantum communication technologies [8]. The advent of QDCs signifies a profound transformation across scientific and industrial sectors, especially in data-intensive fields like machine learning and big data analytics. The fusion of quantum computing with traditional data center technologies promises to unlock new scientific frontiers, drive innovation, and catalyze breakthroughs across various disciplines. At the vanguard of the quantum revolution, QDCs encapsulate the convergence of quantum and classical technologies. As exploration into quantum computing's vast landscape advances, QDCs are set to play a pivotal role in sculpting the future contours of computing, communication, and sensing, marking a leap into an era of untold possibilities [9].

7.2.2 QUANTUM NETWORK AND QUANTUM RANDOM ACCESS MEMORY

In the quantum domain, the development of QDCs depends on two essential technologies, QRAM and QNs. These technologies are foundational for realizing efficient, secure, and precise quantum computing, communication, and sensing applications.

7.2.2.1 QRAM

QRAM is a complex type of quantum memory that enables superposition states to address, thus allowing for the retrieval of data elements from a database in a quantum superposition. This capability is crucial for quantum algorithms demonstrating significant advantages over their classical counterparts by leveraging query models involving quantum inputs. QRAM could also be seen as a theoretical memory system designed for quantum computing that extends the concept of classical RAM into the quantum domain. Unlike classical RAM, which stores and retrieves information in binary form (0s and 1s) at specific memory locations, QRAM can access superpositions of memory sites. This means it can operate on quantum states, where each memory location contains either classical or quantum information (qubits). The key feature of QRAM is its ability to access and manipulate information stored in quantum superpositions and entanglements. This allows for parallel processing on an exponential scale compared to classical systems, significantly enhancing the efficiency and speed of certain computational tasks, such as searching databases, pattern recognition, and executing quantum algorithms [10].

Like classical RAM, a QRAM with n-bit addresses can access 2^n memory sites. However, it leverages quantum mechanics principles to achieve quantum parallelism. It is a critical component for developing large-scale quantum computers and performing complex quantum algorithms requiring efficient data retrieval and storage mechanisms.

7.2.2.1.1 Theoretical Concepts

QRAM operates on the principle of superposition states to access different elements within the database, which can be either classical or quantum data. It facilitates mapping superposed addresses to corresponding data entries, creating entangled states between the data and the addresses. Given an example of a database of N elements, a QRAM is designed to implement a unitary operation U_{QRAM} that acts on an address register $|\alpha\rangle$ and a data register $|d\rangle$ as follows:

$$U_{QRAM}|a\rangle|0\rangle = |a\rangle|d_a\rangle$$

where $|a\rangle$ is the quantum state representing the address in superposition, and $|d_a\rangle$ is the quantum state of the data corresponding to address a.

In the context of QDCs, QRAM enables the execution of complex quantum algorithms that require rapid access to a vast database of quantum states. This is particularly beneficial for tasks such as quantum machine learning, where QRAM can significantly reduce the complexity and execution time of algorithms. Both classical RAM and QRAM are critical in storing and retrieving information processes. However, the underlying principles and the efficiency of these two types of memories differ significantly due to the quantum mechanical nature of QRAM. Classical RAM uses n bits to address $N = 2^n$ distinct memory cells. Each cell can be accessed individually by specifying its unique address in the address register. The conventional architecture involves $O(N^{1/d})$ switches, where d is the dimensionality of the memory array, to access one out of N memory slots when QRAM uses n qubits to address any quantum superposition of N memory cells. This quantum mechanical capability allows QRAM to exponentially reduce the requirements for a memory call to $O(\log N)$ switches, compared to the N used in conventional RAM designs. This represents a significant improvement in computational complexity and power consumption.

7.2.2.1.2 Comparison

The key distinction between RAM and QRAM lies, certainly, in their addressing schemes and the research complexity:

Classical RAM: Requires $O(N^{1/d})$ switches for accessing memory, leading to high power consumption and slower speeds for large N.

Quantum RAM: Reduces the number of switches required for a memory call to $O(\log N)$, significantly decreasing the computational complexity and energy usage.

The QRAM offers an exponential improvement over classical RAM in computational complexity and energy efficiency. This advancement could be pivotal in developing quantum computing technologies, enabling more efficient data retrieval and storage mechanisms.

7.2.2.2   QN

A QN forms the backbone of QDCs, enabling the distribution and sharing of quantum information across different quantum processors and devices within the data center (see Figure 7.2). QNs revolutionize how information is processed and transmitted by enabling fundamentally secure communication, distributed quantum computing, and enhanced measurement and sensing capabilities beyond the limits of classical physics [11]. Central to this revolution are QDCs and the infrastructure for quantum cloud computing, which promise to scale quantum computing power and offer unprecedented computational services to clients [12].

In the following, we explore the challenges, solutions, and potential applications of dynamic entangled QNs, showing what is essential for realizing scalable QDCs and future quantum cloud computing infrastructures [13].

7.2.2.2.1   QDCs and Cloud Computing

QDC is envisioned to scale quantum computing power by utilizing networked few-qubit quantum processors in a structure analogous to today's classical mega data centers. These facilities are critical for realizing quantum cloud computing, where many users can securely access remote quantum computing resources. Unlike classical data centers, QDCs use quantum processor communication and dynamic quantum networking to function effectively.

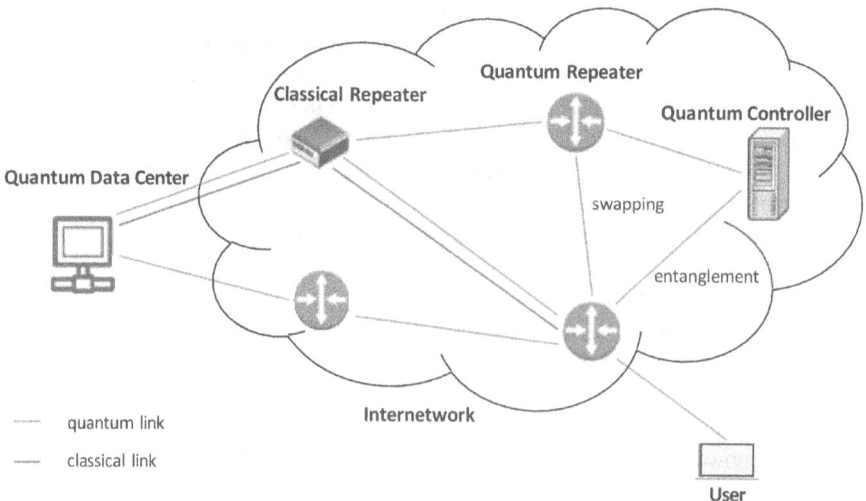

FIGURE 7.2   Quantum network illustration.

7.2.2.2.2   Theoretical Concepts

QNs rely on quantum entanglement and quantum teleportation to achieve secure and efficient transmission of quantum states. These networks utilize entangled pairs of qubits as channels for quantum communication, allowing for the direct transfer of quantum states without the physical movement of the particles. Quantum teleportation, a key process in QNs, can be described mathematically given an unknown quantum state $|\psi\rangle$ to be teleported and an entangled pair shared between the sender (Alice) and the receiver (Bob); the process involves three main steps:

1. Alice performs a Bell state measurement on $|\psi\rangle$ and her part of the entangled pair.
2. The measurement outcome is communicated to Bob through a classical channel.
3. Bob applies a corresponding unitary operation on his part of the entangled pair based on the received classical information, successfully reconstructing the state $|\psi\rangle$.

QNs within QDCs require inter-processor communication and collaboration, such as distributed quantum computing and multi-party quantum cryptographic protocols. By leveraging the principles of quantum entanglement and teleportation, QNs ensure secure and efficient data transmission across the QDC. Integrating QRAM and QNs in QDCs is a significant step toward realizing the full potential of quantum technologies. These advancements enhance the capabilities of QDCs and open new avenues for research and application in quantum computing, communication, and sensing.

7.2.2.2.3   Challenges in Quantum Networking

Despite significant progress in quantum computing and networking technologies, several challenges hinder the deployment of networked quantum processors and the realization of QDCs:

Multitenancy: Sharing quantum computing resources among multiple applications and users in a cloud environment requires a flexible and dynamically reconfigurable QN that preserves quantum states during allocation and clustering.

Entanglement Distribution and Teleportation: A core functionality of intra-data center QNs supports entanglement distribution and teleportation, which is crucial for connecting quantum processors at the quantum state level.

Secure Quantum Cloud Computing: Ensuring security and isolation between tenants in a multi-tenant environment is paramount, especially given the inherently secure nature of QNs benefiting from the no-cloning principle of quantum mechanics.

Developing a dynamic entangled QN that supports the interconnection of qubit processors within a data center and quantum-secured communications is a promising solution to the above challenges. Such a network would employ broad-band entangled photon sources, demultiplexers for dividing the photon spectrum into multiple entangled channels, and optical fiber switches for dynamically distributing entangled photons among qubit processors.

7.2.3 HYBRID COMPUTATION

While classical computation forms the backbone of current technological advancements, it faces inherent limitations, especially when tackling problems involving immense computational complexity or those requiring the simulation of quantum phenomena. Classical computers operate within the bounds of classical physics, making them less efficient for tasks like factoring large numbers, simulating quantum systems, or solving certain optimization problems where the solution space exponentially grows with the problem size [14].

In contrast, quantum computing processes information in ways fundamentally unattainable by classical systems [15]. This quantum approach offers exponential speedups for specific problems, but it also introduces new challenges, including error rates, qubit coherence times, and the complexity of quantum algorithm development [16]. Bridging the gap, hybrid quantum-classical computation emerges as a compelling solution, leveraging quantum computing's strengths for specific tasks while relying on classical computing's robustness for general computation and error correction [17]. This synergy could unlock practical quantum advantages sooner by integrating the best of both worlds to tackle complex problems more efficiently than either could alone.

7.2.3.1 Client Benefits

Running programs across quantum and classical resources involves leveraging the distinct capabilities of both computing paradigms to solve problems more efficiently than could be done with either alone. This hybrid approach integrates the processing power of quantum computers for specific tasks where they excel, such as complex simulations and optimization problems, with the versatility and reliability of classical computers for general-purpose computing and managing quantum computations. Below is a summary of how programs are run and executed across these resources:

1. Quantum programs, often controlled by classical computers, require sophisticated mathematical tools and algorithmic techniques for analysis. Studies involve examining quantum while loops and quantum Markov chains and developing algorithms for reachability analysis of quantum Markov chains. A notable application is computing the average running time of quantum walks, which can be integral in optimizing quantum algorithms.

2. Hybrid quantum-classical computing frameworks, where these hybrid frameworks were proposed for future network optimization and other applications. This involves discussing the fundamentals of quantum computing and its parallelism, detailing the hybrid computing paradigm, and exploring potential applications like network function virtualization and cloud computing. Such algorithms' design and implementation challenges are also

addressed, highlighting the interdisciplinary effort required to make hybrid computing a reality.

3. Formal approaches have been developed to study quantum programs' resource consumption and expected runtime. This involves a calculus for systematically deriving the expected runtime of quantum programs, including a notion of loop runtime invariants to estimate their runtime. Such analyses are crucial for understanding quantum algorithms' efficiency and practical feasibility.

Developing quantum programs that run across quantum and classical systems requires optimizing compilers and software design flows specific to quantum computing. This entails creating software architectures that compile high-level language programs to hardware-specific instructions, enabling scalable quantum computation. These methodologies support rapid innovation and facilitate the compilation of complex quantum algorithms. Hence, running programs across quantum and classical resources is a multifaceted challenge encompassing program analysis, hybrid computing frameworks, runtime analysis, and specialized software methodologies. These efforts pave the way for leveraging quantum computing's potential alongside classical computing's versatility, promising significant advancements in computing capabilities.

7.2.4 QDC Application Domains

QDCs revolutionize various application domains. These centers are at the forefront of quantum computing, communication, sensing, machine learning, and big data industries, promising enhanced efficiency, security, and precision. This section gives some of the common applications of QDCs.

7.2.4.1 Quantum Computing and Communication

QDCs are pivotal in deploying Quantum Key Distribution (QKD) technologies, which are crucial for ensuring future-proof data security. Quantum computing introduces a new paradigm of computation that leverages the principles of quantum mechanics, offering exponential speedups for certain computational problems. In contrast, quantum communication, particularly QKD, utilizes the principles of quantum mechanics to secure communication channels against eavesdropping.

QKD technologies span many applications, from protecting short-range consumer communications to securing global communication networks. These technologies are not just theoretical constructs but are being actively deployed and tested in various settings worldwide. Works such as [18, 19] provide insights into the versatility of QKD applications, from metropolitan to inter-city scales, highlighting their potential to transform the security landscape of modern communication networks.

7.2.4.1.1 Example of QKD in Practice

One notable example of QKD in action is developing and deploying a quantum communication network between cities or within a metropolitan area. In such a setup, QDCs are the backbone for distributing quantum keys among network nodes.

These keys are generated and distributed so that any attempt at eavesdropping by an unauthorized party can be detected due to the fundamental properties of quantum mechanics, such as the no-cloning theorem and the principle of quantum measurement.

For instance, a QN connecting data centers across multiple cities can utilize QKD to ensure the secure transmission of information. Each data center is equipped with QKD systems that generate and share encryption keys made of qubits. These qubits are sent through dedicated quantum communication channels, such as fiber optic cables specifically designed for transmitting quantum states.

As the qubits travel from one QDC to another, any attempt by an eavesdropper to measure the quantum state of the qubits would inevitably disturb their state, alerting the communicating parties to the presence of a potential security breach. This way, QKD enables a level of security that is fundamentally unachievable with traditional cryptographic methods, which rely on the computational difficulty of certain mathematical problems rather than the laws of physics.

By leveraging QKD, QDCs can achieve unprecedented levels of data security, making them an indispensable part of the infrastructure for secure communications in the quantum era.

7.2.4.2   Quantum Software Engineering

Quantum software Engineering (QSE) is an emerging discipline that aims to apply systematic, disciplined, and quantifiable approaches to developing, operating, and maintaining quantum software. Unlike classical software, quantum software leverages new paradigms for information processing and computation. The integration of quantum mechanics with software engineering practices through QSE principles, as shown in Figure 7.3, aids in designing, developing, and evolving quantum software systems and applications [20, 21].

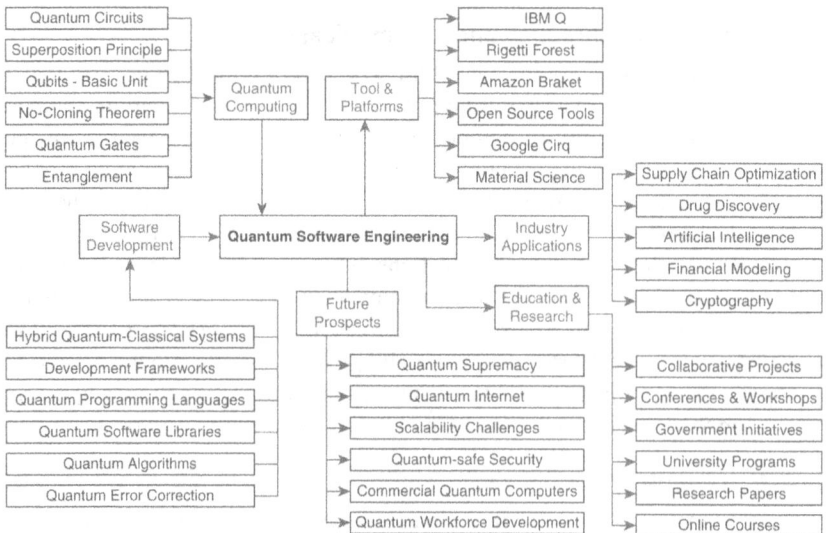

FIGURE 7.3   QSE fundamentals and applications.

7.2.4.3   Definition of QSE

QSE refers to the systematic application of engineering principles to design, develop, and validate quantum computer software. This includes the creation of quantum algorithms, developing software that runs on quantum hardware, and simulating quantum algorithms on classical computers for testing and validation purposes.

QSE Methods, Tools, and Processes: The unique characteristics of quantum computing necessitate specialized methods, tools, and processes tailored for quantum software development. These include:

- *Methods:* QSE methods encompass a range of activities, from quantum algorithm design to quantum program debugging and performance optimization. For instance, quantum algorithm design often requires a deep understanding of quantum mechanics and the ability to translate quantum computational problems into quantum circuits or quantum programs.
- *Tools:* Tools in QSE include quantum programming languages like Q#, Qiskit, and Cirq, which provide high-level abstractions for quantum programming, as well as Integrated Development Environments (IDEs) and simulators that enable developers to write, test, and debug quantum software in a familiar setting.
- *Processes:* Quantum software development processes adapt classical software development life cycles to accommodate the iterative nature of quantum algorithm development, simulation, testing, and deployment on quantum hardware. This includes quantum-specific versions of requirements analysis, design, implementation, testing, and maintenance phases.

A generic view of QSE integrates quantum-specific considerations into traditional software engineering frameworks. This perspective acknowledges the dual nature of quantum software development, which involves both quantum and classical components, and the necessity for quantum software to interact seamlessly with classical software systems.

7.2.4.3.1   Quantum Software Life Cycle

The Quantum Software Life Cycle (QSLC) adapts classical software development phases to the quantum context, incorporating:

- *Quantum Software Requirements Analysis:* Defining what quantum computational problem the software needs to solve and the quantum computational resources available.
- *Quantum Software Design:* Designing quantum algorithms and the classical software interface for interacting with the quantum hardware.
- *Quantum Software Implementation:* Implementing the quantum algorithm using a quantum programming language and developing classical software components for input, output, and control.

Quantum Software Testing: Testing the correctness of quantum algorithms through simulation on classical computers and validation on quantum hardware.

Quantum Software Maintenance: Updating and optimizing quantum software as quantum hardware evolves and new quantum algorithms are developed.

7.2.4.3.2   Example: Quantum Software for Cryptographic Applications

A practical example of QSE is the development of quantum cryptographic software, which leverages quantum algorithms for secure communication. This process involves:

7.2.4.3.3   Requirements Analysis

Defining security requirements and the quantum cryptographic protocol to be implemented.

- *Design:* Designing a QKD algorithm and its integration with classical cryptographic protocols.
- *Implementation:* Coding the QKD algorithm using a quantum programming language and developing classical interfaces for key exchange.
- *Testing:* Simulating the quantum cryptographic software to test its security properties and performing trials on quantum hardware.
- *Maintenance:* Updating the software as new quantum-resistant cryptographic algorithms are developed and quantum hardware capabilities improve.

This example illustrates the multidisciplinary nature of QSE, requiring expertise in quantum mechanics, software engineering, and cryptography.

7.2.4.4   Quantum Cloud Computing and Cybersecurity

Quantum cloud computing merges the revolutionary potential of quantum computing with the accessibility and scalability of cloud computing. As quantum computers become more powerful, they promise to solve complex computational problems much faster than classical computers. However, quantum hardware remains expensive and technically challenging to maintain, making direct access difficult for most users and organizations. Quantum cloud platforms emerge as a solution, offering remote access to quantum processors, simulators, and tools over the cloud. This accessibility accelerates research and development in quantum computing and its application across various fields, including cybersecurity. Essential for scalable quantum cloud computing infrastructures and the next generation of cybersecurity systems, QDCs cater to a wide audience, promising solutions for distributed quantum computing [22, 23]. Table 7.1 provides a comparison of IBM Quantum Experience, Amazon Braket, and Google Quantum AI.

7.2.4.4.1   Quantum Cloud Computing

Quantum cloud computing provides on-demand access to quantum computing resources via the internet. Major technology companies and some startups have

TABLE 7.1

Comparison of IBM Quantum Experience, Amazon Braket, and Google Quantum AI

Feature	IBM Quantum Experience	Amazon Braket	Google Quantum AI
Cloud Access	Available	Available	Limited
Quantum Hardware	Superconducting qubits	Ion Trap and Super-conducting qubits	Superconducting qubits
Programming Languages	Qiskit	SDK supports Python, Jupyter notebooks	Cirq, TensorFlow Quantum
Simulation Support	Included	Included	Included
Quantum Algorithms	Basic algorithms available	Various algorithms available	Various algorithms available
Quantum Computing Resources	Open access to public devices	Pay-per-use model	Limited access

launched quantum cloud services, allowing users to run quantum algorithms without owning quantum computing hardware. These platforms often offer integrated development environments, libraries, and tools tailored for quantum programming, facilitating the development and testing of quantum algorithms in a cloud-based ecosystem.

7.2.4.4.2 Quantum Cloud Platforms and Services

Several key players in the technology sector have introduced quantum cloud platforms, including IBM's Quantum Experience, Amazon Braket, and Google Quantum AI. These platforms serve as a bridge, connecting researchers, developers, and organizations to quantum computing resources. Users can explore quantum algorithms, conduct experiments, and develop new quantum applications. The platforms continuously evolve, integrating more powerful quantum processors and enhancing their services to support complex quantum computing tasks.

7.2.4.4.3 Cybersecurity Implications

The advent of quantum computing introduces both opportunities and challenges for cybersecurity. On one hand, quantum algorithms, such as Shor's algorithm, threaten to break many of the cryptographic schemes currently in use, including RSA and ECC, which underpin the security of digital communications worldwide. On the other hand, quantum computing also paves the way for quantum cryptography, offering theoretically unbreakable encryption methods, such as QKD.

7.2.4.4.4 Quantum Cryptography and QKD

Quantum cryptography utilizes the principles of quantum mechanics to secure communication channels. QKD, a well-known application of quantum cryptography, allows two parties to generate a shared secret key securely, which can then be used to encrypt and decrypt messages [24]. The security of QKD is grounded in the laws of quantum physics, which ensure that any attempt to eavesdrop on the key distribution will inevitably alter the quantum states involved, thus revealing the presence of an interceptor.

7.2.4.4.5   Preparing for the Quantum Threat to Cybersecurity

The potential of quantum computers to break current cryptographic systems has led to the development of Post-Quantum Cryptography (PQC). PQC encompasses cryptographic algorithms believed to be secure against quantum attacks and designed to work on classical computers. Governments and industry standards organizations are actively researching PQC to develop and standardize quantum-resistant cryptographic algorithms, ensuring the continuity of secure digital communications in the quantum era.

7.2.4.4.6   Example: Secure Cloud Communications via Quantum Cryptography

An example of the integration of quantum cloud computing and cybersecurity is the implementation of QKD protocols over cloud services to secure communication channels. In this scenario, a quantum cloud platform could facilitate the distribution of quantum keys among users, leveraging cloud infrastructure to extend the reach of quantum-secured communications. This approach combines the scalability and accessibility of cloud computing with the unparalleled security of quantum cryptography, showcasing a future where quantum cloud services play a critical role in securing digital communications against quantum threats.

7.2.5   QDC Limitations, Complexity, and Challenges

Despite their revolutionary potential, QDCs are faced with significant limitations, complexities, and challenges that stem from the nascent state of quantum technology, the peculiarities of quantum mechanics, and the high demands of quantum computation.

7.2.5.1   Technological Limitations

Quantum Coherence and Decoherence: One of the primary limitations is maintaining quantum coherence for sufficient durations. Qubits are susceptible to decoherence, losing their quantum state due to interactions with the environment. This limits the time available for performing quantum operations and requires sophisticated error correction techniques to preserve the integrity of quantum information.

Error Rates and Correction: Quantum systems currently exhibit higher error rates compared to classical systems, stemming from both gate errors and measurement errors. Developing efficient quantum error correction codes that do not require prohibitive overhead for additional qubits and operations is a significant challenge.

Scalability: Scaling up quantum systems to many qubits, necessary for practical and commercially viable quantum computing, presents formidable engineering and technological challenges. These include maintaining the quality of qubits, interconnecting them with high-fidelity quantum gates, and managing the cooling requirements of such systems.

7.2.5.2 Complexity in Quantum Software and Algorithms

Algorithmic Development: The design and implementation of quantum algorithms that can outperform classical algorithms for practical problems are still in their infancy. The counterintuitive nature of quantum mechanics makes algorithm development highly non-trivial, requiring deep insights into both the problem domain and quantum computational models.

Software Infrastructure: Building the software infrastructure for QDC, including quantum programming languages, compilers, and debugging tools, is complex. These tools must accommodate the nuances of quantum computation while being accessible to programmers without a deep background in quantum physics.

7.2.5.3 Operational Challenges

Integration with Classical Systems: QDC needs to work in tandem with classical computing resources, necessitating robust and efficient interfaces between quantum processors and classical systems. Designing such hybrid systems involves addressing challenges in data transfer, synchronization, and the orchestration of computational tasks.

Environmental Sensitivity: Quantum systems are extremely sensitive to their physical environment, including temperature fluctuations, electromagnetic fields, and vibrations. Ensuring the operational stability of QDCs requires overcoming substantial engineering challenges related to isolation and environmental control.

Energy Consumption: While quantum computers promise significant computational speedups for certain tasks, the energy requirements for cooling and maintaining the quantum hardware environment, especially at cryogenic temperatures, pose sustainability concerns.

7.2.5.4 Example: QKD in QDCs

A practical example illustrating operational limitations and challenges is the deployment of QKD systems in QDCs. QKD systems exploit the principles of quantum mechanics to secure communication channels. Despite their theoretical security advantages, practical QKD implementations face challenges related to decoherence, error rates, and the need for integration with existing classical cryptographic infrastructure. Overcoming these hurdles requires advancements in quantum repeater technology, error correction, and the development of standardized protocols for quantum-classical integration.

7.3 CONCLUSION

QDCs mark a significant milestone in the journey of computational sciences, where the once-theoretical aspects of quantum mechanics are harnessed to solve real-world problems with unprecedented efficiency. As shown throughout this chapter, QDCs embody the synergy of quantum computing, communication, and sensing, offering solutions that transcend the capabilities of classical computing infrastructures.

Despite the potential of QDCs, we are in the early stages of realizing their full potential. The technological limitations, such as maintaining quantum coherence, error rates, and scalability, pose significant challenges. Moreover, the complexity inherent in quantum software and algorithm development and operational challenges like integration with classical systems and environmental sensitivity emphasizes the multidisciplinary effort required to advance this field.

Challenges facing QDC are manageable due to the collaborative response from physicists, engineers, computer scientists, and industry leaders to innovate and refine the quantum technologies that underpin QDCs. As scientists continue to explore and expand the boundaries of what QDCs can achieve, it is critical to build an ecosystem that encourages experimentation, learning, and adaptation. The integration of quantum and classical computing resources in a hybrid computational approach presents a pragmatic pathway to harness quantum advantages while leveraging the robustness of classical systems.

REFERENCES

1. Junyu Liu, and Liang Jiang. Quantum data center: Perspectives. *arXiv preprint arXiv:2309.06641*, 2023.
2. Andy Kuszyk, and Mohammad Hammoudeh. Contemporary alternatives to traditional processor design in the post Moore's law era. In *Proceedings of the 2nd International Conference on Future Networks and Distributed Systems*, ICFNDS '18, New York, NY, USA, 2018. Association for Computing Machinery.
3. Khabat Heshami, Duncan G England, Peter C Humphreys, Philip J Bustard, Victor M Acosta, Joshua Nunn, and Benjamin J Sussman. Quantum memories: Emerging applications and recent advances. *Journal of Modern Optics*, 63(20):2005–2028, 2016.
4. KF Reim, J Nunn, VO Lorenz, BJ Sussman, KC Lee, NK Langford, D Jaksch, and IA Walmsley. Towards high-speed optical quantum memories. *Nature Photonics*, 4(4):218–221, 2010.
5. Michael James Martin, Caroline Hughes, Gilberto Moreno, Eric B Jones, David Sickinger, Sreekant Narumanchi, and Ray Grout. Energy use in quantum data centers: Scaling the impact of computer architecture, qubit performance, size, and thermal parameters. *IEEE Transactions on Sustainable Computing*, 7(4):864–874, 2022.
6. Kishor Bharti, Alba Cervera-Lierta, Thi Ha Kyaw, Tobias Haug, Sumner Alperin-Lea, Abhinav Anand, Matthias Degroote, Hermanni Heimonen, Jakob S Kottmann, and Tim Menke, et al. Noisy intermediate-scale quantum algorithms. *Reviews of Modern Physics*, 94(1):015004, 2022.
7. Yoon-Ho Kim, Sergei P Kulik, and Yanhua Shih. Quantum teleportation of a polarization state with a complete bell state measurement. *Physical Review Letters*, 86(7):1370, 2001.
8. Raju Valivarthi, Samantha I Davis, Cristián Peña, Si Xie, Nikolai Lauk, Lautaro Narváez, Jason P Allmaras, Andrew D Beyer, Yewon Gim, and Meraj Hussein, et al. Teleportation systems toward a quantum internet. *PRX Quantum*, 1(2):020317, 2020.
9. Xiu-Xiu Xia, Qi-Chao Sun, Qiang Zhang, and Jian-Wei Pan. Long distance quantum teleportation. *Quantum Science and Technology*, 3(1):014012, 2017.
10. Vittorio Giovannetti, Seth Lloyd, and Lorenzo Maccone. Architectures for a quantum random access memory. *Physical Review A*, 78(5):052310, 2008.
11. Stephanie Wehner, David Elkouss, and Ronald Hanson. Quantum internet: A vision for the road ahead. *Science*, 362, 2018.

12. H. J. Kimble. The quantum internet. *Nature*, 453:1023–1030, 2008.

13. Stefano Pirandola, Samuel L. Braunstein, Seth Lloyd, Tobias Gehring, Christian Weed-brook, Samuel J. Dolinar, Richard J. Glauber, Jeffrey H. Shapiro, Zheshen Zhang, Zhizhong Yan, Franco N.C. Wong, Jeffrey H. Shapiro, Franco N.C. Wong, and Stefano Pirandola. Unite to build a quantum internet. *Nature*, 532:169–171, 2016.

14. Peter W. Shor. Polynomial-time algorithms for prime factorization and discrete loga-rithms on a quantum computer. *SIAM Journal on Computing*, 26(5):1484–1509, 1997.

15. Michael A. Nielsen, and Isaac L. Chuang. *Quantum computation and quantum infor-mation*. Cambridge University Press, 2000.

16. John Preskill. Quantum computing in the NISQ era and beyond. *Quantum*, 2:79, 2018.

17. Edward Farhi, Jeffrey Goldstone, and Sam Gutmann. A quantum approximate optimi-zation algorithm. *arXiv:1411.4028*, 2014.

18. Nitin Jain, Ulrich Hoff, Marco Gambetta, Jesper Rodenberg, and Tobias Gehring. Quantum key distribution for data center security – a feasibility study, 2023.

19. Timothy P Spiller. The EPSRC quantum communications hub. In *Emerging imaging and sensing technologies for security and defence V; and advanced manufacturing technologies for micro-and nanosystems in security and defence III*, volume 11540, pages 1154005. SPIE, 2020.

20. Aakash Ahmad, Arif Ali Khan, Muhammad Waseem, Mahdi Fahmideh, and Tommi Mikkonen. Towards process centered architecting for quantum software systems. In *2022 IEEE International Conference on Quantum Software (QSW)*, pages 26–31. IEEE, 2022.

21. Manuel A Serrano, José A Cruz-Lemus, Ricardo Perez-Castillo, and Mario Piattini. Quantum software components and platforms: Overview and quality assessment. *ACM Computing Surveys*, 55(8):1–31, 2022.

22. Ivan B Djordjevic. Cluster states-based quantum networks. In *2020 IEEE Photonics Conference (IPC)*, pages 1–2. IEEE, 2020.

23. Reza Nejabati, Rui Wang, and Dimitra Simeonidou. Dynamic quantum network: from quantum data centre to quantum cloud computing. In *Optical Fiber Communication Conference (OFC) 2022*, page Th3D.1. Optica Publishing Group, 2022.

24. Mohammed Elhabib Kahla, Mounir Beggas, Abdelkader Laouid, Mostefa Kara, and Muath AlShaikh. Asymmetric image encryption based on twin message fusion. In *2021 International Conference on Artificial Intelligence for Cyber Security Systems and Privacy (AI-CSP)*, pages 1–5. IEEE, 2021.

8 Quantum as a Service in Cloud Computing

Abdelkader Laouid, Mostefa Kara,
and Khaled Chait

8.1 INTRODUCTION

Quantum as a Service (QaaS) is a new paradigm in the field of Cloud Computing (CC), offering access to quantum computing resources via the cloud [1]. This innovative service model democratizes access to quantum computing, enabling businesses, researchers, and developers to perform complex computations that are beyond the reach of classical computers, without the need to own and maintain costly quantum hardware. This chapter aims to provide a comprehensive introduction to QaaS, exploring its foundations, technological underpinnings, potential applications, and the challenges it faces. Quantum principles enable performing certain types of computations much more efficiently than classical computers, particularly in fields such as cryptography, material science, and complex system simulation.

The chapter explores the architecture of QaaS platforms, discussing how quantum computing resources are made available over the cloud. This includes an examination of the infrastructure required to support quantum computing, including qubit technologies, quantum error correction, and the integration of quantum processors with classical computing resources to form a cohesive cloud service. The potential applications and benefits of QaaS are vast and transformative across various sectors. This chapter explores how customers gain from the enhanced computational capabilities of quantum computing.

Despite its promise, QaaS also presents significant challenges, including technical hurdles related to qubit coherence, error rates, and scalability, as well as broader issues concerning security, privacy, and the development of quantum-resistant encryption methods. This chapter examines these challenges and others related to them, such as Homomorphic Encryption (HE) and blockchain. Moreover, this chapter addresses the current state of the QaaS market, including key players, service models, and the evolving ecosystem of startups, research institutions, and traditional computing giants. We discuss the strategic implications of QaaS for businesses and how they can prepare for a future where quantum computing plays a central role in solving complex problems. Last, the chapter explores solutions to the challenges posed by QaaS.

8.2 CLASSICAL CLOUD COMPUTING

CC is a technology that provides on-demand access to computing and storage resources such as servers, databases, networking, software, analytics, and intelligence

DOI: 10.1201/9781003537243-8

over the Internet, colloquially designated "the cloud". This paradigm shift cultivates faster innovation, flexible resource allocation, and economies of scale.

Typically, the client only pays for his cloud services, helping lower operating costs, run infrastructure more efficiently, and scale as his business needs change [2]. Mainly, there are three deployment models of CC. In a public cloud, services are delivered over the public Internet and shared across organizations. In a private cloud, the cloud infrastructure is exclusively used by a single organization. It offers more control and security. A hybrid cloud combines public and private clouds, allowing data and applications to be shared between them for flexibility and more deployment options. The general use cases of CC are hosting websites and applications, storing, backing up, and recovering data, streaming audio and video, delivering software on demand, and analyzing data for patterns and making predictions.

8.2.1 SERVICE MODELS

CC services offer a wide array of resources via the Internet, tailored to help businesses and individuals use software, store data, and access powerful computing infrastructure without the need for significant capital investment in physical hardware. These services are categorized into three main types, each serving different needs and use cases:

1. Infrastructure as a Service (IaaS) provides fundamental computing, storage, and networking resources on-demand, on a pay-as-you-go basis. This allows clients to rent virtual machines, storage space, and network capabilities without having to invest in and manage the physical infrastructure themselves. It offers flexibility, scalability, and control over IT resources. Examples of IaaS providers include Amazon Web Services (AWS) EC2, Microsoft Azure Virtual Machines, and Google Compute Engine (GCE).
2. Platform as a Service (PaaS) offers a cloud-based environment with everything required to support the complete lifecycle of building and delivering web-based applications and services, without the complexity of building and maintaining the infrastructure typically associated with developing and launching an app. PaaS solutions provide a framework that developers can build upon to develop or customize applications. Examples include Google App Engine, Microsoft Azure App Services, and Heroku.
3. Software as a Service (SaaS) delivers software applications over the Internet, on a subscription basis. SaaS providers manage the infrastructure, middleware, app software, and application data. This model frees clients from installing, managing, and upgrading software on individual devices. SaaS applications are accessible from any Internet-connected device, which makes them highly accessible and convenient. Examples include Google Workspace, Salesforce, Dropbox, and Microsoft Office 365.

Beyond these primary service models, the CC landscape continually evolves, introducing novel services to address specific technological advancements and business needs. Function as a Service (FaaS), often termed serverless computing, empowers developers to execute code triggered by events without managing the underlying infrastructure, with platforms like AWS Lambda and Azure Functions leading the charge. Database as a Service (DBaaS) streamlines access to databases without requiring physical hardware setup or software configuration, exemplified by offerings such as Amazon RDS and MongoDB Atlas. AI as a Service (AIaaS) democratizes AI capabilities to individuals and businesses, providing tools and computational power for seamless integration into applications, thereby circumventing substantial research and development investment. QaaS pioneers access to quantum computing resources via the cloud, allowing clients to leverage quantum algorithms without owning dedicated quantum hardware.

CC services engender transformative capabilities, enabling businesses and developers to leverage vast computing resources and sophisticated software solutions flexibly and cost-effectively. The choice among IaaS, PaaS, SaaS, and newer models depends on the specific needs, technical expertise, and business goals of the client.

8.2.2 System Weaknesses

Classical CC (CCC) has indeed revolutionized business operations by providing flexible resources and fostering innovation. Continuously evolving, CCC incorporates emerging technologies like Artificial Intelligence (AI) and Machine Learning (ML) to offer increasingly advanced services. However, despite its transformative potential, CCC harbors inherent weaknesses and challenges [3, 4].

While this chapter doesn't delve into general cloud challenges such as cost management, data sovereignty and compliance, vendor lock-in, and technical complexity, it concentrates on performance-related issues, including, (1) latency, which poses a significant concern in cloud environments, particularly in scenarios reliant on real-time processing. The physical distance between end-users and cloud data centers can introduce delays, especially critical for high-speed data access or real-time interactions. Even milliseconds of delay can prove problematic in such contexts. (2) Bandwidth limitations remain a potential bottleneck, especially for data-intensive applications, impacting performance and leading to higher operational costs despite significant network capacity. Transferring large volumes of data to and from the cloud can be slow and costly, exacerbating these challenges further. (3) Resource contention in multi-tenant environments, where shared resources such as CPU, memory, and storage experience performance fluctuations due to varying demands, often referred to as "noisy neighbors". Despite the implementation of various isolation and resource management techniques by cloud providers, the demands of one tenant can still significantly impact the performance of others. (4) Input/Output (I/O) performance variability, often stemming from the shared infrastructure and complex storage systems in cloud environments, making it challenging to predict application behavior and ensure consistent user experiences. (4) Cold start issues for serverless functions, where delays occur as the cloud provider allocates resources and initiates functions upon invocation after periods of inactivity, impacting the responsiveness of serverless applications, particularly for sporadic or infrequent workloads. (5) Network dependency inherent in CC, where issues like congestion, downtime, or poor quality of service can directly affect cloud-based application performance, necessitating investments in high-quality Internet services or direct connect solutions. (6) Scaling delays, despite cloud services' scalability, can occur, especially for services that don't automatically adjust to load changes, resulting in performance bottlenecks during peak demand periods. Addressing these performance weaknesses is vital for optimizing cloud environments and ensuring consistent service delivery.

8.3 QUANTUM CLOUD COMPUTING

Quantum CC (QCC) is an exciting fusion of quantum computing and cloud technology, poised to democratize access to quantum computing resources via the Internet [5]. Unlike classical computers, which rely on bits as the fundamental unit of information, quantum computers harness quantum bits, or qubits. These qubits can exist in a superposition of states, representing 0, 1, or both concurrently, and can be entangled, enabling correlations between distant qubits, no matter the distance between them. This unique capability empowers quantum computers to tackle complex computations more efficiently, revolutionizing fields such as cryptography, material science, and system simulation.

QCC seamlessly integrates the prowess of quantum computing with the accessibility and scalability of cloud technology. Clients gain access to quantum processors through cloud platforms, eliminating the need for intricate quantum infrastructure setup, which often demands stringent environmental conditions such as ultra-low temperatures.

Numerous companies and research institutions have embraced the paradigm of quantum computing services via the cloud, democratizing access and catalyzing the development of quantum algorithms and applications. This inclusive approach empowers users from academia, industry, and research to conduct experiments, pioneer new algorithms, and delve into the boundless potential of quantum computing without the prohibitive costs associated with owning and maintaining dedicated quantum hardware.

While QCC is still in its early stages, ongoing research endeavors are dedicated to enhancing qubit coherence times, reducing error rates, and advancing scalability. Despite the formidable challenges ahead, QCC holds the potential to unveil solutions to challenges currently deemed insurmountable for classical computers.

Figure 8.1 illustrates the pivotal role of quantum cloud services and its intricate connections to a multitude of components, encompassing quantum processors, classical computers, data storage, and end-user devices such as smartphones, laptops, and tablets. This visual depiction underscores the symbiotic relationship between quantum and classical computing paradigms, orchestrating the delivery of cutting-edge computing services to users through a compelling fusion of modern technology.

8.3.1 QaaS Model

The QaaS model represents a burgeoning paradigm in the quantum computing landscape, offering access to quantum computing resources via the cloud [6]. Analogous to established cloud service models like SaaS, PaaS, and IaaS, QaaS is tailored explicitly to deliver quantum computing capabilities. Imagine unlocking the

FIGURE 8.1   QCC ecosystem: Interplay of components.

immense potential of quantum computing without the prohibitive costs or needing to possess advanced knowledge of quantum physics. QaaS significantly lowers the barrier to entry for both individuals and organizations, enabling them to explore and potentially leverage the transformative problem-solving capabilities of quantum computing. Central to QaaS are its core features:

Accessibility: QaaS platforms grant diverse clientele, from researchers and scientists to businesses and developers, access to quantum computing resources without the necessity of owning or directly managing quantum computers. Given the specialized and costly nature of quantum hardware, this accessibility plays a pivotal role in democratizing quantum computing.

Scalability: Clients can seamlessly scale their quantum computing needs in alignment with project requirements, liberated from concerns about the underlying physical infrastructure. This inherent scalability ensures that projects spanning from modest experiments to expansive quantum computing initiatives can be accommodated within the same adaptable framework.

Cost-effectiveness: Leveraging shared quantum computing infrastructure, clients can significantly mitigate the financial overheads associated with quantum computing experiments and development, paying only for the resources they actively utilize.

Innovation and collaboration: QaaS platforms serve as catalysts for innovation by broadening access to quantum computing for researchers and developers alike. This accessibility accelerates the exploration of new quantum algorithms, applications, and solutions across a myriad of domains, including cryptography, drug discovery, optimization, and beyond.

8.3.2 Efficiency and Precision

The QaaS model is designed to elevate efficiency and precision in computational tasks by leveraging the unparalleled capabilities of quantum computing. This model's benefits in efficiency and precision are most pronounced where quantum computing exhibits superiority over classical methods [7].

In terms of efficiency, QaaS offers several advantages. Quantum computers harness the phenomenon of superposition, enabling them to process multiple possibilities simultaneously. This unique capability translates into expedited problem-solving, outperforming classical algorithms in tasks requiring parallel processing. Additionally, quantum algorithms excel in tackling complex optimization problems prevalent in logistics, finance, and materials science. By efficiently navigating vast solution spaces, quantum computing identifies optimal solutions, a feat challenging for classical counterparts. Notably, for critical cryptographic tasks like integer factorization, quantum algorithms such as Shor's algorithm have the potential to drastically reduce computational time from millennia to mere seconds or minutes, given sufficiently robust quantum hardware.

In terms of precision, QaaS offers unparalleled capabilities. Quantum computers, operating on quantum mechanics principles, excel in simulating other quantum systems with exceptional accuracy. This precision is particularly invaluable in fields like materials science and pharmaceuticals, where understanding molecular quantum behavior drives groundbreaking discoveries. Despite current quantum computers' susceptibility to errors, ongoing research in quantum error correction, particularly for Noisy Intermediate-Scale Quantum *(NISQ) computers*, holds promise for significantly enhancing precision in quantum computations. Moreover, quantum technologies enable high-precision measurements applicable across diverse fields, from metrology to environmental sensing. While not a direct application of QaaS, these technologies share foundational principles with quantum computing.

In summary, QaaS holds immense potential for significantly enhancing computational efficiency and precision, particularly in tasks suited to quantum computation. However, realizing these transformative benefits necessitates overcoming current technological barriers and advancing the field of quantum computing.

8.3.3 Advantages of QaaS

QaaS brings forth numerous advantages that extend beyond mere technological capabilities, spanning economic and educational dimensions [8]. These advantages are pivotal in reshaping the landscape of quantum computing.

By democratizing technology, QaaS empowers organizations and researchers to tap into quantum computing resources without the overwhelming expenses associated with acquiring and maintaining quantum hardware. This democratization broadens the horizons of exploration and utilization within the quantum computing realm. Moreover, QaaS transcends geographical constraints, offering global access to quantum computing resources via the Internet. This encourages international collaboration and breaks down barriers that impede innovation and progress.

The rapid prototyping and experimentation capabilities of QaaS accelerate the pace of innovation and discovery in quantum computing and related fields. Researchers and developers can swiftly test theories and algorithms on real quantum hardware, expediting the cycle of innovation.

Furthermore, QaaS facilitates the development of specialized applications in fields where quantum computing holds immense promise, such as cryptography, drug discovery, materials science, and optimization problems. QaaS platforms often provide educational tools, tutorials, and communities, supporting the next generation of quantum scientists, engineers, and programmers. By making quantum computing more accessible, QaaS bridges the existing skill gap, enabling more individuals to gain expertise in this transformative field.

Businesses leveraging QaaS stand to gain a competitive edge by solving complex problems more efficiently or by innovating in ways that were previously unimaginable with classical computing alone. Additionally, QaaS has the potential to give rise to new business models and services, particularly in sectors poised to benefit most from quantum computing's unique capabilities.

In the domain of cryptography, QaaS plays a pivotal role in both posing challenges and presenting opportunities. It facilitates the development of quantum-resistant encryption methods, thereby enhancing data security in an era dominated by quantum computing.

Moreover, QaaS empowers organizations to remain agile, allowing them to experiment with quantum computing applications and integrate them into their operations without committing to specific hardware.

Overall, QaaS signals a new era in accessing and leveraging quantum computing resources, stimulating innovation, lowering barriers to entry, and nurturing a global ecosystem of quantum research and application development. As the field of quantum computing continues to advance, the crucial role of QaaS in enabling access, reducing costs, and facilitating collaboration will only become more pronounced.

8.3.4   POTENTIAL APPLICATIONS OF QAAS

QaaS heralds exciting possibilities for applying the formidable computational prowess of quantum computing across diverse fields [9]. The following paragraphs highlight the envisioned potential applications of QaaS across various domains.

In the realm of cryptography and cybersecurity, QaaS can fortify communication networks by enabling Quantum Key Distribution (QKD), leveraging quantum mechanics to secure channels against eavesdropping. Additionally, QaaS accelerates the development of post-quantum cryptography, ensuring cryptographic standards are resilient to quantum attacks. In the energy sector, quantum computing facilitated by QaaS holds promise for optimizing smart grids, and efficiently managing energy distribution in real-time. Furthermore, QaaS could expedite material science breakthroughs, facilitating the discovery of advanced materials for energy storage, such as high-performance batteries. For drug discovery and healthcare, QaaS enables molecular simulations at a quantum level, paving the way for the discovery of novel drugs and materials with tailored properties. Moreover, QaaS-driven analyses of genetic data offer potential for personalized medicine, revolutionizing disease treatment strategies.

In financial services, QaaS offers avenues for solving complex optimization problems like portfolio optimization and enhancing fraud detection capabilities, leveraging quantum algorithms for efficient data analysis. Supply chain and logistics stand to benefit from QaaS-enabled optimization, streamlining operations and routing decisions to save time and resources. AI/ML could see advancements through Quantum ML (QML), accelerating model training and data processing tasks. In environmental science, QaaS-driven quantum simulations hold the potential for precise climate modeling, aiding climate research and mitigation efforts. Manufacturing processes could be optimized using QaaS, leading to cost savings and efficiency gains across production and logistics.

Quantum software development stands to benefit from QaaS platforms, facilitating algorithm testing, refinement, and the development of quantum software solutions. Educational institutions can leverage QaaS to impart quantum computing concepts and skills, nurturing the next generation of quantum researchers and professionals. The potential applications of QaaS span nearly every industry, promising significant advancements and innovations. As quantum computing technology matures and becomes more accessible through QaaS, we anticipate solving complex global challenges more efficiently than ever before (Figure 8.2).

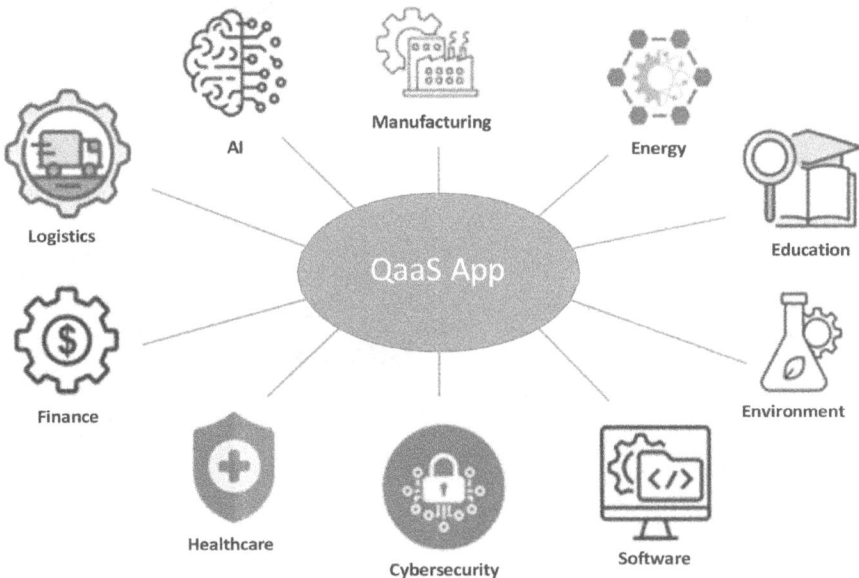

FIGURE 8.2 Potential real-world applications of QaaS model.

8.4   RESTRICTIONS AND CHALLENGES

In the realm of QCC, the emergence of QaaS promises on-demand access to quantum computing resources, yet it faces several limitations (Figure 8.3) and challenges (Figure 8.4) to its widespread adoption [10].

At present, quantum hardware is still in its nascent stages, marked by noise, errors, and limited qubit counts and coherence times, imposing constraints on problem complexity and necessitating error correction techniques. However, reliable error correction methods are still under development, potentially yielding inaccurate results from quantum computations run through QaaS. Moreover, the complexity of quantum algorithms demands expertise in quantum mechanics, linear algebra, and quantum computing principles, hindering accessibility to clients lacking a strong quantum background. Furthermore, efficiently mapping real-world problems onto quantum algorithms is non-trivial and often requires significant expertise. Addressing this educational and skill gap requires substantial investment in education, training, and research initiatives to cultivate a workforce capable of leveraging QaaS effectively.

QaaS is currently constrained by a limited number of applications where quantum computers offer a significant advantage over classical counterparts, making finding suitable applications challenging. Adding to this, the dearth of QaaS providers and service variety compared to established cloud services presents another hurdle. Cost is another significant consideration, as the development and maintenance of quantum hardware incur substantial expenses, potentially rendering QaaS less accessible to certain businesses.

In terms of challenges, security concerns loom large, with the potential for quantum computers to break current cryptographic standards, such as RSA and ECC, through algorithms like Shor's algorithm, requiring robust security measures in QaaS platforms to safeguard sensitive data [11, 12].

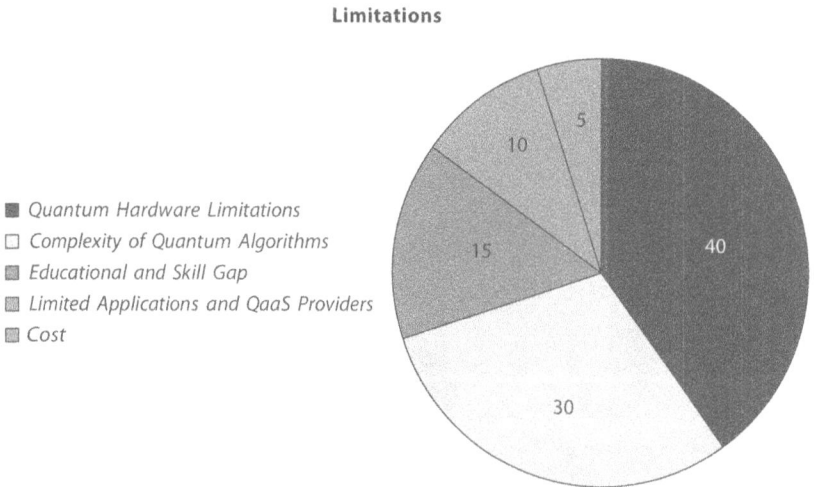

Limitations

- ■ Quantum Hardware Limitations
- □ Complexity of Quantum Algorithms
- ▨ Educational and Skill Gap
- ▨ Limited Applications and QaaS Providers
- ▨ Cost

FIGURE 8.3   QCC limitations.

Challenges

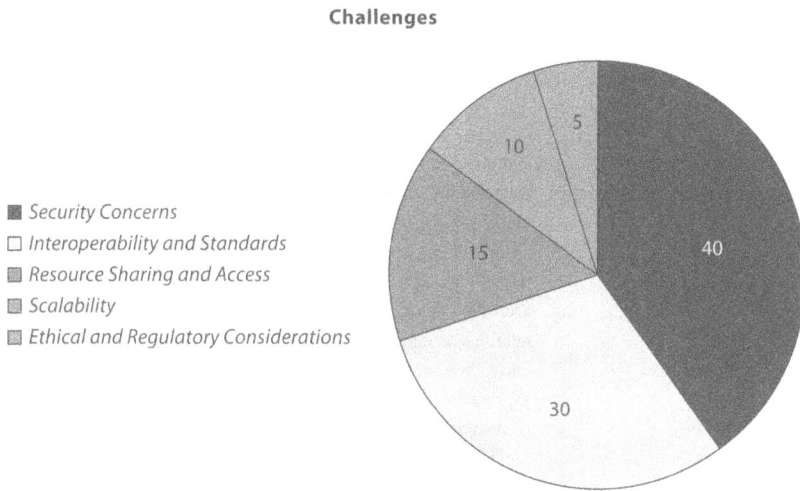

Security Concerns
Interoperability and Standards
Resource Sharing and Access
Scalability
Ethical and Regulatory Considerations

FIGURE 8.4   QCC challenges.

Interoperability and standards remain elusive, hindering client transitions between different QaaS providers and impeding ecosystem development, as there is currently a lack of standardized programming languages, tools, and interfaces for quantum computing. Resource sharing and access pose another challenge, with quantum computers' high costs necessitating fair and equitable resource utilization and allocation amid increasing demand. Scalability remains a significant obstacle. Achieving the scaling of quantum systems to large problem sizes, involving hundreds or thousands of qubits with minimal error rates, is particularly daunting due to persistent obstacles such as decoherence and error propagation. Ethical and regulatory considerations also weigh heavily, with QaaS raising concerns regarding data privacy, surveillance, and weaponization, mandating careful navigation of these complexities by providers.

Despite these challenges, QaaS holds great promise for accelerating quantum computing technology development across industries. Overcoming these obstacles demands collaborative efforts from academia, industry, and policymakers to address technical, ethical, and societal concerns. Additionally, privacy and security within QCC require meticulous attention. This encompasses areas such as quantum-safe cryptography, data privacy, quantum network security, secure Multi-Party Computation (SMPC), and regulatory compliance. Establishing resilient frameworks and practices becomes imperative to shield sensitive data and uphold regulatory standards. Notably, QCC, entailing the utilization of quantum computing resources and algorithms through cloud services, unveils distinctive privacy and security concerns [13]. Refer to Table 8.1 for a detailed exploration of these challenges.

Mitigating these privacy and security challenges demands a comprehensive, multi-disciplinary strategy, drawing upon expertise in quantum computing, cryptography, cybersecurity, and regulatory compliance. Quantum cloud providers are

TABLE 8.1
Privacy and Security Considerations

Item	Consideration
Quantum-safe cryptography	As quantum computers advance, they may be able to break traditional cryptographic algorithms, such as RSA and ECC, using algorithms like Shor's algorithm. To address this threat, organizations need to transition to quantum-resistant cryptographic techniques, also known as post-quantum cryptography, to secure their data in transit and at rest within cloud environments.
Data privacy	Quantum computing has the potential to enhance data processing capabilities significantly. However, this also raises concerns about the privacy of sensitive data stored or processed in quantum cloud environments. Robust encryption techniques and access control mechanisms must be implemented to protect sensitive information from unauthorized access, both in classical and quantum domains.
Quantum network security	Quantum networks, which use quantum communication protocols like QKD, offer the promise of ultra-secure communication channels. However, these networks are vulnerable to various attacks, such as interception and man-in-the-middle attacks. Quantum cloud providers need to implement robust security measures to safeguard quantum communication channels and prevent data interception or tampering.
SMPC	QCC enables distributed computation among multiple parties, allowing them to collaborate on sensitive tasks without revealing their inputs. SMPC protocols [14] play a crucial role in ensuring the privacy and integrity of computations performed in quantum cloud environments. These protocols need to be designed and implemented carefully to mitigate the risk of data leakage or manipulation.
Physical security of quantum hardware	Quantum cloud providers must ensure the physical security of their quantum computing infrastructure to prevent unauthorized access, tampering, or sabotage. This includes implementing strict access controls, monitoring systems, and physical safeguards to protect quantum processors and other sensitive components from potential threats.
Quantum software security	Quantum software development introduces new security challenges, such as vulnerabilities in quantum algorithms and programming frameworks. Quantum cloud providers need to adopt secure software development practices, including code reviews, vulnerability assessments, and penetration testing, to identify and mitigate potential security flaws in their quantum software stack.
Regulatory compliance	QCC may be subject to various regulatory requirements related to data privacy, security, and compliance with industry standards. Cloud providers need to ensure compliance with relevant regulations, such as GDPR, HIPAA, and ISO/IEC 27001, to maintain the trust and confidence of their customers and stakeholders.

tasked with fostering collaboration among industry partners, researchers, and poli-cymakers. Together, they must devise resilient security frameworks and best practices to uphold the confidentiality, integrity, and availability of data within quantum cloud environments.

8.5 QUANTUM-ENHANCED PRIVACY

Innovative advancements in quantum computing are reshaping the landscape of data security and privacy. Within QaaS frameworks, the fusion of HE and blockchain technology emerges as a potent force. This section explores the synergy between these cutting-edge concepts, unravelling their transformative impact on data security and privacy in quantum computing environments.

8.5.1 HOMOMORPHIC ENCRYPTION

HE is a cryptographic technique that allows computations to be performed on encrypted data without decrypting it first [15, 16]. This property is particularly relevant to QCC, where sensitive data may be processed on remote quantum computers. HE enables computations to be performed on encrypted data, preserving the privacy of sensitive information. In the context of QCC, users can encrypt their data before uploading it to the cloud, ensuring that the cloud provider cannot access or view the plaintext data during computation. For secure outsourcing of quantum computations, clients can securely outsource quantum computations to cloud providers without exposing their data or algorithms to potential adversaries. The cloud provider can perform the computations on encrypted data and return the results without accessing the underlying plaintext.

HE facilitates the integration of quantum and classical computing resources in a privacy-preserving manner [17]. Clients can leverage quantum cloud services for executing quantum algorithms on encrypted data while also utilizing classical cloud services for processing classical data or executing classical algorithms, all within the same secure computing environment. HE can be used as part of SMPC protocols in QCC environments. SMPC allows multiple parties to jointly compute a function over their respective private inputs while preserving the privacy of those inputs. By combining HE with quantum computing resources, SMPC protocols can be implemented securely in a distributed quantum cloud environment. As quantum computing advances, traditional cryptographic techniques may become vulnerable to quantum attacks. HE provides a potential solution for achieving post-quantum security in QCC environments. By encrypting data using HE schemes that are resistant to quantum attacks, clients can protect their data against future quantum threats.

It is important to note that HE comes with limitations and performance overheads. The computational complexity of HE schemes can be high, which may impact the efficiency and scalability of quantum computations performed on encrypted data. Additionally, not all types of computations are well-suited for HE, and careful consideration is needed when designing applications and algorithms for use in quantum cloud environments. Despite these challenges, HE remains a valuable tool for achieving privacy-preserving computation in QCC.

8.5.2 Blockchain

QCC and blockchain have a complex relationship, presenting both opportunities and challenges. A major concern for blockchains is their vulnerability to future quantum computers that could break current encryption standards [18]. QCC could be used to develop and implement quantum-resistant cryptography algorithms, making blockchains more secure in the quantum era. To improve efficiency, quantum algorithms might offer ways to optimize blockchain processes, potentially leading to faster transaction times and lower fees. Moreover, the combination of QCC and blockchain could unlock entirely new applications, such as secure and transparent supply chain management or complex financial calculations.

Overall, the intersection of QCC and blockchain holds immense promise for the future of secure and efficient distributed ledger technology. However, significant challenges need to be addressed before this potential can be fully realized such as early-stage technology, technical expertise, integration complexity, cost, standardization, and uncertain regulatory landscape.

8.6 QUANTUM CLOUD SERVICES PROVIDERS

Several technology companies and research institutions have launched QaaS platforms, offering access to quantum processors and simulators through cloud-based interfaces. These platforms often provide additional tools and services to aid in the development of quantum algorithms, including software development kits, user friendly interfaces, and extensive documentation and support, while access can be expensive for corporate users, some offer access free to researchers. According to Omdia chief quantum analyst Sam Lucero,[1] access to quantum computing resources can cost about $1,000 to $2,000 an hour for cloud access, compared with $20 million to $40 million for an on-premises hardware sale. Here are some of the notable companies offering quantum cloud services [19–21]:

> *IBM Quantum:* IBM's (Armonk, New York) quantum system features a 127 qubit processor and the company's Qiskit quantum development toolkit for construction and deploying applications. Users can even create and run quantum computing circuits.
>
> This company provides access to quantum hardware as well as HPC simulators. These can be accessed programmatically using the Python-based Qiskit framework, or via a graphical interface with the IBM Q Experience GUI. Launched in May 2016 as the IBM Quantum Experience, both Qiskit and the graphical interface with the IBM Q Experience GUI are based on the OpenQASM standard for representing quantum operations. There is also a tutorial and online community. Currently, available simulators and quantum devices are multiple transmon qubit processors. Those with 5 and 16 qubits are publicly accessible. However, devices up to 65 qubits are available through the IBM Q Cloud Network.
>
> *Google Quantum AI:* The Quantum AI Lab was established by Google Research in May 2013 (Mountain View, California). Google's quantum

computing service provides clients access to Google's quantum computing hardware through Cirq, an open-source quantum computing program language. This service allows for running programs on quantum computers in Google's quantum computing lab.

Amazon Braket: With beginnings that date back to the early 2000s, by the mid-2010s AWS has become the market leader in the sector. Amazon Braket clients can try their algorithms on a local simulator. Also, they can utilize the Amazon Braket software development kit for making quantum applications and executing algorithms on quantum computers.

Microsoft Azure Quantum: Microsoft (Redmond, Washington) delivers cloud-based access to algorithms built by 1QBit and Microsoft. The Microsoft Quantum Computing Kit comprises chemistry, ML, and numeric libraries.

Alibaba Cloud: Founded by Chinese business magnate, investor, and philanthropist Jack Ma in 1999, 2017 saw Alibaba release its cloud service subsidiary Aliyun. Alibaba Cloud offers access to an 11-qubit quantum computer through its cloud services. The platform is available for scientific researchers. Public users can learn about basic quantum information details on the cloud platform and interact with scientists online.

D-Wave Leap: Founded in 1999, D-Wave is a Canadian company based in Burnaby, British Columbia, Canada. D-Wave's Leap quantum cloud service delivers developers access to a cloud-based quantum processor to make quantum-hybrid applications in real-time. Developers can also employ a feature called the hybrid solver service, which merges both quantum and classical resources to solve computational problems.

Xanadu Cloud: Canada-based Quantum Cloud consists of cloud-based access to three fully programmable photonic quantum computers. Xanadu Cloud provides clients with free access to software and support. Its free plan delivers clients with credits for executing small workloads on its Borealis quantum hardware. It also gives a full-stack Python library for constructing, simulating, and running programs on photonic quantum computers.

QuTech Inspire: Quantum Inspire by Qutech was launched in May 2020 by Minister Ingrid van Engelshoven and European Commissioner Mariya Gabriel. QuTech's Inspire claims to be Europe's first public-access quantum-computing platform. It delivers clients a two-qubit semiconductor electron spin processor, a five-qubit superconductor Transmon processor, and three simulators. This platform incorporates IBM's QisKit.

QC Ware Forge: QC Ware is a Palo Alto, California-based startup founded in 2014. Its Forge cloud platform offers a 30-day free trial including one minute of quantum computing time. QC Ware delivers quantum engineers with circuit building blocks to build and execute algorithm simulations for data scientists, financial analysts, and engineers. It concentrates on binary optimization, linear algebra, Monte Carlo methods, and ML.

Quantinuum AI: Formed when Honeywell Quantum Solutions and Cambridge Quantum Computing came together in late 2021 (Broomfield, Colorado). Quantinuum's AI platform includes quantum natural language processing, cloud-based QML services, and quantum deep learning. It also delivers a quantum computing software development kit, TKET, to build and run programs for gate-based quantum computers.

AQT: AQT is an Innsbruck, Austria-based QCC company founded in 2018 and sponsored by the Federation of Austrian Industries Tyrol, the FFG Austrian Research Promotion Agency, and the University of Innsbruck. AQT's ion-trap platform is a freely open online quantum simulator, with or without noise, for the office environment. It aims to bridge the gap between exploratory academic research and highly specialized, commercially obtainable, cloud-based resources.

Oxford Quantum Circuits: Launched in 2017 and founded in Reading, the UK, OQC is producing quantum computers and utilizing quantum cloud software to assist its clients solve some of humanity's most significant challenges, from climate change to new drug discoveries. Last summer OQC also launched the UK's first Quantum Computing as-a-Service (QCaaS), taking the QCC system to the enterprise, at the fingertips of its clients and partners.

Forest: Rigetti Computing (Quantum Cloud Services): Another startup, Rigetti Computing, a Berkeley, California-based company, offers its QCS, Rigetti's quantum-first CC platform. With QCS, its Quantum Processors Units (QPUs) are tightly combined with classical computing infrastructure and made obtainable over the cloud. Its Forest SDK is a set of software tools that permit clients to write quantum programs in Quil, and then compile and run them via QCS or a simulator. The SDK comprises pyQuil, a Python library for construction and running Quil programs, quilc, an optimizing Quil compiler and QVM, a quantum virtual machine (simulator).

IonQ Quantum Cloud: The IonQ (College Park, Maryland) Quantum Cloud offers access to the company's trapped-ion systems through the Quantum Cloud API. The company claims to be consistent with all major quantum software development kits, such as QisKit and Cirq.

Terra Quantum: Based in Germany, Terra Quantum offers clients access to a library of algorithms, such as hybrid quantum optimization and quantum neural networks. The company also delivers high-performance simulated QPU and solutions for secure quantum and post-quantum communications.

Although this list does not cover every provider, it highlights the wide range and depth of companies delivering quantum computing as a service. As the field progresses, providers are expected to offer an expanded array of resources and services to developers.

For more information, there are many other companies like Toshiba (New York, New York, 2003): which started research into quantum cryptography in 1999; Intel (Santa Clara, California, 2015): which announced the release of its newest quantum research chip, Tunnel Falls, a 12-qubit silicon chip; Baidu: which was founded in 2000 by Internet pioneer Robin Li, its quantum computer, Qianshi, featuring a 10-qubit processor, and says it also developed a 36-qubit quantum chip; Atos: which is a leader in cybersecurity; ColdQuanta (Boulder,

Colorado); Quantum Circuits (New Haven, Connecticut, 2019); Atom Computing (Berkely, California); Strangeworks (Austin, Texas, 2018); Zapata Computing (Cambridge, Massachusetts); Bleximo (Berkeley, California); 1QBit (Vancouver, British Columbia, 2012); ISARA Corporation (Waterloo, Ontario); ProteinQure (Toronto, Ontario); etc.

8.7   CONCLUSION

In conclusion, QCC represents a significant step forward in the computational capabilities available to researchers, developers, and businesses. By harnessing the principles of quantum mechanics, this emerging technology offers the promise of solving complex problems that are currently beyond the reach of classical computing systems. The availability of quantum computing through cloud-based services democratizes access to this cutting-edge technology, allowing users worldwide to explore quantum algorithms and applications without the need for substantial upfront investment in quantum hardware.

As the industry continues to evolve, we anticipate further advancements in quantum computing technologies, along with an expansion of the ecosystem of quantum cloud services. These developments will not only enhance computational power but also inspire new algorithms, applications, and solutions across various sectors, including cryptography, materials science, pharmaceuticals, and more. The journey of QCC is just beginning, and its full potential is yet to be realized. The coming years will undoubtedly witness the transformative impact of quantum computing on the world, as it opens new horizons in the realm of computational science.

NOTE

1. https://omdia.tech.in f orma.com/om029041/evolving–quantum–computing–access–models

REFERENCES

1. Jose Garcia-Alonso, Javier Rojo, David Valencia, Enrique Moguel, Javier Berrocal, and Juan Manuel Murillo. Quantum software as a service through a quantum API gateway. *IEEE Internet Computing*, 26(1):34–41, 2021.
2. Sumit Kumar, Arup Kumar Pal, SK Hafizul Islam, and Mohammad Hammoudeh. Secure and efficient image retrieval through invariant features selection in insecure cloud environments. *Neural Computing and Applications*, 35(7):4855–4880, 2023.
3. Sana Belguith, Nesrine Kaaniche, and Mohammad Hammoudeh. Analysis of attribute-based cryptographic techniques and their application to protect cloud services. *Transactions on Emerging Telecommunications Technologies*, 33(3):e3667, 2022.
4. H Kanakadurga Bella, and S Vasundra. A study of security threats and attacks in cloud computing. In *2022 4th International Conference on Smart Systems and Inventive Technology (ICSSIT)*, pages 658–666. IEEE, 2022.
5. Reza Nejabati, Rui Wang, and Dimitra Simeonidou. Dynamic quantum network: from quantum data centre to quantum cloud computing. In *Optical Fiber Communication Conference*, pages Th3D–1. Optica Publishing Group, 2022.

6. Md Masudul Islam, and Mijanur Rahaman. A review on progress and problems of quantum computing as a service (QCaaS) in the perspective of cloud computing. *Global Journal of Computer Science and Technology*, 15(B4):23–26, 2015.

7. Hoa T Nguyen, Muhammad Usman, and Rajkumar Buyya. Qfaas: A serverless functionas-a-service framework for quantum computing. *Future Generation Computer Systems*, 154:281–300, 2024.

8. Lalitha Nallamothula. Quantum ecosystem development using advanced cloud services. In *Ubiquitous Networking: 7th International Symposium, UNet 2021, Virtual Event, May 19–22, 2021, Revised Selected Papers 7*, pages 163–171. Springer, 2021.

9. Javier Romero-Álvarez, Jaime Alvarado-Valiente, Enrique Moguel, José Garcia-Alonso, and Juan M Murillo. Quantum services: A tutorial on the technology and the process. In *International Conference on Service-Oriented Computing*, pages 335–342. Springer, 2023.

10. Enrique Moguel, Javier Rojo, David Valencia, Javier Berrocal, Jose Garcia-Alonso, and Juan M Murillo. Quantum service-oriented computing: Current landscape and challenges. *Software Quality Journal*, 30(4):983–1002, 2022.

11. Aissaoua Habib, Abdelkader Laouid, and Mostefa Kara. Secure consensus clock synchronization in wireless sensor networks. In *2021 International Conference on Artificial Intelligence for Cyber Security Systems and Privacy (AI-CSP)*, pages 1–6. IEEE, 2021.

12. Mostefa Kara, Abdelkader Laouid, Ahcene Bounceur, Mohammad Hammoudeh, Muath Alshaikh, and Romaissa Kebache. Semi-decentralized model for drone collaboration on secure measurement of positions. In *The 5th International Conference on Future Networks & Distributed Systems*, pages 64–69, 2021.

13. Kazuki Ikeda. Security and privacy of blockchain and quantum computation. In *Advances in computers*, volume 111, pages 199–228. Elsevier, 2018.

14. Mostefa Kara, Abdelkader Laouid, and Mohammad Hammoudeh. An efficient multi-signature scheme for blockchain. *Cryptology ePrint Archive*, 2023.

15. Mostefa Kara, Abdelkader Laouid, Mohammed Amine Yagoub, Reinhardt Euler, Saci Medileh, Mohammad Hammoudeh, Amna Eleyan, and Ahcène Bounceur. A fully homomorphic encryption based on magic number fragmentation and el-gamal encryption: Smart healthcare use case. *Expert Systems*, 39(5):e12767, 2022.

16. Saci Medileh, Abdelkader Laouid, Mohammad Hammoudeh, and Mostefa Kara. Tarek Bejaoui, Amna Eleyan, and Mohammed Al-Khalidi. A multi-key with partially homomorphic encryption scheme for low-end devices ensuring data integrity. *Information*, 14(5):263, 2023.2023.

17. Hongfeng Zhu, Chaonan Wang, and Xueying Wang. Quantum fully homomorphic encryption scheme for cloud privacy data based on quantum circuit. *International Journal of Theoretical Physics*, 60(8):2961–2975, 2021.

18. Mostefa Kara, Abdelkader Laouid, Ahcene Bounceur, Farid Lalem, Muath AlShaikh, Romaissa Kebache, and Zaoui Sayah. A novel delegated proof of work consensus protocol. In *2021 International Conference on Artificial Intelligence for Cyber Security Systems and Privacy (AI-CSP)*, pages 1–7. IEEE, 2021.

19. James Dargan. 13 quantum cloud computing companies, 2022.

20. Stephen Gossett, and Jessica Powers. Top 20 quantum computing companies, 2022.

21. John Potter. 13 quantum cloud computing companies, 2023.

9 Future Directions and Challenges, Quantum Supremacy, and Beyond

Harbaksh Singh

9.1 INTRODUCTION

Quantum computing stands at the forefront of a technological revolution, promising to redefine the boundaries of processing power and computational capabilities. As researchers and industry giants push towards achieving quantum supremacy—the point at which quantum computers can perform tasks beyond the reach of even the most powerful classical supercomputers—the field is abuzz with excitement and anticipation. However, this journey is not without its hurdles.

Future directions in quantum computing encompass the refinement of quantum algorithms, the scaling up of qubit systems, and the mitigation of error rates, while challenges include maintaining quantum coherence, ensuring reliable qubit interconnectivity, and developing user-friendly quantum programming languages. As we venture beyond quantum supremacy, the implications for cryptography, material science, and complex system modeling are profound, yet the path is fraught with both technical obstacles and philosophical quandaries about the nature of computation itself.

This chapter explores the future trajectory of quantum computing, examining both the potential advancements and the challenges that lie ahead. It delves into the concept of "Quantum Supremacy," the point at which quantum computers surpass classical computers in computational capabilities. The discussion revolves around the implications of reaching this milestone, particularly for cybersecurity, due to the potential vulnerabilities in current cryptographic systems. The chapter also addresses the challenges that impede the full-scale practical implementation of quantum computers, such as error correction, stability, and the development of quantum algorithms. Additionally, it explores quantum-resistant algorithms and cryptographic systems, recognizing the importance of post-quantum cryptography in preparing for a world where quantum computers reign supreme.

The chapter concludes by underscoring the need for active research, innovation, and collaboration across government, academia, and industry globally to effectively navigate these challenges and fully harness the transformative benefits of the quantum revolution.

9.2 PRACTICAL QUANTUM COMPUTING

Practical quantum computing is fraught with significant challenges, particularly concerning hardware and software. Developments are moving at an exciting pace,

DOI: 10.1201/9781003537243-9

141

but translating these into practical use cases requires more than just scientific break-throughs; it also requires navigating a chain of technical obstacles.

9.2.1 HARDWARE CHALLENGES

The stability of qubits presents a substantial challenge for quantum computing. Unlike classical bits, qubits are highly sensitive to their environment. Even minor external interference can cause a state transition, in a phenomenon known as 'decoherence'.

Superconducting circuits, trapped ions, topological qubits, and photonic qubits are different types of physical qubits that are currently being studied and developed. Each of these types come with its own set of challenges and advantages. For instance, superconducting qubits, which is the preferred design by computing giants like IBM, are sensitive to changes in temperature, electromagnetic radiation, and electrical noise. Alternatively, trapped-ion qubits, which involve trapping ions using an electromagnetic field and manipulating them with lasers, demonstrate remarkable coherence times but face difficulties in scaling up.

Topological qubits, a less mature but promising area of research, aim to circumvent the instability issue by encoding information in a way that is robust against local errors. However, the experimental realization of these qubits poses significant challenges.

Below is a summary of the hardware challenges facing quantum technologies.

- *Quantum Bits (Qubits):* These are the fundamental building blocks of quantum computers. Ensuring qubit stability, coherence, and scalability remains a challenge. Researchers are exploring various physical implementations, such as superconducting circuits, trapped ions, and topological qubits, to address these challenges.
- *Quantum Gates:* Quantum gates perform operations on qubits. Designing efficient gates that minimize errors and maximize fidelity is crucial for qubit manipulation. Researchers are developing gate sets that allow universal quantum computation while minimizing gate errors. Additionally, optimizing gate sequences for specific algorithms is an ongoing area of research.
- *Quantum Error Correction:* Mitigating noise and decoherence to maintain reliable qubits. Implementing QEC requires additional qubits and sophisticated error-detection protocols. Researchers are exploring surface codes, color codes, and other approaches to achieve fault tolerance.
- *Cooling and Isolation:* Operating quantum computers at ultra-low temperatures to reduce thermal noise and interference. Cryogenic systems and dilution refrigerators are used to achieve these conditions. Isolation from external electromagnetic interference is equally critical. Shielding quantum processors from environmental noise ensures reliable qubit operations.

9.2.2 SOFTWARE CHALLENGES

In parallel with progress in hardware, significant challenges exist on the software side. Harnessing qubits for various computational tasks requires tailored algorithms designed to exploit the properties of a complex quantum system. Furthermore, these algorithms must consider inherent quantum properties like superposition and entanglement and inherent quantum limitations such as 'no-cloning theorem' and 'quantum uncertainty'.

From a programming perspective, there are not yet well-established standards or practices in quantum computing as there are with classical computing. While a few quantum programming languages and SDKs like Qiskit from IBM, Q# from Microsoft and Cirq from Google have emerged, most have steep learning curves and pose significant differences from classical programming languages.

Compounding these issues is the challenge of translating real-world problems into the quantum context or finding problems that can benefit from a quantum solution. A great deal of creativity, innovation, and effort is needed to design quantum algorithms that can solve real-world problems faster than classical computers.

Below, we summarize the key software challenges facing quantum technologies.

- *Quantum Algorithms:* Developing algorithms that outperform classical counterparts by exploiting quantum parallelism. Shor's algorithm for factoring large numbers and Grover's search algorithm demonstrate quantum speed-up. Researchers are exploring applications in optimization, cryptography, and simulation.
- *Quantum Compilation:* Mapping high-level quantum programs to specific hardware architectures is non-trivial. Quantum compilers translate abstract quantum code into gate-level instructions. Optimizing compilation strategies is crucial for efficient execution.
- *Quantum Programming Languages:* Creating user-friendly languages like Qiskit, Cirq, and Quipper that simplify quantum programming. These languages abstract low-level details, allowing researchers and developers to focus on algorithm design. Improving language features and tooling is an ongoing effort.

9.2.3 Error Correction

Dealing with noise and errors in quantum systems is another major problem that needs to be addressed. Traditional error correction methods used in classical computing can't be directly applied to quantum computing due to the 'no-cloning theorem' which states that an arbitrary unknown quantum state can't be exactly duplicated.

Moreover, the act of reading a quantum state (measurement) alters that state, hence conventional techniques which involve copying and checking data for errors can't work. This has necessitated the development of quantum error correction methods, such as the surface code, to correct for errors without causing additional errors in the process.

9.2.4 Cybersecurity Challenges

While the concept of quantum computing is thrilling, it brings with it new security challenges that could prove calamitous if not properly addressed. Quantum computers are expected to render current encryption systems useless by factoring large integers rapidly, a capability with significant implications for online security protocols.[1]

Public Key Infrastructure (PKI) which forms the basis of many modern internet security protocols such as RSA depends on the fact that factoring large numbers is computationally expensive for classical computers. However, once sufficiently powerful quantum computers are realized, they could factor these large numbers in negligible time, breaking the RSA cryptosystem and laying bare the internet's 'secure' communications.[1-3]

On the flip side, Quantum Key Distribution (QKD) provides a new secure method for distributing cryptographic keys. Unlike classical key distribution, QKD's security is based on the principles of quantum mechanics where any attempt at eavesdropping on the key would disturb its quantum state and hence, can be detected by legitimate users.

The double-edged nature of quantum computing in cybersecurity places us in a race between developing quantum-resistant algorithms and the realization of a powerful enough quantum computer that can break current cryptosystems.

9.2.5 SCALABILITY CHALLENGES

Scalability is yet another hurdle that stands in the way of developing practical quantum computers. As mentioned earlier, many quantum computing models are hard to scale due to the fragility of qubits. The number of physical qubits on chips has been increasing; however, the quality of those qubits in terms of error rates, coherence times, and successful two-qubit gates has to be exceptional to be of practical use.

9.3 THE FUTURE OF PRACTICAL QUANTUM COMPUTING

While the above challenges may seem daunting, they are steadily being overcome. Companies are investing heavily in research and development, scientists are relentlessly pushing the boundaries of what's possible, and policymakers are fostering cooperation between academia, government, and industry to accelerate progress toward practical quantum computing. The potential pay-off of overcoming these challenges is massive, not just in terms of economic value but also in the transformational societal benefits that would come with such powerful computational tools.

Quantum supremacy refers to the point at which a quantum computer can perform a task that is practically impossible for classical computers to achieve within a reasonable time frame. Key aspects of this race include the following:

The Qubit Race:
- Companies and research institutions are competing to build quantum computers with a large number of qubits.
- Google's achievement of quantum supremacy in 2019 with its 53-qubit Sycamore processor.

The Quantum Advantage:
- Beyond quantum supremacy, quantum computers promise advantages in optimization, cryptography, and simulation tasks.
- *Noisy Intermediate-Scale Quantum (NISQ)* devices bridge the gap between classical and fault-tolerant quantum computers.

Investments and Focus Areas:
- IBM, Microsoft, D-WAVE, PASCAL, PsiQuantum, and other players are investing in quantum hardware and software.
- Research focuses on error correction, qubit stability, and quantum algorithms.

Companies and research institutions compete to build quantum computers with more qubits. Google's Sycamore processor claimed to have achieved quantum supremacy by solving a specific problem in 200 seconds that would take today's most powerful classical supercomputers about 10,000 years.[4]

IBM's popular 133 qubit Heron processor, introduced in 2024, fits well into their 'IBM Quantum System Two' architecture. This architecture combines quantum communication and computation, assisted by classical computing resources, and leverages a middleware layer to appropriately integrate quantum and classical workflows. IBM is focused on achieving has 'quantum advantage', rather than 'quantum supremacy'.[5]

A view of qubit counts as of Jan'2022 across different types of quantum computing systems is depicted in Figure 9.1.

Beyond quantum supremacy, quantum computers offer advantages in specific applications:

- *Optimization:* Solving complex optimization problems (e.g., portfolio optimization, supply chain logistics).
- *Cryptography:* Quantum-safe encryption and decryption.
- *Simulation:* Modeling quantum systems (e.g., materials, chemical reactions).

Major players like IBM, Microsoft, D-WAVE, and PsiQuantum invest in quantum hardware and software. Research focuses on error correction, qubit stability, and quantum algorithms.

This need for a scalable quantum computing model has led to significant research in various qubit types and quantum computing models, leading to innovative approaches like topological quantum computing and photonic quantum computing that offer potential scaling advantages.

Realizing the potential of quantum computing gives way to a variety of use cases that could revolutionize numerous sectors. For instance, computational chemistry looks to be one of the first direct benefits of quantum computing. By allowing precise simulation of molecules, it could accelerate drug discovery, enzyme engineering, the development of solar cells, and many other areas.

Google, for example, is utilizing its Sycamore quantum processor to simulate chemical reactions. Their experiment on the reaction between Hydrogen and Nitrogen potentially paves the way to understanding nitrogen fixation, the process

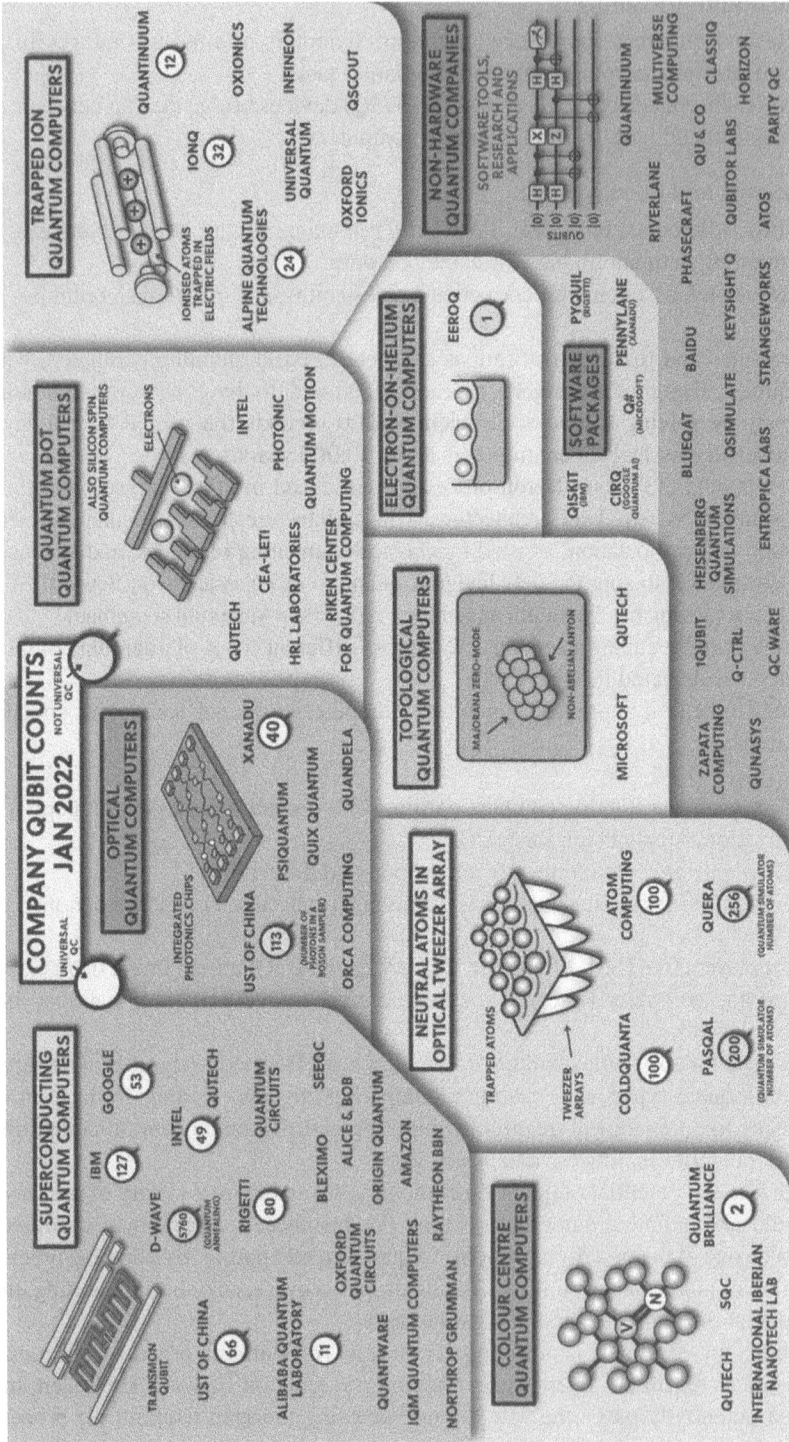

FIGURE 9.1   The map of quantum computing poster (*Source:* https://miro.medium.com/v2/resize:fit:1358/1*YteMIhM860MgR0GqHgZ4Gg.png.)

by which nitrogen in the atmosphere is converted into ammonia – a key process for the production of fertilizer.

9.4 PROMINENT USE-CASES ACROSS SECTORS

1. *Climate Change Modeling:* Quantum computers have the potential to enhance weather predictions and climate forecasting by simulating complex atmospheric reactions that are currently out of reach for classical computers. IBM, for instance, is working on algorithms for quantum simulation that could be used to understand cloud formation, an important factor in climate models that is currently not well understood due to its complexity.
2. *Space Exploration:* Quantum computing could aid in solving complex numerical problems to analyze space data and improve space exploration. Under NASA's Quantum Artificial Intelligence Laboratory (QuAIL), researchers have been studying the application of quantum algorithms for scheduling and planning problems, Machine Learning (ML), data analysis, and complex system optimization problems in aeronautics and space missions.
3. *Material Discovery:* The ability of quantum computers to accurately simulate complex molecules could revolutionize material science and engineering. For instance, Microsoft is using its Quantum Development Kit to simulate exotic states of matter and understand superconductivity, a phenomenon that has major implications for energy transmission.
4. *Precision Medicine:* Quantum computing has potential implications for drug discovery and genomics. Cambridge Quantum Computing (CQC), for example, is pioneering efforts to use quantum computers to understand protein folding – a process that could aid in drug discovery and combat diseases like Alzheimer's.

9.5 COMPANIES IN THE RACE TO QUANTUM SUPREMACY

The application of quantum technologies across sectors has accelerated the international competition to attain quantum supremacy. Notable leading tech companies such as IBM, Microsoft, and Google are heavily investing in research, hardware, and software for quantum technologies.[6]

1. IBM is a major player in the field of quantum computing with its quantum system model, IBM Q. IBM also offers the cloud-based quantum computing service, IBM Quantum Experience, allowing users to run algorithms and experiments on IBM's quantum processor. IBM's quantum roadmap includes reaching 1,121 qubits by 2023 (see Figure 9.2).
2. Similarly, Google is exploring superconducting qubits and has successfully demonstrated quantum supremacy with its 53-qubit quantum computer named Sycamore. Google's Quantum AI team has proposed a roadmap

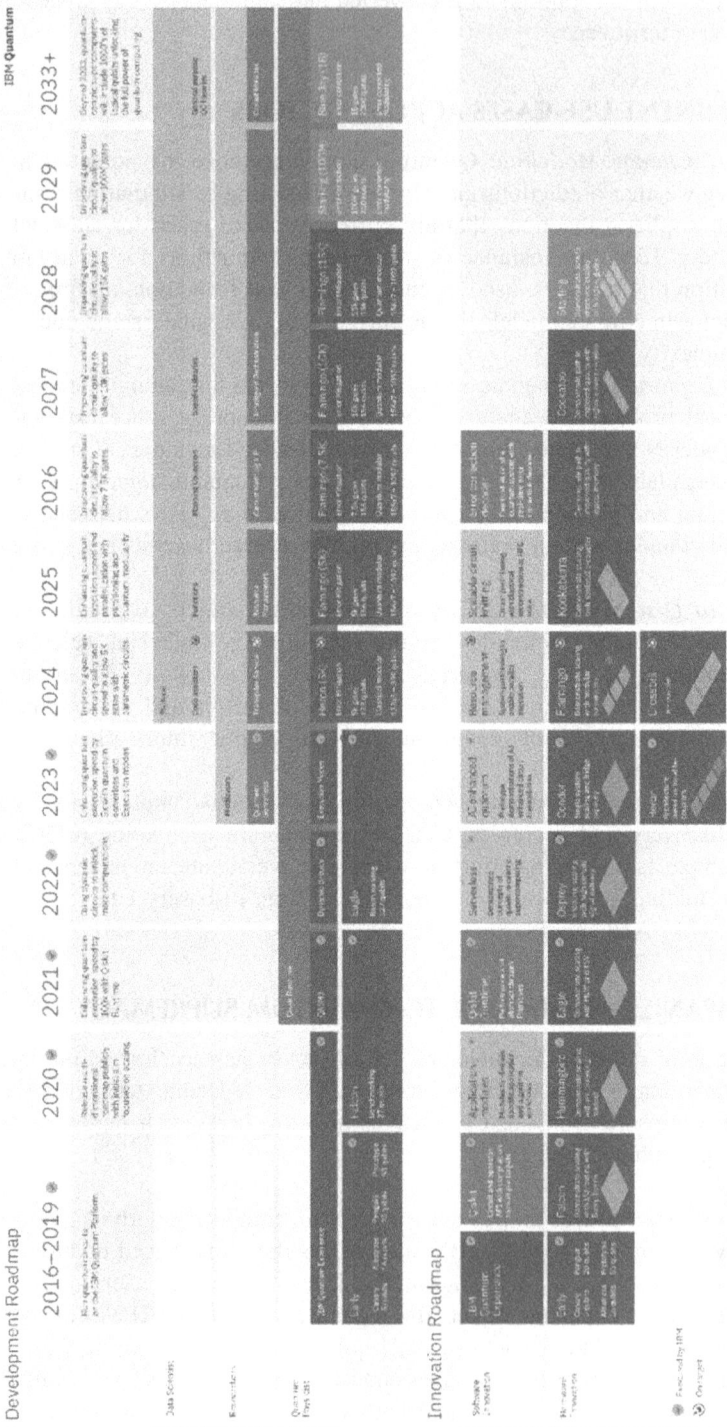

FIGURE 9.2   At IBM Quantum Summit 2023, the company extended the IBM Quantum Development Roadmap to 2033 and has established an IBM Quantum Innovation Roadmap through 2029. (Source: IBM.)

toward a fault-tolerant quantum computer but hasn't committed to a specific timeline yet.

3. Microsoft is taking a different path by investing in topological quantum computing which theoretically allows for more stable qubits. Though Microsoft hasn't yet produced a working topological qubit, they've been contributing to the quantum community through their Quantum Development Kit and Q# programming language.

4. *Alibaba:* Alibaba's DAMO Academy collaborates with the Chinese University of Science and Technology in the world of quantum cryptography and quantum computing. They are investing in both hardware and software research to build useful quantum machines.

5. *Intel:* Intel is exploring various studio lines in quantum research. They collaborate with research partners on creating 'silicon spin qubits' that might be manufactured with the same processes used to create traditional computer chips.

The discussion so far provides an idea of the technicalities and current developments in quantum computing. The subsequent sections will address the potential of a quantum internet and its implications on communications as we know them.

9.6 QUANTUM INTERNET AND A NEW ERA OF COMMUNICATIONS

The emergence of quantum technology promises to revolutionize future communication networks. The quantum internet can be described, in its simplest form, as a network that allows quantum devices to exchange some amount of quantum information and collaborate on quantum computing tasks.

Research and development in quantum information science and technology are gradually escalating and are set to advance the next-generation communication networks. Primarily, the concept of quantum internet is based on the principles of quantum teleportation and entanglement.

The quantum internet promises secure and ultra-fast communication. Key aspects include the following:

- *Quantum Channels: Optical vs. free space (wireless/satellite):*
  - *Optical Channels:* Fiber-based quantum communication using entangled photons.
  - *Free Space Channels:* Satellite-based quantum communication for global coverage.
  - Challenges include distance limitations and scalability.
- *Protocol Enhancements:*
  - QKD enables secure communication using quantum entanglement.
  - *Entanglement Swapping:* Quantum repeaters for extending entanglement over long distances.
  - *Quantum Teleportation:* Instantaneous transfer of quantum states.

- *Quantum for 6G:*
  - Quantum-enhanced communication will play a role in the next generation of wireless networks (6G). Quantum-enhanced sensing, secure communication, and network optimization are potential applications. Quantum-enhanced communication for the next generation of wireless networks.

Quantum entanglement, one of the cornerstones of quantum mechanics, occurs when particles become interconnected, and the state of one instantly influences the state of the other, no matter the distance separating them, and *quantum teleportation* are key solutions that enable the quantum enabled internet.

Quantum teleportation is a protocol that utilizes the principles of entanglement to transport qubits from one location to another. This is the cornerstone of a quantum network – a fundamental requirement of a quantum internet. Chinese researchers have already achieved quantum teleportation across a 1,400-kilometer network and are in the process of developing a full-fledged quantum internet.[7]

In trying to implement quantum communication, two main channels are being extensively studied: optical fiber-based and free-space (optics and/or satellite) quantum communication.

In fiber-based quantum communication, single-photon sources and detectors are coupled with fibers to transport the qubits. However, photon loss and interference in the fiber pose significant challenges.

In contrast, free-space communication involves encoding information on photons and beaming them through open spaces or through the vacuum of space. This technique has been proven over long distances, even from orbiting satellites to ground stations, but atmospheric turbulence, pointing errors, and loss pose substantial challenges.

QKD is being developed alongside the study of these channels to enhance the security of quantum networks. As discussed in earlier chapters, QKD guarantees secure communication by employing a cryptographic protocol involving components of classical and quantum encryption. It assures that the presence of any third party intercepting quantum data will be noticed by the communicating users. In addition, the idea of quantum repeaters and entanglement swapping is being explored to potentially connect multiple users across a longer distance. Quantum repeaters use entangled pairs of qubits to extend the range of quantum channels, ensuring secure and efficient transmission of quantum information over longer distances.

The quantum internet, leveraging the principles of quantum mechanics, is expected to usher in an era of ultra-secure communications and distributed quantum computing. The potential applications of a quantum network are vast, ranging from highly secure communication, enhanced precision sensing, to efficient problem-solving.

Applications such as Quantum Digital Signatures (QDS) use the principles of quantum mechanics to certify and authenticate the origin and integrity of specific information. This not only ensures security but also authorizes access to classified information to designated individuals.

A functional quantum internet would lead to the advent of distributed quantum computing. This could be a game-changer in terms of scalability and computational power for major industries. For example, a quantum cloud-based service could solve complex computational problems involving traffic flow, complex financial models, logistics, or even AI model training which classical systems would struggle with.

Furthermore, a quantum internet could support the creation of a 'quantum cloud', a quantum-computing-as-a-service platform. Quantum cloud could be a means to provide computational abilities to players who lack the financial resources to develop their own quantum systems. For instance, IBM already offers quantum computing services to the public through its IBM Q Experience, which provides online access to quantum processors and simulators.

In the field of sensing and metrology, quantum phenomena tend to offer higher precision than classical methods. Quantum internet might propagate the use of these phenomena across distances. Quantum sensors could have applications like gravitational wave detection, high-precision chronometers, and ultra-sensitive magnetometers.

The pathway to a quantum internet is layered with numerous technological challenges, including the need for quantum memory and error correction methods to maintain the fidelity of transmitted quantum data. Furthermore, there is a need for the development of quantum repeaters to scale up the quantum network. Multiple research groups and companies worldwide are rigorously working toward the realization of a quantum internet. For instance, QuTech, a research center in the Netherlands, aims to develop a five-node (city-scale) quantum network by 2022.[7]

As quantum technology advances and a quantum internet becomes more feasible, standardization in protocols, quantum systems, security, privacy will be crucial for a successful global, interoperable quantum internet.

9.7   QUANTUM MACHINE LEARNING AND AI

9.7.1   QUANTUM MACHINE LEARNING POTENTIAL

Quantum Machine Learning (Quantum ML or QML) is an area that merges quantum physics with ML to create hybrid methods that are potentially more powerful than classical ML algorithms. Quantum ML models capitalize on the computational superiority of quantum computing to expedite the processing of information, offering the potential for speed-ups in data analysis and the capacity to handle big data.[8]

Quantum ML incorporates quantum algorithms into the process of training and implementation of ML models, which can infuse new possibilities into the field of artificial intelligence. Quantum AI includes QML as a subfield and broadly integrates quantum techniques into AI, including quantum simulations and optimization.

Quantum algorithms can accelerate ML tasks. Quantum neural networks, Quantum support Vector Machines (QSVMs), and quantum variational circuits are being explored. Quantum computing's potential impact on *Artificial General*

Intelligence (AGI) remains an open question. Quantum-enhanced optimization and training deep neural networks are areas of interest.

Quantum ML is helping unlock quantum algorithms for optimization, pattern recognition, and ML. Optimization problems are classic use-cases where quantum ML is anticipated to shine. Many ML tasks boil down to optimization. For instance, the training process of a neural network involves optimizing the network's parameters to minimize a loss function. Given the exponential nature of quantum systems, quantum algorithms like Quantum Approximate Optimization Algorithm (QAOA) might help in navigating large, complex optimization landscapes much faster than classical algorithms.

QML could also lead to speed-ups in ML algorithms. Prominent quantum algorithms such as Harrow-Hassidim-Lloyd (HHL) algorithm or the QSVM suggest exponential speed-up over their classical counterparts. With the HHL algorithm, quantum computers could solve linear systems of equations exponentially faster, a technique that could be beneficial for image and pattern recognition tasks. QSVM could help in accelerating kernel methods in ML.

While researchers look toward the era of fault-tolerant quantum computers, many efforts are currently being directed toward reaping the benefits from near-term quantum computers, or 'NISQ' devices. Quantum ML algorithms are being designed, keeping in mind the limited number of qubits and the noise in the present quantum processors. Variational Quantum Eigensolver (VQE), QAOA are some algorithms designed for NISQ era machines.

One exciting area of quantum ML is Quantum Natural Language Processing (QNLP) where quantum mechanics is used to understand and manipulate human language. CQC recently demonstrated a method that involves the direct encoding of a sentence's grammatical structure into a quantum state. By operating in this state, they could obtain quantum information about the sentence's structure. This is a nascent area of research, but results suggest that quantum-enhanced NLP has the potential to outperform classical algorithms in certain tasks.

A caveat with quantum ML, despite its transformational potential, is the lack of 'quantum readiness'. This refers to the need for awareness, understanding, and the necessary skills among data scientists and ML practitioners to exploit quantum computing. The steep learning curve of quantum physics concepts and the novel programming models currently limit the usability of quantum resources. In addition, there are open questions about the practical advantage of a quantum speed-up, given that quantum computers are nowhere near as developed as classical computers today. Also, physical limitations like error rates, the performance of quantum gates, and the number of qubits in existing quantum machines limit the size of problems that can be solved.

To address this, researchers propose a co-design approach where quantum physicists, data scientists, and domain experts work in tandem to groom future 'quantum-ready' data scientists. This approach involves incorporating quantum courses into data science curriculums and promoting the development of user-friendly quantum programming languages and tools.

The development of ML algorithms that can operate within these limitations, without substantial computational overhead, is an area of ongoing research. As quantum technology matures, tech giants are playing a crucial role in shaping the future of quantum ML. Companies like IBM, Google, and Microsoft are investing in quantum research to create quantum processors, develop quantum programming languages, and explore the potential of quantum ML. For instance, IBM's Quantum Experience encompasses their Qiskit Aqua library, which includes algorithms for QML like the VQE, the QAOA, and more.

PennyLane, a Python-based software library developed by Xanadu, is focused on enabling and facilitating the union of quantum computing and ML, also known as QML. The solutions offered by PennyLane are practical yet forward-looking. The seamless integration with ML libraries like 'Pytorch' and 'TensorFlow'; creation of hybrid quantum-classical models, which combine traditional neural networks with quantum computations; support for a variety of quantum hardware and simulators, including those from Rigetti, IBM, Google, and trapped-ion quantum computers from AQT; and 'differentiable quantum computing' that offers pipelines in ML workflows enables creation of quantum circuits and quantum computations simple on this platform.

Google's TensorFlow Quantum (TFQ) is an open-source library for rapid prototyping of quantum ML models. It combines quantum computing concepts from Cirq (a Python library for creating, editing, and invoking NISQ circuits) and ML capabilities of TensorFlow, thereby providing a framework for both quantum and classical ML.

Microsoft has developed the Quantum Development Kit which incorporates the Q# programming language for quantum computing. The QDK provides a full-stack approach with solutions for quantum-inspired optimization, providing developers and customers access to the most competitive quantum algorithms.

While the field of quantum ML is still in its infancy, its potential to revolutionize information processing creates an exciting area for future innovation. The ability of quantum systems to carry out complex computations at unprecedented speeds could lead to significant advancements in many areas, including pattern recognition, optimization problems, and natural language processing.

- *Implementation Challenges:* Building quantum models that provide an advantage over classical models remains a daunting task. Overcoming noise and increasing the stability of qubits, while also maximizing their numbers, is key to developing effective quantum machines. Furthermore, there are challenges in error correction and the development of robust quantum gates.
- *Quantum Advantage:* Given the complexities involved and the advancement of classical computing techniques, it is still unclear where and when quantum techniques will provide a significant practical advantage over classical methods in ML or AI.
- *Quantum Machine Learning Interpretability:* Like classical ML models, quantum ML models also face the challenge of interpretability. It can be even more complex to understand why a quantum model is making certain predictions due to the underlying quantum phenomena involved.

Despite these challenges, the research community is optimistic that we may soon see practical applications of quantum ML and quantum AI. Interestingly, quantum ML and AI could also help in the advancement of quantum computing itself. For instance, AI techniques can be used to optimize the configuration of quantum devices or to error-correct quantum computations. Moreover, reinforcement learning models could potentially learn to devise new quantum computing tactics or quantum algorithms. This concept that AI could help in quantum computing, and vice versa, forms an exciting 'Quantum-AI feedback loop'.

The advent of QML heralds a new era in computation, which combines classical computers' power and the exponential potential of quantum computing. It promises to resolve complex computational problems much faster and more efficiently than classical systems.

9.7.2 THE ROLE OF ETHICS AND REGULATION IN QUANTUM AI

As the field of Quantum AI strides forward, it brings forth a host of ethical, societal, economic, and strategic considerations. With the introduction of any transformative technology, appropriate regulatory and ethical frameworks must be established to guide its use and manage potential risks.

1. *Privacy:* Quantum computing can potentially crack current encryption methods, making our present-day internet communications vulnerable. While QKD promises ultra-secure encryption, it's crucial to note that its benefits will initially be accessible to only a select few due to its high cost and limited availability. It thus raises ethical issues around privacy and the digital divide.
2. *Quantum AI and warfare:* The military application of Quantum AI could accelerate advances in autonomous weaponry, surveillance, and cybersecurity threats. International cooperation and agreements, similar to nuclear treaties, need to be considered to ensure the peaceful use of quantum technology.
3. *Legal and regulatory matters:* Quantum technologies present several legal and regulatory challenges. These range from international collaboration and sharing of quantum resources, to patenting quantum algorithms, governing quantum internet, and handling cybersecurity threats. Legislators will need to understand the nuances of quantum technology to develop effective laws and regulations.
4. *Workforce transition and economic inequalities:* Quantum technology will disrupt the job market, requiring a workforce skilled in quantum physics and quantum computing. Policymakers need to institute educational policies to promote quantum literacy and mitigate potential economic inequalities.

9.7.3 WHAT POSSIBILITIES DOES QUANTUM AI OPEN UP?

Quantum-enhanced algorithms could greatly accelerate ML tasks, pushing the boundaries of what AI can accomplish. Quantum AI could revolutionize data analysis, ease optimization problems, empower natural language processing, and propagate other AI applications to unprecedented levels of capability.

As we read in Chapter 10, industries that could benefit from the merger of these two powerful fields are the following:

- *Cryptography:* Quantum algorithms might crack many of the encryption systems currently in use, leading to a reboot of cryptographic techniques with quantum-resistant algorithms and new security schemas based on quantum encryption.
- *Pharmaceutical Industry:* Quantum computing can simulate quantum systems such as molecular structures and interactions, providing massive speed-ups in drug discovery and biomedical research.
- *Finance:* Quantum systems' power to solve complex mathematical problems could be exploited to optimize trading strategies, asset pricing, risk management, and other areas in finance.
- *AI and Data Analysis:* Quantum algorithms could outperform classical ones in sorting and searching through massive amounts of data, providing considerable benefits to the field of big data and AI.

9.8   EDUCATING THE QUANTUM GENERATION

Creating awareness and developing skills for quantum technology has become an international priority. Countries around the globe are incorporating quantum science and computing in their academic curriculum. Major tech players also offer quantum computing courses, to foster a 'Quantum Ready' workforce.

- IBM provides Qiskit Global Summer School, a two-week intensive quantum computing course.
- Google AI quantum team collaborate with universities and offer internship programs.
- Microsoft offers the Quantum Development Kit, which includes comprehensive documentation and self-paced tutorials for learning quantum computing and their Q# programming language.

9.9   THE QUANTUM REALM: MYTH OR REALITY?

The quantum realm, with its counterintuitive properties, holds immense promise and challenges. As we have learnt in previous chapters, the concepts enable some very exciting possibilities:

Superposition and Entanglement:
- *Superposition:* Quantum systems can exist in multiple states simultaneously. A qubit can be both 0 and 1 at the same time. This property enables quantum parallelism, which is harnessed in quantum algorithms.
- *Entanglement:* When two qubits become entangled, their states become correlated, regardless of the distance between them. Instantaneous changes in one qubit affect the other, even if they are light-years apart. Entanglement enables quantum teleportation and secure communication via QKD.

Quantum Simulation:
- Quantum computers can simulate quantum systems that are impossible to model classically. Applications include the following:
  - *Materials Science:* Predicting material properties, discovering new materials, and optimizing catalysts.
  - *Chemistry:* Simulating molecular interactions, drug discovery, and protein folding.
  - *Quantum Field Theory:* Understanding fundamental particles and their interactions.

Quantum Cryptography:
- Quantum-safe encryption using principles of quantum mechanics.
- *QKD:* Securely exchanging cryptographic keys based on entanglement. QKD ensures information-theoretic security against eavesdropping.

Quantum Sensing:
- Ultra-precise measurements using quantum-enhanced sensors.
- *Quantum Metrology:* Improving accuracy in fields like geophysics, navigation, and gravitational wave detection.

Quantum Imaging:
- Quantum-enhanced imaging techniques, such as ghost imaging and quantum radar.
- Applications in medical imaging, remote sensing, and security.

Quantum Machine Learning (QML):
- Quantum algorithms for ML tasks.
- *Quantum Neural Networks:* Enhancing pattern recognition and optimization.

Quantum Communication Networks:
- Building a quantum internet for secure communication.
- *Quantum Repeaters:* Extending entanglement over long distances.
- *Quantum Teleportation:* Instantaneous transfer of quantum states.

Quantum Computing Beyond Bits:
- *Qutrits and Qudits:* Exploring higher dimensional quantum systems.
- *Topological Quantum Computing:* Robust against local noise.

Quantum Ethics and Philosophy:
- Debates on the nature of reality, consciousness, and the observer effect.
- *Many-Worlds Interpretation:* Parallel universes branching with every quantum measurement.

Debunking misconceptions and exploring the true potential of quantum technologies. Quantum mechanics challenge our classical intuition but offer other exciting possibilities that so far have been the themes of science fiction.

Extracting energy from the quantum realm using quantum annealers:
- Quantum annealing for optimization problems.
- Applications in energy extraction from the quantum realm.

The concept of the quantum realm has captivated the scientific world for over a century. It is a branch of physics that remains as paradoxical and perplexing as it was when first discovered by Max Planck in 1900. However, amid its complexities and peculiarities, one question continues to bewitch scientific and public imaginations alike – is the quantum realm a myth or a reality?

The quantum realm or quantum world refers to the microscopic scale at which quantum mechanics come into play, typically the scale of atoms, electrons, and photons. It is a world that defies our conventional understanding of reality – particles can exist in multiple states at once (known as superposition) and can be 'entangled' such that the state of one instantly affects another, no matter the distance, and the very act of observing a particle alters its nature.

This is a world that seems to have leapt straight from the pages of science fiction. Yet, scientists have recorded and experimented with these phenomena extensively. Technologies like Magnetic Resonance Imaging (MRI), lasers, superconductors, and even the modern computer owe their existence to our understanding of the quantum world.

Challenges abound in validating and developing quantum mechanics further. The inherent randomness and indeterminacy in quantum systems, quantum decoherence, and the difficulty in observing quantum phenomena without disturbing them are just a few. However, these obstacles have not dampened the scientific community's enthusiasm for exploring this mesmerizing realm.

The quantum realm is characterized by a set of phenomena that seem to contradict our everyday experiences and deeply held perceptions of the world.

Superposition, a defining feature of quantum mechanics, posits that a quantum particle can exist in multiple states at once. Only when measured or observed does the particle 'collapse' into one of its possible states. This concept, when applied on a macro scale, can produce thought experiments as bewildering as Schrödinger's Cat, where a cat could be simultaneously dead and alive, until observed.

Another phenomenon is **quantum entanglement**, where particles become inherently linked regardless of the distance separating them. Change the state of one, and the other, instantly reflects this change, defying the speed of light. This 'spooky action at a distance', as Einstein famously called it, continues to puzzle scientists today.

Wave-particle duality, which suggests that particles like electrons and photons exhibit both particle-like and wave-like characteristics, further defies our classical understanding of the world. A single electron, when passed through a double-slit apparatus, generates an interference pattern typical of waves, suggesting that particles can behave as waves and vice versa.

While these phenomena seem to stretch credulity, they have been validated through rigorous experimentation and are widely accepted by the scientific community. They also form the backbone of numerous technologies we take for granted today, from lasers and semiconductors to GPS systems and MRIs.

9.10   SCIENTIFIC INVESTIGATIONS AND CONFIRMATIONS

The bizarre behaviors in the quantum realm were first revealed through mathematical equations. Eventually, a surge of experimental data validated these theoretical predictions, providing concrete evidence that these quantum phenomena are real, albeit strange.

One such critical experiment was the double-slit experiment, demonstrating the wave-particle duality of light and matter. In 1927, by firing individual electrons at a photosensitive screen through two thin slits, the research team observed an interference pattern indicative of a wave. This exists even when only one electron is fired at a time, leading to the shocking implication that each electron interferes with itself – suggesting that particles can indeed behave as waves.

Quantum entanglement was another theoretical prediction famously tested and confirmed. In the 1960s, physicist John Bell derived 'Bell's Theorem' to decide if entanglement could be explained by 'hidden variables' as Einstein suggested and made certain predictions for experimental outcomes. Multiple experiments have since been conducted to test Bell's Theorem, including Alain Aspect's groundbreaking work in 1982. The outcomes have invariably matched predictions, reinforcing the reality of entanglement.

Superposition was tested and confirmed through the famous Schrödinger's Cat thought experiment and other quantum experiments that used delicate apparatus to minimize any disturbance to the system. Nowadays, superposition is routinely utilized in quantum computing, with 'qubits' existing in several states simultaneously.

These scientific investigations give weight to the reality of the quantum realm. While the narrative seems to imply a world of myth, these phenomena have a firm grounding in experimental science and are a testament to the uncanny, yet undeniable realm of the quantum.

The principle of quantum entanglement stands at the heart of quantum communication and quantum cryptography. Quantum entanglement can be harnessed to transfer information securely between distant parties, as any attempt at eavesdropping would disrupt the delicate quantum states and be readily detected.

In medicine, the technology used in MRI scanners is rooted in quantum physics. The machine manipulates the spin states of individual atoms in the human body using a large magnet, creating detailed images of human tissues and organs.

The accuracy of the GPS system also relies on quantum mechanics. The clocks in GPS satellites use the principles of quantum mechanics for precise timekeeping, which immensely improves the accuracy of location positioning.

While the quantum realm is undoubtedly a reality, it still poses numerous unresolved questions and mysteries that continue to fuel scientific curiosity and drive ongoing research.

One of the significant debates revolves around the interpretation of quantum mechanics. Prominent interpretations like the Copenhagen interpretation, the Many-Worlds interpretation, or the Pilot Wave theory, each come with their own set of philosophical implications and continue to be hotly debated within scientific circles.

The prospect of quantum gravity, aiming to reconcile quantum mechanics with General Relativity, remains another area of intense research. String theory, Loop Quantum Gravity (LQG), and quantum foam are all proposals that seek to address this, but a conclusive theory of quantum gravity is still elusive.

Decoherence, where quantum systems lose their quantum behavior due to interactions with the environment, poses a significant roadblock in the scalability of quantum technologies. Research to develop methods to mitigate decoherence is critical to the advancement of technologies like quantum computers and quantum communication systems.

The relationship between quantum mechanics and consciousness, spurred by the role of observers in the collapse of quantum states, is another area that fascinates researchers and stirs controversy.

9.11 BEYOND QUANTUM – WHAT LIES AHEAD?

Having embarked on a thrilling journey from the realm of quantum mechanics, we now approach the exciting frontier of what lies beyond quantum. While quantum physics has recalibrated the lens through which we perceive the universe, it is appreciated that our voyage into the unknown has only just begun. The question persists – what lies beyond the captivating world of quantum?

Physicists today grapple with the challenging task of reconciling Quantum Mechanics, governing the extraordinarily small, with General Relativity, explaining the unimaginably large. The quest for a quantum theory of gravity, or what is often referred to as a theory of everything, is the holy grail of theoretical physics. Various theories such as string theory, LQG, and M-theory have been proposed to bridge this gap.

But the exploration does not stop there. As we learn more about the universe, we encounter tantalizing mysteries such as dark matter and dark energy, enigmatic entities that pervade the cosmos yet remain unseen. The search for understanding these phenomena is forging new paths in physics.

Innovations in technology are propelling us forward as well. With the rise of quantum computing, we are on the cusp of a computational revolution that could unlock answers to some of our universe's biggest questions. Quantum artificial intelligence could augment this further, offering unprecedented problem-solving capabilities.

In the following sections, we delve into these potential trajectories, exploring the tantalizing possibilities that might lie beyond the quest for a Grand Unified Theory.

Additional topics that continue to be researched but are not covered in more detail in this book are the following:

1. Blind Quantum Signature *(BQS)* and Blind Quantum Computation (BQC) BQS
   - *Concept:*
     - BQS allows a signer to sign a quantum state without knowing its content.
     - The signature remains blind, ensuring privacy.
   - *Applications:*
     - *Secure Voting:* BQS can be used for verifiable and anonymous voting systems.
     - *Digital Contracts:* Blind signatures enhance privacy in digital contracts.

- *Example:*
  - Researchers at the University of Science and Technology of China demonstrated BQS using entangled photons.

BQC

- *Concept:*
  - BQC enables a client to delegate quantum computation to a server without revealing the input or output.
  - Privacy-preserving quantum cloud computing.
- *Applications:*
  - *Secure Cloud Quantum Computing:* Clients can perform quantum computations without exposing sensitive data.
- *Example:*
  - Researchers implemented BQC protocols using trapped ions.

2. Quantum Blockchains: Unbreakable, decentralized protection
   - *Quantum-Resistant Blockchains:*
     - Designing blockchain protocols resistant to quantum attacks (e.g., Shor's algorithm).
     - *Example:*
       - Quantum-secure hash functions (e.g., XMSS) are being integrated into blockchain platforms like IOTA.

3. Quantum in the Web3.0
   - *Decentralized Finance (DeFi):*
     - Quantum-safe smart contracts for DeFi platforms.
     - *Example:*
       - Researchers are exploring quantum-resistant cryptographic primitives for Ethereum and other DeFi ecosystems.

4. Quantum in the Metaverse
   - *Quantum-enhanced Virtual Reality (VR):*
     - Simulating complex quantum systems within virtual environments.
     - *Example:*
       - Quantum-inspired simulations for drug discovery in VR.

One of the principal pursuits in modern physics is synthesizing quantum mechanics and General Relativity into a comprehensive 'Theory of Everything'. This elusive theory would coherently explain the behavior of objects ranging from subatomic particles to the vast cosmos.

One of the leading candidates in this regard is string theory. It proposes that fundamental particles are not point-like, but rather tiny, vibrational strings of energy. Different modes of vibration give rise to different particles. String theory also implies the existence of extra, hidden dimensions, offering a radical shift in our understanding of reality.

LQG is another pioneering theory attempting to quantify space-time itself. In LQG, space-time is not continuous but consists of discrete loops or 'quanta', offering a novel way to reconcile gravity with quantum mechanics.

M-theory, an extension of string theory, unifies different versions of string theory along with the concept of supergravity. It tantalizingly proposes an

11-dimensional reality, with strings replaced by higher dimensional membranes or 'branes'.

However, these theories are mathematically intense and experimental confirmation remains challenging. Investigations and research are ongoing, with the scientific community eager to find the cohesive framework that harmoniously unifies these disparate forces of nature.

9.12 UNLOCKING THE MYSTERIES OF DARK MATTER AND DARK ENERGY

Another realm that beckons physicists beyond the quantum world is uncovering the enigmatic entities known as dark matter and dark energy. Despite not detecting these directly, their profound impact on the universe is unmistakably evident.

Dark matter, which scarcely interacts with ordinary matter yet exerts gravitational effects, is thought to provide the 'missing mass' in the universe that binds galaxies together. Several particle candidates, such as *Weakly Interacting Massive Particles (WIMPs)*, axions, and sterile neutrinos, have been proposed, but direct detection of dark matter remains one of the most compelling unsolved mysteries in physics.

Dark energy, on the other hand, is hypothesized to drive the accelerating expansion of the universe. The Cosmological Constant, quintessence fields, and modifications to General Relativity are among the many theories proposed to explain this mysterious phenomenon.

Understanding these elusive components could have profound implications, potentially ushering in new physics that surpasses the Standard Model and quantum field theory. As experimental techniques advance and observatories like the Large Hadron Collider and James Webb Space Telescope press onward, there is renewed hope for shedding light on these cosmic enigmas.

9.13 THE FUTURE OF QUANTUM COMPUTING AND QUANTUM AI

The advent of quantum technology opens up an exciting pathway to the future, promising unprecedented computational and problem-solving capabilities. Quantum computers, employing superposition and entanglement, hold the potential to outperform classical computers in solving complex problems in areas like optimization, materials science, and cryptography. Quantum supremacy, the point where quantum computers perform a task no classical computer feasibly can, could herald a new era of computing.

Beyond machine computations, we are also on the threshold of quantum artificial intelligence. Quantum AI has the potential to elevate ML operations to unprecedented efficiency. Training complex AI models, which currently require extensive computational resources, could be significantly optimized using quantum algorithms.

As we seek to harness the full power of quantum technology, challenges related to coherence times, error correction, and scalability need to be surmounted. The development of quantum software, quantum programming languages, quantum networking, and other supporting infrastructure will be pivotal to the realization of a quantum future. Unfathomable as it sounds now, we might soon command computing power that will stimulate scientific breakthroughs, revolutionize industries, and propel our understanding of the universe toward new horizons.

REFERENCES

1. Cyber Intelligence, Cyber Conflicts, and Cyber Warfare. (2015). In Cybersecurity. https://doi.org/10.1201/b18335-9
2. Rohith, C., & Batth, R. S. (2019). Cyber Warfare: Nations Cyber Conflicts, Cyber Cold War between Nations and its Repercussion. Proceedings of 2019 International Conference on Computational Intelligence and Knowledge Economy, ICCIKE 2019. https://doi.org/10.1109/ICCIKE47802.2019.9004236
3. Christiansen, L. V., Bharosa, N., & Janssen, M. (2023). Policy Guidelines to Facilitate Collective Action towards Quantum-Safety: Recommended Policy Guidelines to Aid and Facilitate Collective Action in Migration towards Quantum-Safe Public Key Infrastructure Systems. ACM International Conference Proceeding Series. https://doi.org/10.1145/3598469.3598480
4. Arute, F., Arya, K., Babbush, R. et al. (2019). Quantum supremacy using a programmable superconducting processor. Nature, 574, 505–510. https://doi.org/10.1038/s41586-019-1666-5
5. IBM Newsroom. (2023). IBM Debuts Next-Generation Quantum Processor & IBM Quantum System Two, Extends Roadmap to Advance Era of Quantum Utility. https://newsroom.ibm.com/2023-12-04-IBM-Debuts-Next-Generation-Quantum-Processor-IBM-Quantum-System-Two,-Extends-Roadmap-to-Advance-Era-of-Quantum-Utility
6. Seetharam, K., & DeMarco, M. (2021). Catalyzing the quantum leap. MIT Science Policy Review. https://doi.org/10.38105/spr.lcbqc1igt5
7. de Forges de Parny, L., Alibart, O., Debaud, J., Gressani, S., Lagarrigue, A., Martin, A., Metrat, A., Schiavon, M., Troisi, T., Diamanti, E., Gélard, P., Kerstel, E., Tanzilli, S., & van den Bossche, M. (2023). Satellite-based quantum information networks: Use cases, architecture, and roadmap. Communications Physics, 6(1). https://doi.org/10.1038/s42005-022-01123-7
8. Boyd, J. H. (2022). The max born symmetry topples the many-worlds theory. Journal of Advances in Physics, 20. https://doi.org/10.24297/jap.v20i.9114

10 A Peek into the Post-Quantum Era—PQA PQC

What Will Happen in 2030

Abdullah Saad Alessa, Mohammad Hammoudeh, and Harbaksh Singh

10.1 LEVERAGING QUANTUM FEAR

Companies have expediently positioned themselves as frontrunners in the quantum-safe future, using the probable vulnerability of standard encryption to quantum computing as a compelling marketing strategy. The storyline often highlights the inescapable nature of quantum computing's propensity to compromise existing cryptographic systems, thereby generating a feeling of urgency among corporations and governments to promptly embrace Post-Quantum Cryptography (PQC) solutions. This strategy exploits the anxiety of not being ready for a quantum future, compelling corporations to promptly invest in quantum-safe technology.

With the competition for dominance in the quantum-safe market intensifying, there has been a surge in the number of claims about items that are described as "quantum-proof" or "quantum-resistant." Although these statements may be impactful in terms of marketing, they have the potential to conceal the intricate truth that the area of PQC is still undergoing development and refinement. Cryptographic professionals advise against accepting absolute security promises without careful consideration, arguing for a nuanced understanding of the concept of quantum-safe. The continuous efforts of standards agencies like as National Institute of Standards and Technology (NIST) are essential in establishing a reference point for assessing these assertions, guaranteeing that PQC systems adhere to a stringent level of security against existing and predicted quantum vulnerabilities.

As previously covered, although the quantum danger is genuine, the exact timeframe for when quantum computers will possess the capability to compromise existing encryption methods is still undetermined. Specialists in the domain have divergent viewpoints on the timeline for quantum computers to attain sufficient capability to present a legitimate threat to encryption techniques like RSA or ECC. Despite this ambiguity, academics, governments, and firms have nevertheless been indicating that the quantum danger is urgent. This might result in premature or wasteful expenditures in PQC technology [1].

As quantum computing progresses, cryptography solutions will also evolve to protect digital communications from quantum attacks. The collaboration between technical advancement and ethical advertising will have a crucial impact in guaranteeing that the shift to PQC is both efficient and practical. Businesses and governments should prioritize the implementation of a proactive but prudent strategy for PQC, based on the most recent research and established protocols [6].

10.2 WHAT THE FUTURE HOLDS—LOOKING BEYOND 2030?

As we stand at the edge of the next computing revolution, looking back at a decade of fast technological evolution, it is clear that we are at the start of a new era: the post-quantum era. This era is characterized not only by the advent of quantum computing into the commercial and academic domains but also going to be known for the substantial developments made in PQC, aimed at ensuring the safety of our digital information against the rising power of quantum machines.

The preceding chapters have outlined the rise of quantum technologies, laying down the complicated events, innovations, and advances that led to the current state-of-the-art. This chapter considers the implications of quantum computing both for our present and our future, it becomes clear that the perspective of what lies ahead is as limitless as it is imaginable.

Today, organizations are at the stage of preparing to move forward into the unfamiliar quantum technologies of the future. In doing so, this chapter revisits the key transformations and predicts how, beyond 2030, the continuous collaboration between industry and academia will not only tackle emerging challenges but also exploit the available opportunities of a post-quantum world. As we investigate deeper into the future of PQC, the possibilities develop into more theoretical areas, yet have a remarkable impact on the world. It is possible that the convergence of PQC with other complex technologies could result in a new era of cybersecurity by the year 2030 and beyond. This would have consequences for all aspects of society, economy, security, and government.

10.2.1 QUANTUM-SAFE HYBRID ECOSYSTEMS: THE FRONTIER OF FUTURE CRYPTOGRAPHY

As we investigate the potential of quantum-safe hybrid ecosystems beyond 2030, it is evident that this emergent notion signifies a substantial change in cryptographic technique. Quantum-safe hybrid ecosystems are created to effortlessly combine the security advantages of both quantum-resistant algorithms and regular cryptographic approaches, resulting in strong protection against a wide range of threats, including present digital exploits and potential quantum assaults in the future.

The fundamental basis of quantum-safe hybrid ecosystems is rooted in their use of a dual-layer strategy. These systems try to ensure reliability by combining both PQC and traditional cryptographic approaches, hence reducing the risk of failure in either method. It is crucial to consider this aspect, especially during the transitional phase when quantum computers are not yet sufficiently capable of decrypting all conventional encryption methods, but are progressing quickly.

10.2.1.1 Technological Synergy in the Adaptive Security Protocols

Within a quantum-safe hybrid system, security protocols have the ability to adjust and modify themselves according to the threat levels. For example, a system may initially use quicker and less resource-intensive classical encryption in typical situations, but it might automatically convert to stronger quantum-resistant approaches when it detects or predicts the presence of quantum-level threats [12].

10.2.1.2 Technological Synergy in Layered Encryption

Data may undergo numerous rounds of encryption using various cryptographic techniques. The use of this layering strategy significantly improves security by guaranteeing that in the event of one encryption layer being compromised, there are other levels in place to safeguard the underlying data.

On the other hand, despite the significant potential benefits, it is important to overcome a number of obstacles in order to successfully implement quantum-safe hybrid ecosystems. The term "interoperability" refers to the capacity of newly developed quantum-resistant algorithms to operate in a seamless manner with existing encryption techniques, without causing any disruptions to the services provided or by degrading the quality of the user experience.

Compared to normal algorithms, quantum-resistant algorithms often have greater performance overheads. This is because quantum-resistant methods demand more computer resources than regular algorithms. The achievement of a balance between the demand for performance and the assurance of security will be of the utmost importance. The creation of systems that are capable of intelligently and automatically transitioning between several cryptographic approaches in response to varying degrees of threat is one of the components that make up dynamic response mechanisms. In order to do this, it is necessary to use complex decision-making algorithms and capabilities for real-time threat interpretation.

It is likely that in the future, the creation of hybrid ecosystems will be secured using quantum computers. The most advanced machine learning models can provide warning about the degrees of quantum threats, and they can also automate the process of selecting the most appropriate cryptographic method. These systems will have the capability to proactively adapt their security mechanisms by analyzing patterns and predicting future attacks. They can achieve this by the monitoring of potential threats. The establishment of worldwide standards for hybrid cryptographic systems requires significant efforts to be made in the direction of standardization. The need for this is essential to ensure compatibility across a broad range of platforms and devices, as well as to promote greater adoption. The integration of QKD with conventional and quantum-resistant encryption algorithms can significantly enhance the security of data transmission, specifically for unauthorized actors to eavesdrop on conversations [12].

The development of quantum-safe hybrid systems is a practical approach to respond to the developments in quantum cryptography. As these systems continue to advance, it is anticipated that they will eventually become fundamental components of the global cybersecurity framework, therefore safeguarding important data from both existing and potential threats. The continued development of new technologies, thorough standardization, and proactive acceptance of new technologies are going to be essential for the survival of these ecosystems [3].

10.3   ACADEMIA AND RESEARCH: TRAILBLAZERS OF QUANTUM INNOVATION

The landscape of technology in the next few years will be marked by the emergence of quantum computing. From its infancy in the early 21st century, when it was a theoretical science limited to the most advanced laboratories, quantum computing will mature into a robust technology in the next six years that will change our approach toward security and computation [4].

By 2030, quantum processors will have eclipsed the tens of thousands of qubits threshold and will be capable of tackling complex simulations and optimization tasks with unparalleled proficiency. One of the most disruptive aspects of quantum computing is its potential to break current encryption paradigms. Public-key cryptographic algorithms used for securing communications today are vulnerable to quantum attacks. Anticipating this, there has been a concerted effort today to transition to PQC—cryptographic systems that are secure against both classical and quantum attacks. PQC is no longer a theoretical construct but a practical necessity, and by 2030, this will be integrated into the fabric of digital security protocols worldwide.

The advancement in PQC systems by 2030 has not been linear; it has been marked by significant collaborative research and development, resulting in standardized algorithms resilient to quantum attacks. The NIST in the United States finalized a set of quantum-resistant algorithms, which are in the process of being widely implemented in cryptographic applications. These algorithms can secure communication, financial transactions, and sensitive data storage against quantum threats.

However, the journey to PQC adoption is faced with several challenges. PQC adoption requires large-scale updates to the existing IT infrastructure and re-education of the current cybersecurity workforce. Entities ranging from small businesses to governments will have to re-assess their security strategies and implement new systems—a task thought to be costly and complex, but one that is essential for maintaining privacy and security in the post-quantum era.

As we look at the innovative advancements that quantum technology is making, it is critical to acknowledge that these will not be the end of our advancement but rather a foundation for the future. Quantum computing and PQC are set to open doors to new possibilities in every field they touch, from logistics to medicine, from finance to space exploration. As robust as our PQC solutions will be in 2030, the quantum horizon continues to expand, and with it, our need to develop, innovate, and protect.

10.4   INDUSTRY REVOLUTION: QUANTUM COMPUTING IN THE MARKETPLACE

The advent of quantum computing and PQC will bring about a seismic shift in the industrial landscape. Industries that once functioned within the bounds of classical computing paradigms will be seen embracing the vast potential of quantum technologies. These changes, which will be both profound and pervasive, are bound to reshape the very fabric of how businesses operate and compete.

Industries such as finance, cybersecurity, pharmaceuticals, and logistics have been at the forefront of integrating quantum computing into their operations. Financial institutions, for instance, exploit quantum algorithms for complex risk assessment and portfolio optimization, achieving insights in minutes that once took days. Meanwhile, the cybersecurity industry leverages PQC to protect data transmission and storage, ensuring a level of security that is unattainable with conventional encryption methods.

In healthcare, the pharmaceutical industry witnesses a quantum revolution in drug discovery processes. Quantum simulations can model molecular interactions at an unprecedented scale and speed, significantly reducing the time and cost of developing new medications. The complexity of human biology, once a barrier to understanding and treatment, is now unraveled layer by layer with quantum-assisted research [11].

One of the most compelling case studies in quantum industrial application is found within the logistics sector. Companies harness quantum optimization to streamline supply chains and distribution networks, addressing previously unsolvable logistics problems. This efficiency gain not only reduces operational costs but also minimizes the environmental footprint of global supply chains—a testament to quantum computing's potential to aid in sustainability challenges.

Another example is the complex problem of weather predictions and climate change. Forecasting relies upon nonlinear differential equations which will greatly benefit from quantum computing power and arguably provide an exponential improvement in such forecasting. This will have significant impacts on industry and governments from logistics routing, emergency management, agriculture, and urban planning.

The transformation into a quantum-informed industry has not been without its hurdles. The initial investment in quantum infrastructure and the retraining of the workforce presented significant challenges. However, these were progressively overcome through strategic planning, government incentives, and the emergence of a quantum-ready workforce, as forecasted by academia's changed curriculums.

Cross-industry collaborations have also played a key role in this revolution, with businesses sharing insights and best practices for quantum integration. Consortia and partnerships have formed, creating ecosystems that promote innovation and accelerate the adoption of quantum technologies [10].

It is anticipated that by 2030, the benefits of early and continued investment in quantum computing and PQC will be realized. Businesses that adopt these technologies will gain significant competitive advantages, driving economic growth and prompting a new wave of quantum entrepreneurship. The industry's evolution is also measured in the societal impacts, impacting everything from job creation to international trade dynamics. Beyond 2030, the expectation is that the industry will continue not just to adapt but also to advance, continuously exploring new frontiers in quantum application and constantly raising the bar for what is achievable.

10.5   INTEGRATION OF ARTIFICIAL INTELLIGENCE WITH PQC

It is anticipated that the combination of Artificial Intelligence (AI) and PQC will bring about a significant change in cybersecurity paradigms. The combination of these advanced technologies gives great outlooks to increase the security and efficiency of cryptographic systems, and this is something that can be expected to happen beyond the year 2030. Currently, PQC is critical to respond to the ever-changing environment of cyber threats [12].

- *The Application of AI to the Improvement of Cryptographic Algorithms*
  The investigation of patterns, the forecasting of potential security weaknesses, and the automation of complex processes are all areas in which AI has the potential to have a significant influence on the enhancement and protection of cryptographic methods.

  Optimization of Algorithms: AI can help in developing and assessing quantum-ready algorithms. AI uses machine learning techniques to rapidly effectively analyze large datasets and identify potential vulnerabilities in cryptographic algorithms. Robust PQC algorithms must be able to withstand the ever-growing quantum capabilities.

  Automatic Security Evaluations: AI systems have the capacity to evaluate the security state of cryptographic implementations on a regular basis, therefore identifying and resolving issues as soon as they appear. This proactive technique ensures that security measures are able to change in unison with future threats, particularly those that are posed by quantum computers.

- *Security Protocols That Are Dynamic*
  The construction of flexible security protocols that are able to automatically adapt their operations in response to changes in the threat environment is made possible by the incorporation of AI into PQC systems.

  Threat Detection and Response: AI can analyze network traffic and other relevant information to detect quantum-level threats. This makes it feasible for cryptographic systems to rapidly switch to modes that are more secure whenever it is necessary. This adaptive feature helps maintain the highest possible level of security while ensuring that the performance of the system is not impacted.

  The Models of Risk Assessment: The degrees of danger that are associated with different kinds of cyberattacks, including those that may be made easier by quantum computing, may be evaluated using sophisticated prediction models. When it comes to assigning security resources and activities, these models provide assistance by tailoring them according to the intensity and characteristics of the threats that have been discovered.

  Despite the fact that the benefits are readily apparent, the process of integrating AI with PQC is also associated with a number of challenges that need careful consideration:

  1. It is of the utmost importance to ensure that AI systems are protected against quantum as well as conventional assaults in order to safeguard the confidentiality and authenticity of data, that AI uses for the purposes

of learning and making decisions. For the purpose of preventing any possible breaches or compromises, this may be accomplished via the use of PQC.

2. The complexity of AI systems and the management of their resources are also important considerations. In order to successfully integrate these systems with PQC, it is necessary to ensure that the processing capabilities of the devices and networks that they protect are not too taxed.

3. For AI systems, unbiased and reliable design is essential. In order to prevent biased or unfair findings, this requires the process of obtaining training on a variety of datasets. This is especially important in security scenarios when the dangers are substantial.

It is anticipated that in the not-too-distant future, the integration of AI with PQC will be a prevalent technique used in the development of advanced cybersecurity systems. The major purpose of the research and development activities is to construct cryptographic systems that are more efficient, intelligent, and capable of regulating themselves when they are implemented. Both AI and technology that are immune to quantum attacks will be used in these systems to take advantage of their respective benefits. The following are some examples of possible developments [12]:

- Quantum machine learning has the potential to improve the capabilities of AI in cryptographic settings. This may lead to the development of more robust security solutions.
- *Cross-disciplinary innovations:* The convergence of quantum computing, AI, and encryption will fuel multidisciplinary innovations, possibly establishing new fields of study and innovative applications.

The motivation behind the integration of AI with PQC is not only to protect against the quantum threat but also to revolutionize the implementation and management of security in an increasingly interconnected society. As these technologies continue to advance, there is little doubt that they will radically change the landscape of cybersecurity, calling for continuous innovation and change [10].

10.6 PQC IN SPACE COMMUNICATIONS

It is becoming clearer that the implementation of PQC into space communications is of the highest significance after taking into consideration the time period that extends beyond the year 2030. Due to the large distances that signals need to travel and the fact that their transmission routes are open to the public, space communication networks, such as satellite communications and interplanetary links, are vulnerable to being intercepted and even eavesdropped on. When it comes to these networks, the use of encryption techniques that are resistant to quantum computing is becoming more important as quantum computing continues its advancement.

Very sensitive information is often sent across great distances by the use of space communication technology. To protect these communications from the possibility of being intercepted by quantum technology, it is vital to implement encryption that is resistant to quantum computing. This will ensure that the data that is sent by satellites and other space-based assets does not compromise their confidentiality or integrity.

Because space missions, such as those involving the exploration of other planets or the surveillance of the Earth from orbit, can last for many years, the cryptographic mechanisms that are currently in place are resistant to the potential threats that could be posed by quantum computing. Even if advances in technology are made in the future, the data will continue to be protected because of the durability of the encryption software against the potential quantum threat.

In the field of space communications, which includes several different international and commercial parties, it is of the utmost importance to achieve compatibility and collaboration between various governments and corporate groups. Establishing a universal security standard could be made possible by the implementation of PQC on a global scale, which allows secure collaboration and the interchange of data across nations and enterprises.

The implementation of PQC in the unique environment of space involves many challenges, including the following:

- The limitations that spaceborne systems, such as satellites, are often referred to as resource constraints, including power, computational capabilities, and memory. Hence, it is challenging to adopt quantum-resistant algorithms by existing space systems as these algorithms need a greater amount of computing power and memory than traditional encryption methods do.
- *Delay in the propagation of the signal:* When it comes to space communications, the large distances involved result in significant delays in the transmission of signals. Under the existence of long latency networks, real-time key exchanges and updates become more difficult to accomplish. As a result, the use of complex protocols that are capable of functioning effectively is required [14].
- *Extremely Dangerous Environmental Conditions:* There is a possibility that the reliability of the computer systems on board might be affected by the radiation and microgravity environments in orbit. It is of the utmost importance to make certain that both the PQC algorithms and the hardware that are used to execute them are resistant to *such circumstances.*

There are a number of significant developments that have the potential to strengthen the use of PQC in space communications. These developments include:

- To build lightweight cryptographic solutions, it is essential to make efforts to design cryptographic algorithms that are both more efficient and less resource-intensive. While at the same time lowering the resource costs that are often associated with current PQC solutions, these algorithms need to guarantee quantum resistance [15].
- Key management systems that include QKD and PQC have the potential to provide increased security via a dual-layer approach. This is true for

advanced key management systems. In order to improve the safety of cryptographic keys, this integration would take advantage of the properties that are exclusive to quantum mechanics, while at the same time using PQC to safeguard the data itself.

- *Collaboration across Disciplines:* In order to tackle the difficult problems associated with implementing PQC in space, it will be essential to have specialists in cryptography, quantum physics, and aerospace engineering work together. There is a possibility that this interdisciplinary approach may promote breakthroughs that are expressly tailored to solve the practical issues of space exploration and communication.

A tremendous potential to improve the safety of space communications is presented by the developing field of quantum computing, which is gaining momentum. Protecting the future of space exploration and satellite communication will require the purposeful incorporation of PQC into space communication systems. In addition to protecting sensitive information, this preventative plan will also strengthen the fundamental infrastructure that is crucial to both the growth of scientific knowledge and the protection of the nation's security. In order to secure space communication networks that are entirely safe against quantum assaults, ongoing innovation, adjustment, and worldwide cooperation are required.

10.7 THE DEVELOPMENT OF UNIVERSAL QUANTUM-RESISTANT STANDARDS

It is becoming more important to have universal standards that are resistant to quantum computing as quantum computing continues to advance. In order to successfully protect against both existing and potential quantum threats across a broad range of platforms and technologies all over the globe, the goal of these standards is to serve as a strong foundation. For the purpose of preserving global security and ensuring compatibility in the quantum era, the adoption of these standards is not only a necessary technical requirement but also an essential strategic imperative.

- *Challenges in Developing Universal Standards*
  Diversification of Technologies: The adoption of quantum-safe algorithms is required across a wide variety of technologies, such as cloud services, space communications, the Internet of Things, operational technology, business systems, and mobile communications. Considering that every platform has its unique requirements and constraints, the development of universal solutions is a complex challenge. Cooperation on a Global Scale is needed to achieve wide adoption and implementation of standards that are widely recognized, it is necessary to have extensive global cooperation across different standardization organizations, governments, and industries [2]. To be successful, this global initiative must not only overcome

technical challenges but also overcome geopolitical and economic conditions. Another significant challenge is the need to ensure that future quantum-resistant standards continue to be compatible with existing systems while also preserving their security. Ensuring compatibility is vital to prevent fragmentation and ensure a smooth transition to new cryptographic systems [5].

- *Multiple endeavors and partnerships are now in progress to tackle these difficulties:*
  Organizations that are responsible for international standards, such as the International Organization for Standardization (ISO) and the International Telecommunication Union (ITU), are now working on the creation and distribution of global standards that are resistant to quantum computing. The collaboration that is required to produce standards that are generally recognized and considered to be robust is provided by these organizations.

  Testing quantum-resistant systems is underway to build best practices that might potentially impact international standards, both national governments and the private sector. Academic institutions and research institutes are at the forefront of the creation of innovative algorithms that are resistant to quantum computing. Before the standardization of these algorithms, their research is an essential component in determining whether or not they are secure, and whether or not they are feasible [2].

The areas essential to future developments in universal quantum-resistant standards:

- The construction of complex cryptographic algorithms that are not only resistant to quantum attacks but also efficient and scalable. This is the subject of ongoing research and development efforts on advanced cryptographic algorithms.
- An increasing need for testing and certification methods to ensure compliance with the appropriate security requirements. Quantum testing and certification will address this demand.
- Educational programs to encourage the broad use of quantum-resistant standards, so that they incorporate quantum cryptography and its implications. By providing the next generation of technologists and policymakers with the information and skills required to effectively implement and control the usage of these standards, these programs hope to accomplish their goals.

An initiative that is not only difficult but also essential to protect future global communications and data security is the development of universal quantum-resistant standards. It is vital to have a plan that is collaborative, interdisciplinary, and transcends both geographical and sectoral restrictions. As time goes on, these standards will not only protect against the possibility of quantum dangers but will also make it easier to increase the digital economy in a way that is sustainable in the quantum age.

10.8   GLOBAL POLICY AND QUANTUM ETHICS

The advancements in quantum technologies demand international coopera-tion in creating policies and ethical guidelines to govern their use. As quantum computing and PQC reshape industries and national security, governments worldwide recognize the need for a coordinated approach to oversight and regulation.

Global policy efforts should be aimed at securing the benefits of quantum advancements while mitigating risks. As nations seek to protect their critical infrastructures from quantum threats by investing in PQC and managing the geopolitical implications of quantum supremacy, a delicate balance will have to be achieved between collaboration and rivalry. International agreements, simi-lar to the cybersecurity accords of the early 21st century, will help facilitate the secure exchange of information and minimize the impact of quantum-enabled cyber warfare. Given that codebreaking and cryptography attacks have a long history of nation-state competitive advantage, reaching such a goal will be dif-ficult [9].

The development of quantum technologies also raised a range of ethical consid-erations that global policy needed to address. Issues of privacy and surveillance took on new dimensions with the power of quantum computing. Without appropriate pro-tections, the quantum data analysis and decryption capabilities present significant threats to individual liberties and privacy. Hence, ethical frameworks are needed to ensure that the use of quantum technology adheres to principles of privacy, consent, and transparency.

Amid these considerations, the role of international regulatory bodies was amplified. Organizations like the United Nations, the ITU, and the World Trade Organization (WTO) took active roles in facilitating dialogues and agreements that transcended national borders. These bodies worked alongside dedicated quantum ethics committees, including voices from civil society, academia, and industry, to address the moral questions arising from quantum capabilities.

Furthermore, quantum ethics extended to considerations of equity and access. As the benefits of quantum technologies became evident, it was imperative to ensure that these advantages did not exacerbate global inequalities. Policies were put in place to promote equal access to quantum education and technology, particularly for developing countries, to prevent a "quantum divide."

The establishment of quantum ethics as a field of study also encouraged the responsible development and deployment of quantum technologies. Researchers and developers were urged to consider the long-term effects of their work, incorporating ethical analysis into the innovation process. This ethos of responsibility is the basis of quantum research, promoting trust and public support for the continued advance-ment of quantum technologies.

By 2030, as the world stands on the edge of further quantum breakthroughs, the groundwork laid by global policy and ethical discourse will provide a frame-work for moving forward responsibly. The quantum technologies governing poli-cies are designed to be adaptive, growing with the technology and its implications on society.

10.9 ETHICAL IMPLICATIONS AND POLICIES FOR PQC

The progress of PQC implementation introduces technical, ethical, and regulatory dilemmas. These problems need careful deliberation to guarantee that the shift to quantum-resistant algorithms is both just and safe, promoting confidence and fairness in the utilization of these potent instruments.

- *Concerns Regarding the Ethical Implications of PQC*
  There are concerns about privacy as the increased capabilities of quantum computers can decode communications that were previously encrypted, which might affect the privacy of individuals. To ethically use PQC, it is essential to ensure that these technologies are developed and used in a way that protects privacy rather than reducing it.

  Because it may result in restricted access to the most effective cryptographic protections for just a select few governments or organizations, the possibility of uneven distribution of the benefits of PQC is a concern that must be addressed. This may make the differences that now exist across countries and within communities even more apparent, particularly in regions that have a limited technological infrastructure.

  It is feasible that the deployment of sophisticated quantum computing technologies by governments and large organizations would increase the amount of monitoring and control that is exercised over individuals' data. There are ethical considerations that arise because of this situation about the trade-off between individual liberty and national security.
- *Determination of regulations and policies for the PQC*
  In order to address these ethical concerns, it is very necessary to have comprehensive regulation and policy frameworks prepared and in place. The security aspects of quantum-resistant algorithms should be included in these rules, but the larger socioeconomic repercussions of these algorithms should also be taken into consideration [8].

There is a need for government bodies to establish regulations that will limit the use and worldwide dissemination of quantum computing technology. These regulations should be comparable to the constraints that are now in place for dual-use technologies that have the potential to be utilized in both civilian and military settings. The goal of these regulations ought to be to create an environment that discourages misuse while simultaneously encouraging innovation and promoting safety.

10.9.1 STANDARDS AND COOPERATION ON A GLOBAL SCALE

Because of the global nature of digital communications and the internet, it is imperative that international cooperation be undertaken in order to develop standards for PQC. In order to ensure that these programs are fair and applicable to a wide range of situations, it is essential to include stakeholders from both developed and developing countries.

When policymakers are discussing the implications of quantum computing and PQC, they should make sure to involve members of the general public in the conversation. This requires not only the disclosure of the benefits and possible downsides transparently and openly but also the solicitation of input from a variety of stakeholders to collect information that can be used to make decisions on policy. Participation from the general public is essential for establishing confidence and ensuring that the development of positive quality control technology is in accordance with the ideals of society [13].

10.9.1.1 Principles of Ethical Conduct Concerning Users and Developers

During the creation and implementation of PQC, it is vital to establish ethical guidelines that uniquely fit the situation. Concerns like as data privacy, ethical use of data, and equitable access to quantum-safe technology might be addressed with the help of these principles, which could offer optimum approaches for handling these issues.

The ethical problems and policy decisions associated with PQC technologies will likely get more complicated as their underlying technology continues to advance. Therefore, it is important to anticipate and address these challenges proactively to ensure that PQC not only enhances security but also maintains high ethical standards. Consequently, to navigate the ethical landscape that is affected by these technologies, engineers, ethicists, legislators, and the general public must engage in continuing talks [8].

Society can maximize the benefits of PQC while minimizing its negative implications, so ensuring a secure and equitable digital future in the quantum era. This would be an effective way to address the ethical and policy issues that face society.

10.10 SOCIETY AND CULTURE: THE QUANTUM LEAP FORWARD

The transformative impact of quantum computing and PQC is expected to reach far beyond the domains of technology and industry by the year 2030, deeply influencing society and culture. As Quantum will exponentially advance technologies of today, i.e., AI will become more integrated into everyday life, changing the way we interact with the world and with each other.

The societal shift is perhaps going to be most visible in the realm of employment. The quantum industry is expected to create a wealth of new job opportunities, ranging from specialized quantum engineers and cryptographers to roles in quantum software development and quantum information security. This will lead to a rethinking of workforce training programs, aimed at equipping individuals with the skills necessary to succeed in a quantum-powered economy.

Culturally, the broader public perception of quantum technologies will undergo a significant evolution in the coming years. Early on, quantum computing was often regarded as science fiction with little day-to-day relevance. By 2030, this narrative would have changed, with quantum breakthroughs being widely reported in media and becoming a part of the public conversation. Quantum literacy efforts will help demystify the science, fostering a general understanding of its principles and potential among the population.

Quantum technology is also expected to influence the arts field, inspiring new forms of digital and creative art, and changing storytelling in film, literature, and television. As people face the implications of this technology, it will unlock new pathways to creative explorations of quantum themes, reflecting society's expectations, fears, and interest in quantum technologies. This cultural change will bring its challenges. The fast development of quantum technologies is likely to lead to discussions around the digital divide and can potentially even lead to a quantum divide—where access to quantum advancements could be faced by socioeconomic, geographical, or educational barriers. Addressing this potential divide in advance should be a priority for policymakers and educators alike to offer inclusive access to the benefits of quantum computing [7].

The integration of PQC into the public domain will have transformed the landscape of digital security. Individuals would have become more confident in the protection of their personal data, knowing it was safeguarded by the most secure cryptographic methods available. This trust in PQC-enabled systems will bolster the rise of a new era of digital services and applications, where privacy and security will no longer be seen as trade-offs but as fundamental guarantees [7].

By becoming a part of the societal fabric, quantum computing and PQC also is expected to influence social norms. Conversations around ethics, privacy, and capability will reflect a deeper understanding and appreciation of the technology's potential risks and benefits. As a result, society will become more critical and conscious of how their data and digital interactions are handled and secured [9].

10.11   THE QUANTUM FUTURE: PROJECTIONS BEYOND 2030

By the year 2030, society will have emerged more connected, informed, and secure, with quantum technologies playing an integral role in shaping a new cultural consciousness. The quantum leap forward is not only a scientific or industrial revolution but a societal development, preparing humanity for the continuous journey into the quantum future.

The year 2030 serves as a significant milestone in the journey of quantum computing and PQC. The quantum future presents a landscape rich with potential, as well as raises fundamental questions about the course of technological advancement and its interaction with the human experience [15]. Several long-term predictions have become part of the discussion among technologists and futurists:

- *Quantum Internet:* One of the most anticipated developments is the emergence of a quantum internet, a network that leverages quantum entanglement for virtually unbreakable communication security and instantaneous data transfer across vast distances. The foundations for such a network, laid in the 2020s, are expected to culminate in the first fully operational quantum networks connecting major hubs around the world.
- *Quantum Artificial Intelligence (AI):* With exponential increases in processing capabilities, quantum AI is predicted to surmount current limits in machine learning, providing unseen computing power for data analysis and problem-solving. The convergence of AI and quantum computing is set

to transform fields as varied as climate modeling, logistics, personalized medicine, and autonomous systems.

- *Quantum Materials and Manufacturing:* The ability to simulate and manipulate materials at the quantum level is projected to unlock a new age of materials science. This could lead to the fabrication of materials with tailored properties, including high-temperature superconductors, advanced photovoltaics, and nanostructured composites, transforming the manufacturing sector, and the associated industry players and consumers.
- *Democratic Access to Quantum Computing:* Efforts to make quantum computing resources widely available through cloud-based platforms are expected to democratize access, e.g., the spread of classical computing in the late 20th century. This democratization will enable a rise in innovation and creativity from individuals and smaller enterprises, challenging the dominance of large corporations and research institutions.

As we investigate the potential future challenges and opportunities that may arise from these quantum advances, a few considerations stand out:

- *Ethical Implications:* The great capabilities of quantum technologies call for continuous evaluation of ethical concerns, particularly relating to surveillance, data privacy, and the impacts on employment and societal structures.
- *Education and Literacy:* Preparing future generations for life in a quantum world requires continued updates to education, with a focus on developing quantum literacy across all levels of society, ensuring that individuals are informed and skilled actors in a quantum-powered society. Quantum poses a challenge to security and defence. As quantum technologies grow more powerful, they will play a critical role in national security and defence strategies. Balancing the benefits of these advances with the need for international peace and stability will be a lasting challenge for policymakers and governments.

Peering beyond the horizon of 2030, it's going to be the time when quantum is integrated and impacts every walk of life will start coming to life. We are likely to find ourselves at the beginning of an era where the theoretical is made tangible, and the impossible becomes achievable. The pathways laid by industry, academia, and researchers will continue to guide us as we navigate the quantum landscape, exploring its vast potential while we remain vigilant stewards of the power it puts in our hands.

10.12   THE JOINT EFFORT TOWARD A QUANTUM-SAFE WORLD

The industrial sector, academic institutions, and academic institutions are all working to improve their readiness for the next quantum period, which is anticipated to take place after the year 2030. The use of the enormous potential of quantum technology while simultaneously minimizing the risks that are associated with it is a collaborative and proactive strategy, as shown by this point.

- *Industry*
  The industrial sector is expanding its investments in quantum computing, with a particular focus on the development of quantum hardware, software, and algorithms. Quantum computing is now being investigated for its potential applications in a variety of sectors, including pharmaceutical research, materials science, and problem optimization. This investigation is being carried out by both well-established technological businesses and rising startups. In addition, industries are preparing themselves by creating quantum divisions a great number of well-known information technology companies have established specialist quantum computing divisions with the intention of integrating quantum technology into their business models. The collaboration between technology companies and startups in the area of quantum technology is on the increase. This cooperation is often made possible by investments from venture capitalists, and the purpose of these investments is to speed up the development of quantum applications and their introduction to the market [15].
- *Academia*
  One of the most important roles that academic institutions play is in fostering the theoretical and practical research that is necessary for the advancement of quantum technology. In addition to expanding existing quantum computing courses, universities all around the globe are also establishing new research centers that are specifically devoted to quantum technology. The primary duties include: universities are now in the process of developing new courses and degree programs that are centered on quantum computing, quantum cryptography, and other disciplines that are relevant to these areas of study. The future generation of quantum scientists and engineers is the target audience for these programs, which are designed to educate and prepare participants.
- *Innovative Research Projects*
  The academic institutions that are at the forefront of quantum research are conducting investigations into a wide range of topics, including quantum algorithms, quantum hardware, and the effects that quantum technology will have on society.
- *Researchers*
  Researchers in the field of quantum physics are often at the forefront of technological and theoretical advancements, pushing the boundaries of what can be accomplished using quantum technologies. Beyond the year 2030, it is expected that researchers enact: collaboration across the fields of physics, computer science, engineering, and mathematics has been more prevalent in the area of quantum research, which has led to the development of interdisciplinary study. The goal of this partnership is to find solutions to complex problems that arise during the development of quantum technology. Dissemination of quantum knowledge researchers are actively

distributing their findings and exchanging ideas via the use of conferences, journals, and public lectures, which are helping to facilitate the dissemination of quantum knowledge all around the globe.

- *Collaborative Efforts*
The convergence of industry, academic institutions, and research is central to preparation for the year 2030 and beyond. Below are some examples of such activities:
  - *Partnerships between government and the private sector:* Several governments are now in the process of establishing national offers of financial support and technical help for collaborative research between universities, national labs, and businesses.
  - *International collaborations:* The creation of transnational agreements and partnerships to facilitate the exchange of research and building of standards. Global cooperation is crucial for the advancement and equitable access to quantum technologies.

Not only are these efforts needed for advancements in the technology itself, but they are also core for ensuring that the workforce is suitably equipped to meet the needs of a new quantum-powered industry. Creating a robust and dynamic system that is prepared to exploit the quantum revolution is the result of a collaborative effort including the business sector, academic institutions, and researchers [16]. Taking this step will ensure that we are well-prepared to face the complex challenges and massive opportunities of quantum technology.

10.13 CONCLUSION

As we conclude this investigation into the post-quantum era beyond 2030, the joint efforts of industry, academia, and researchers have paved the way for a future that is quantum-powered and quantum-prepared. The transition to a quantum-safe world is a challenging task that is only possible if the community sets initiatives for collaboration, innovation, and resilience.

The protection of our digital infrastructures through PQC is a proactive response to mitigate the quantum threat, ensuring that we transition further into this new landscape while guaranteeing the security and integrity of our information. The widespread adoption of quantum technologies across industries provides a revolutionary approach to efficiency, economic growth, and societal advancement.

Looking ahead, the constant progress toward quantum supremacy draws an exciting picture of the future. Yet, with great power comes great responsibility. The choices we make as a global community, in exploiting quantum technologies for the common good, will be crucial in shaping a thriving, equitable, and secure world.

REFERENCES

1. Lindsay, J. Why Quantum Computing Will Not Destabilize International Security: The Political Logic of Cryptology (June 29, 2018). Available at SSRN: https://ssrn.com/abstract=3205507 or http://dx.doi.org/10.2139/ssrn.3205507

2. D'Anvers, J. P., Karmakar, A., Roy, S. S., & Vercauteren, F. SABER: Mod-LWR Based KEM. NIST Post-Quantum Cryptography Standardization: Round 2 (2019). https://www.esat.kuleuven.be/cosic/publications/article-3055.pdf

3. Diffie, W. (1976). New direction in cryptography. IEEE Trans Inform Theory. 22(6):644–54. doi:10.1109/TIT.1976.1055638

4. Steane, A. (1998). Quantum computing. Reports on Progress in Physics. 61(2):117. doi:10.1088/0034-4885/61/2/002

5. Kumar, A., Ottaviani, C., Singh Gill, S., & Buyya, R. (2022). Securing the future internet of things with post-quantum cryptography. Security and Privacy. 5(2):e200. doi:10.1002/spy2.200

6. Pirandola, S., Andersen, U. L., Banchi, L., et al. (2020). Advances in quantum cryptography. Advances in Optics and Photonics. 12(4):1012–1236.

7. Ghosh, S., Misoczki, R., & Sastry, M. R. Lightweight post-quantum-secure digital signature approach for IoT motes. IACR Cryptology ePrint Archive; 2019: 122.

8. Kong, I., Janssen, M., & Bharosa, N. (2024). Realizing quantum-safe information sharing: Implementation and adoption challenges and policy recommendations for quantum-safe transitions. Government Information Quarterly. 41(1):101884.

9. Baseri, Y., Chouhan, V., & Hafid, A. (2024). Navigating Quantum Security Risks in Networked Environments: A Comprehensive Study of Quantum-Safe Network Protocols. arXiv preprint arXiv:2404.08232.

10. Coccia, M., Roshani, S., & Mosleh, M. (2022). Evolution of quantum computing: Theoretical and innovation management implications for emerging quantum industry. IEEE Transactions on Engineering Management.

11. Gupta, S., Modgil, S., Bhatt, P. C., Jabbour, C. J. C., & Kamble, S. (2023). Quantum computing led innovation for achieving a more sustainable Covid-19 healthcare industry. Technovation. 120:102544.

12. Yavuz, A. A., Nouma, S. E., Hoang, T., Earl, D., & Packard, S. (2022, December). Distributed cyber-infrastructures and artificial intelligence in hybrid post-quantum era. In 2022 IEEE 4th International Conference on Trust, Privacy and Security in Intelligent Systems, and Applications (TPS-ISA) (pp. 29–38). IEEE.

13. Zeydan, E., Turk, Y., Aksoy, B., & Ozturk, S. B. (2022, February). Recent advances in post-quantum cryptography for networks: A survey. In 2022 Seventh International Conference on Mobile and Secure Services (MobiSecServ) (pp. 1–8). IEEE

14. D'Oliveira, R. G., Cohen, A., Robinson, J., Stahlbuhk, T., & Médard, M. (2021, November). Post-quantum security for ultra-reliable low-latency heterogeneous networks. In MILCOM 2021-2021 IEEE Military Communications Conference (MILCOM) (pp. 933–938). IEEE.

15. Mashatan, A., & Heintzman, D. (2021). The complex path to quantum resistance: Is your organization prepared? Queue. 19(2):65–92.

16. Chen, L., Chen, L., Jordan, S., Liu, Y. K., Moody, D., Peralta, R., & Smith-Tone, D. (2016). Report on post-quantum cryptography (Vol. 12). Gaithersburg, MD: US Department of Commerce, National Institute of Standards and Technology.

Index

For Product Safety Concerns and Information please contact our EU
representative GPSR@taylorandfrancis.com
Taylor & Francis Verlag GmbH, Kaufingerstraße 24, 80331 München, Germany

www.ingramcontent.com/pod-product-compliance
Lightning Source LLC
Chambersburg PA
CBHW070716220326
41598CB00024BA/3179